Mn

No

x53
159 top
199

202

Ambon

GSG Sketches
p 44 Nos 1 & 4
140   12 & 14/15

RIVER KWAI RAILWAY

The Story of the Burma–Siam Railroad

The Wampo Viaduct, 1973

RIVER KWAI RAILWAY

The Story of the
Burma–Siam Railroad

CLIFFORD KINVIG

BRASSEY'S (UK)

LONDON · WASHINGTON · NEW YORK

First English edition 1992

UK editorial offices: Brassey's, 165 Great Dover Street, London SE1 4YA
orders: Marston Book Services, PO Box 87, Oxford OX2 ODT

USA editorial offices: Brassey's, 8000 Westpark Drive, First Floor, McLean, VA 22102
orders: Macmillan Publishing Company, Front and Brown Streets, Riverside, NJ 08075

Distributed in North America to booksellers and wholesalers by the Macmillan Publishing Company, NY 10022

Library of Congress Cataloging in Publication Data
Available

British Library Cataloguing in Publication Data
A catalogue record for this book is available from the British Library

ISBN 0-08-037344-5 Hardcover

Printed in Great Britain by B.P.C.C. Wheatons Ltd., Exeter

For Shirley

Contents

List of Maps

List of Plates

A Note On Names and Spelling

SIAM became Thailand in 1939 and I have given the state this latter
name throughout; but I have preferred 'Siam' in the compound title of
the railway by which it is more commonly known. Similarly the river
Kwai of the story is correctly 'Kwae Noi' (little Kwae) but 'Kwai' has
been the popular label at least since 1960 and I have adopted it
throughout the book. But there are two Kwais, the other being the
'Kwae Yai' (big Kwae) which is generally called the Maekhlaung,
especially south of the confluence with its smaller brother. There is, in
any case, a particular difficulty for English speakers in the spelling of
Thai names. Our alphabet of 26 letters and five vowels can do scant
justice to the Thai language with its 44 consonants, 30 vowels and five
tones. There is a similar though lesser difficulty with Burmese, but in
Burma English was more widely understood and commonly used.
Besides, many of the place names used in this account, particularly of
camps, do not appear on conventional maps in a land which was, in
any case, poorly surveyed. The precise derivation of place names used
by the prisoners is at times obscure. Thus spelling of place names
often varied significantly; Konkoita was also referred to as Concreeta
and Konhuita, Kanyu as Konyu and Thanbyuzayat as Taung Bazaar;
even the Kwae Noi appears sometimes as Gwenoi. I hope my choice of
spelling sufficiently resembles what the reader may remember or
recognise for the locations to be identifiable.

Preface

As RIVERS GO there is nothing particularly remarkable about the River Kwai. By comparison with the great waterways of the world, the Nile, the Amazon or the Mississippi, it is a mere stream. Even in the regional context it remains relatively insignificant; in Thailand alone it is dwarfed by many mightier flows. Nor can it claim the dignity of an independent existence from source to sea, surrendering its tributary waters after 240 kilometres of separate identity to the currents of the mightier Maekhlaung. The Kwai nevertheless has a modest impressiveness. In 1942 it bore a quiet beauty throughout its course and its occasional rapids and waterfalls provided an arresting contrast to an otherwise regular and even flow. Its littoral offered plenty of variety; at times flanked by flat, sandy banks, at others jungle-covered to the water's edge, on occasions with rocks rising steeply and cliff-like on one bank while the land rose only slowly and bamboo-clad on the other, the Kwai accepted all riverine challenges without demur. Moreover, like every other river subject to the full intensity of the south west monsoon, for the five months of the rainy season the Kwai was transformed in size and strength and impressiveness; turgid and dramatically risen, it carried a hugely increased weight of water down to the confluence with the Maekhlaung. It was then navigable by modest river craft for about 200 kilometres north of the junction, a water highway in a roadless land.

There must be a thousand rivers of average proportions like the Kwai which remain nameless and unknown to all but the local population and the community of geographers. In this respect the Kwai claims its uniqueness, for its name is probably more widely known than that of any other river of comparable size and significance on the surface of the globe, a name familiar throughout most of the English-speaking world, in South East Asia, in Holland and of course in

Japan. It is known less for its physical characteristics than for its association with the monumental struggle which took place along its eastern bank in 1942 and 1943 as a third of a million men strove to build a railway linking Thailand with Burma. What gave this railroad its gruesome notoriety was not its uniqueness as an engineering achievement, remarkable feat though it was, but the ruthless detemination of its architects to have it completed on time, however daunting the task in the inhospitable climate and topography of the region, regardless of the cost in human life. The railway along the Kwai was built like the pyramids of old, with the labour and lives of a multitude.

A second feature gave the Kwai railway its worldwide reputation. This was the film *The Bridge on the River Kwai* by David Lean and Sam Spiegel, released in 1960 and based on Pierre Boulle's novel of the same title. The film's theme tune, the old 'Colonel Bogey' refrain, became familiar the world over. Its powerful images left an abiding if erroneous impression of the nature and consequences of the confrontation between the Japanese military and their prisoner labour force which was as far removed from the novel's portrayal as Boulle's own story had been from the reality of the bridge-building operation at Tamarkan which provided the setting for the film's theme. *The Bridge on the River Kwai* has proved one of the most durable of the films to come out of the Second World War, still attracting a television audience of seven and a half million at its eighth BBC showing in Britain in March 1990 and retailing for a fresh generation of viewers its quite misleading account of the railway bridge-building episode. Although Boulle's book was quite clearly a novel, the film is presented as a recreation of the wartime reality. The building of the bridges at Tamarkan was indeed a quite spectacular undertaking, though it involved the spanning of the Kwae Yai (Big Kwai) otherwise known as the Maekhlaung, rather than Kwae Noi (Little Kwai) whose course the railway followed for much of its length. Moreover, few of the prisoners who worked on the Tamarkan bridge would have recognised their commanding officer in Alec Guinness's Colonel Nicholson; while the bridge itself was destroyed not by commandos as the film would have us believe but, as many prisoners knew to their cost, by B-24 Liberators flying down from eastern India on long haul interdiction missions. According to one of the film's special advisers the British prisoner of war commander portrayed in the film was an amalgam of Pierre Boulle's recollection of collaborationist officers he had known in Indo-China (he was a Gaullist himself), David

Lean's conception of the military mind and his wish not to turn the film into an anti-Japanese tract, and Guinness's own interpretation, which was that Nicholson was not a quisling but quite simply mad.[1] This characterisation hardly explored the true dilmema of the Allied commander of a labour force in Japanese hands, but it is the one which has left the most abiding impression of the nature of the clash between the Japanese military and the forces of the West. It is noteworthy that the prisoners of war who laboured on the railway were not the only ones who found its portrayal unrealistic: the Japanese took particular exception to it as well, but for quite different reasons. A second film has recently rewakened the memories of this wartime episode, though *Return from the River Kwai*, again based on a book of the same title, tells a different prisoner of war story, albeit one every bit as harrowing as the railway episode itself; the journey to Japan of many ex-railway labourers who now had to run a fresh gauntlet as American submarines unwittingly attempted to sink the transports in which the prisoners were travelling.

Long before David Lean's film transformed the river Kwai railway episode into a piece of Western folklore, the main events of the railway's construction had already been recorded and published. Numerous prisoners who laboured on the track had kept secret diaries of their incarceration, often risking their lives in the process. Quite a number of them published their stories once they were repatriated at war's end. There has been a steady stream of such eye-witness accounts ever since. These personal memoirs vary enormously in quality, balance and perspective. Some are outpourings of bitterness and hate at the appalling treatment meted out to the prisoners by their Japanese captors. This can be as typical of accounts written forty years after the event as of those produced in the immediate aftermath of the experience itself. Others, however, display a remarkable balance on the part of the authors, as critical at times of their own frailty as of their captors' harshness, and as full of compassion for Japanese wounded as for the ordeals of their own sick men. Candour and courage shine out like beacons from some accounts, while others are the work of men whose entire lives have plainly been blighted by their experience as prisoners of the Japanese. Some authors admit that the act of recording their war experiences as prisoners has provided the final release from the bitter and recurring memory of their incarceration. Several such accounts were written on the advice of psychiatrists trying to treat ex-railway prisoners for nightmares, depression or a range of personality and behavioural problems which had developed from the physical and psychological bruising they had suffered on the line.[2] Such emotion recollected in something other than tranquillity is not without is significance for the historian; but from his viewpoint the main limitation of those personal accounts is the inevitably restricted experience and limited perspective of the individual prisoners telling their story. Despite the generalised titles which such works often carry, they usually centre on the activity in the one or two camps in which the author served. His knowledge of what was happening along the rest of the line was generally anecdotal and fragmentary, coming as irregularly and insubstantially as fresh meat with the rice ration. The Japanese were obsessively secretive about their operations and seldom passed on accurate information to the prisoners, even when they knew it themselves. Furthermore the prisoners' knowledge of the larger strategic enterprise into which the railway project fitted was a patchwork of gossip and rumour occasionally supplemented by genuine war news gleaned at great risk from one or another of the wireless sets operated clandestinely in many camps along the railway. There was often a huge gap in comprehension and experience between the 'big picture' of the war as the wireless portrayed it and as it was passed on to the individual captive in furtive whispered conversations and the restricted, jungle-bound reality of the prisoner's daily existence. Furthermore there is only brief mention in the Allied POWs' accounts of the activity of that other great labour force on the railway, the huge number of civilian labourers recruited in Burma and Malaya and elsewhere in South East Asia; the 'coolie forces' as the prisoners called them. These pitiful masses were largely illiterate and in any event too busy trying to survive their ordeal to produce a coherent record of their railway tribulations for the benefit of posterity. But their story is as much a part of the railway enterprise as is that of the Allied POWs themselves.

The British and American official histories of the war against Japan do not devote a great deal of space to an account of their prisoners of war in Japanese hands. In one sense this is natural; prisoners are by definition *hors de combat*, not part of the fighting forces and, therefore, outside the account of the main struggle. Besides, for the POW experience there existed nothing comparable to the war diaries and operational records that are available as the basic source material for the campaign sections of the official war histories. However, the numbers of servicemen captured by the Japanese were so vast, 130,000 in Singapore alone, and their treatment by the captors was so much at variance with Western norms, that some explanation and evaluation of their experience is historically vital. Moreover, whatever the Geneva Convention on the treatment of prisoners of war may have enjoined upon its signatories, the Japanese of the Southern Army still regarded the prisoners as part of their war, their bodies as an element of their war *matériel*. The role which the prisoners' exertions played in Japanese success or failure, particularly in such a large-scale enterprise as the building of the Burma–Siam railway, deserves the telling. The Australian and New Zealand official histories accord the prisoners' story a more prominent place. New Zealand, with about 9,000 of its nationals taken prisoner during the Second World War, devoted an entire volume of its official history to their story; Australia, with 22,000 captured by the Japanese alone, recounted their treatment in 170 pages; Britain, with 136,000 prisoners in Japanese hands had only ten pages in the five volumes of *The War Against Japan* recording their not uneventful incarceration. It is an odd contrast. Furthermore all three official accounts are largely a record of Japanese ill-treatment rather than an explanation of the POW experience as an aspect of the war itself, which in the Far East it certainly was. In few instances were the prisoners of Japan immured for the duration with little to note except for their attempts to escape from captivity. In the particular circumstances of the Japanese camps the odds against escape were very high; but the Japanese attitude to the fact of their prisoners' captivity was interesting in itself and their determination to see that their charges played a part in the war made leadership and courage as much prerequisites for captivity as they had been for combat.

Japanese accounts of the Burma–Siam railway do exist but their official record of the railway's building and operation do not. Just as the Japanese authorities had forbidden the POWs to keep unit records during their time on the railway, they were also unwilling to leave any records of their own. When the war turned against them and its end in Indo-China was imminent, they destroyed their main records of the railway's construction. We are left, therefore, with the recollections and memoirs of some of the principals involved together with the interrogation reports and compilations produced by or at the behest of the Allied intelligence staff at the end of the war, together with a few official documents. These are far from comprehensive but substantial enough to confirm the main outline of the daunting logistical enterprise which they saw through to completion in the most difficult circumstances. A balanced account of the subject is, therefore, possible, taking into consideration the Japanese perspective, incorporating something of the story of the oriental as well as the occidental labour force and relating the facts of the railway's construction to the larger strategic purposes it was designed to serve. The present volume attempts to provide it and also to take account of the railway experience as a clash of cultures as well as an episode in a bitterly-contested war.

Burma was said to have been the least popular campaigning theatre for the Japanese and it was the scene of one of their greatest defeats of the Pacific War. Consideration of the critical events of the Burma campaign naturally focusses on the thwarting of General Mutaguchi's ambitions at Imphal and Kohima, the shattering of the campaigning potential of Burma Area Army in the battle of the Mandalay plain and the destruction of its defeated remnants in the Sittang breakout battle. Before the ultimate test of battle could occur, each side had to attempt to solve immense logistical problems to get their forces to the battlefield and to keep them supplied there, for Burma was a uniquely isolated land. The Japanese Burma–Siam railway was one attempt at a solution; the British and United States' high commands each undertook a similar major logistical enterprise to surmount the problems which this aspect of the land battle presented for them. The United States had little intrinsic interest in Burma as a theatre of war and even less in returning it to the imperial ownership of the British; for them it provided the last landward lifeline to the beleaguered Chinese. The Burma Road to Kunming and Chungking in China had been cut when the Japanese first occupied Burma and the major communications enterprise for the Americans was the building of a fresh highway linking Ledo in the north-eastern corner of India with the upper part of the original Burma Road still in Chinese hands. Along this new highway, Chiang Kai-Shek's embattled forces could be supplied. The 'Ledo Road' across the southern slopes of the Himalayas, through dense jungles, and on via Myitkyina and Bhamo to join up with the Chinese end of the enterprise north of Lashio, was a massive undertaking and one of the major engineering feats of the war. The amount of road-making equipment the Americans had available for it General Slim, Commander of Britain's 14th Army, noted, 'made our mouths water'. They also had skilled US Army engineers to direct the project and an almost inexhaustible supply of Indian labour to support it. As General 'Vinegar Joe' Stilwell and his Chinese Armies pushed down the Hukawng valley towards Kamaing, so the Ledo Road, sustained and developed by these immense material resources, inched southwards behind them. This new overland umbilical for the Chinese was finally opened when the Japanese were cleared from northern Burma in January 1945, by which time the enterprise was largely superfluous. During the next ten months it carried only 38,000 tons of *matériel* into Yunnan, compared with the 39,000 tons flown each month by the huge US airlift to China over the mountains of the 'Hump Route'. Furthermore, the Chinese armies which the road was designed to sustain played no important part in defeating the Japanese.

Aside from the efforts of six battalions of US railway troops which turned the diminutive 600 tons-a-day tea gardens railway running from Calcutta to Dimapur and Ledo into an arterial military route carrying more than ten times that tonnage, the major logistical project on the British part on the front was also a road-building one. It entailed creating a highway across Manipur province and another one down to the Arakan front. This too was a massive undertaking, but it was attempted without the substantial equipment support which characterised the Ledo Road enterprise. The more important of the two roads was driven through Manipur to serve General Slim's vital central front. It first climbed the hills from Dimapur railhead to Imphal and then snaked down again, providing a magnificently-surfaced two-lane highway almost to the Burma border. The other road constructed in the Arakan ran from south of Chittagong to Cox's Bazaar. This was a less mountainous route but it had to cope instead with many tidal creeks and the fact that the region afforded no stone for roadmaking. 14th Army's engineers therefore built it with bricks, countless millions of them, shipping coal across from India to bake them and setting up a brick kiln every 20 miles or so along the road's route. Both roads were built with primitive equipment, picks, shovels and baskets and with the aid of a huge Indian labour force, much of it provided by the great tea estates of north east India whose business organisation, the Indian Tea Association, supplied and marshalled 40,000 of its workers for the operation. These roads were vital for the success of the Allied campaign; the Manipur highway in particular, except for a short period when the Japanese managed to cut it, carried traffic day and night down to the central front of 14th Army.

It is with these great engineering projects that the third major communications enterprise of the theatre, the Burma–Siam railway, must be compared. It was certainly not to prove such a superfluous undertaking as the American Ledo Road and, in the light of the ultimate outcome of the campaign, it was certainly not as successful in supporting Burma Area Army as were 14th Army's roads in supplying its fighting divisions. It was also different in being not a road but a railway. There was a service road running alongside it but the railway had priority for very good local reasons. The railway's construction made different demands on the Japanese Army's engineering skills but its ultimate purpose was very similar to the other two ventures; keeping the armies reinforced and supplied. No doubt in building the railway the Japanese engineers would have known that their adversaries, the British, had been the first to develop railways and the earliest to put them to military employment; but they would also have known that it was their own military mentors, the Prussians, who had first put railways to decisive strategic use. Not for nothing had the great Prussian military theorist Von Moltke noted, in a remarkably prescient judgement, exactly a hundred years before the Japanese opened their railroad to Burma, that 'every development of railways is a military advantage'. How costly this Japanese development was to be and how significant any advantage it conferred are the essential subjects of this book.

Acknowledgements

I MUST first of all record my gratitude to that courageous band of railway prisoners who took the considerable personal risk of keeping diaries, notes or other records of their time on the line. Their accounts do much to flesh out the official post-war reports and interrogation records of some of the principals involved; without them the story of this infamous railway would be a colourless affair. I owe similar respect and thanks to the railway artists whose pictorial records, produced in the same hazardous circumstances and generally with the most inadequate materials, have added so much to our understanding of the conditions in which the inmates of the Kwai camps lived, worked and often died; but have also reminded us of the scenic beauty which surrounded them. I am particularly grateful to those whose work is reproduced here and should like to thank Stanley Gimson, Jack Chalker, Philip Meninsky and William Wilder for allowing me to include their drawings. Similar thanks are due to Mrs Hilda Thrale for permission to include her late husband's work. Ronald Searle's drawings appear by permission of the Tessa Sayle Agency and that by Leo Rawlings is included with permission from a private collection. The reproductions are by courtesy of the Imperial War Museum. The frontispiece photograph was kindly supplied by P A Tyler.

Numerous ex-prisoners have helped me with advice and additional information. I would like to express particular thanks to that meticulous documenter, the late C E Escritt, for invaluable discussions and for the use of some items in his private collection of Japanese works. His translation of the various recollections of Futamatsu Yoshihiko have greatly aided my understanding of the Japanese perspective on events recorded herein. I owe similar thanks to Stanley (Sheriff Principal G S) Gimson for, in addition to his sketches, personal recollections and advice so generously offered.

I am in the debt of several military libraries for their help with reference material and should like to thank the staff of the Ministry of Defence Library London, Prince Consort's Library Aldershot and the RAEC Centre Library Beaconsfield for their invaluable assistance. I am grateful too for the research facilities of the Imperial War Museum and particularly for the help of Philip Reed of the Department of Documents and Jenny Wood of the Department of Art. The staff of the Ministry of Defence Army and Air Historical Branches have also been most helpful. The forbearance, advice and encouragement of the staff of Brassey's, especially Jenny Shaw and Jim Pipe I must also gratefully acknowledge. Finally my sincere thanks are due to Valerie Paddon for her immaculate typing of a scrappy manuscript. Errors which remain, typographical, factual or perceptual are, of course, mine.

London 1991 Clifford Kinvig

1

The Explosion of Japanese Power

Japan the Saviour of Asia, Japan the Leader of Asia,
Japan the Light of Asia
Slogan launching 1942 Japanising Campaign in Java.

JAPAN'S GEOSTRATEGIC situation has been likened to that of the United Kingdom; each country consists of medium sized islands close to a major continental land mass but protected from it by a band of sea. The relative freedom from invasion which this position has historically conferred has resulted, in the United Kingdom's case, in security concerns occupying a secondary position in national affairs and in the military being very much subordinated to the civil power. That the very opposite should have resulted in Japan is due in part to its internal geography – limited coastal plains separated from each other by mountain ranges encouraged the development of local power centres and violent clan-based politics with continuous struggles for overall control. In such a situation military forces played a crucial and enduring role and developed into an entrenched and privileged military caste, the *samurai*, who dominated feudal Japanese society until that social structure foundered in the nineteenth century under Western commerical and political pressure, backed by the threat of vastly superior military force.[1]

This concern with internal politics and local feuding is perhaps one reason why the energetic and resourceful Japanese made such a late appearance on the imperial scene. It is certainly one of the ironies of history that the Tokugawa government should have decided, early in the seventeenth century, to withdraw Japan from contact from the rest of the world and particularly from Western Christian influence. For this was the very time when Japan might have created a modest empire for itself, should it have been so minded, with relative ease and

1

without too much opposition from the European powers. Instead Japan chose to indulge its imperial ambitions in the twentieth century when European empires were already well established in South East Asia and a powerful and influential, if ideologically anti-colonial USA had substantial political and commercial interests in client Asian states which it did not wish to see disturbed. In consequence, although Japan was able to extend an empire remarkably rapidly in late 1941 and early 1942, this was not a durable expansion. Indeed, the enlarged Japanese Empire was one of the shortest-lived in history; by September 1945 the newly-won territories had all been surrendered along with those overseas possessions acquired earlier. But the process of gaining this empire and then losing it changed for all time the face of South East Asia and wrested it permanently from European control.

Japan's integration into the international system after two centuries of virtual isolation had come rapidly after the country was forcibly opened up to foreign trade by the American Commodore Perry and his naval squadron in 1854. Other European trading delegations rapidly followed the American lead. The disparity in power and technological sophistication between the Japanese and these Western missions was so enormous that the Japanese had little choice but to accede to their commercial demands and to accept the changes to Japanese society which they made inevitable. These enforced contacts produced a profound shock to the entire political, cultural and social system, and to no social group more so than the *samurai*. Japan's determination to follow a similar path of modernisation as had its Western trading partners was not pressed to a conclusion without enormous difficulty. The restoration of central Imperial authority in 1868 was the first critical step, and after it came the creation of a modern army to enforce the Emperor's will. A system of universal conscription on the Prussian model, and quite alien to the Japanese tradition, was introduced in 1870 and a French military mission was brought in in the following year to advise on the training of the new national force. This attempt to inculcate the military virtues into peasants and townspeople was a direct threat to the skills and position of the *samurai*, and many of them resisted it. Indeed the early purpose of the embryonic Imperial Army was not to execute any grand colonial plan but to protect the security and authority of the new regime from internal challenge. After several minor skirmishes, the first great test came in 1878 when the new peasant-manned army put down the rebellion of the Satsuma clan led by the famous ex-

Commander-in-Chief Saigo Takamori. It is tempting to conclude from this victory (and not a few writers have) that Japan's military revolution was now complete and the path to modernisation assured, but the reality was somewhat different.[2] In the first place the peasants were far from being the enthusiastic supporters of the new order that might be supposed. They resented the new taxation that central authority required and they resisted the conscription which took labourers from the fields and increased the workload of the remainder. More importantly, they lacked the martial values and special skills of the *samurai*. Saigo and his men, though armed only with antiquated matchlocks and the *samurai*'s traditional two swords, resisted ferociously and took a terrible toll of the national army, a quarter of its force becoming casualties. The government had to commit its entire resources including reserves, some armed police, young cadets and even hastily recruited *samurai* from other clans before its victory was assured. The rebellion was finally quashed not as a result of the superiority of the peasant conscript soldier over the *samurai* but by dint of greater numbers, equipment and resources. Much needed to be done before this embryonic Imperial Army was an appropriate instrument for Japan's aggrandisement. Moreover for several decades the *samurai* continued to provide its officer corps. There was some dilution over time but as late as 1927 50–60 per cent of officers were still of *samurai* stock. In the intervening period the task was to inculcate their military values into the largely peasant rank and file, to train the whole army in the use of modern military technology and to guarantee the loyalty of the force to the nation and the Emperor.

The first major external test of the army came in 1894 when a rebellion in Korea provided the occasion for both China and Japan to intervene. The Japanese installed a compliant Korean government and drove out the Chinese, winning battles in Korea itself and at Port Arthur on the Liaotung Peninsula in north eastern China. Naval victories accompanied these land engagements and the Chinese, defeated in every department, sued for peace. The Japanese terms were harsh. They took Formosa and the Pescadore Islands from China, secured the independence of Korea and additional trading concessions from the Chinese. However the diplomatic pressure of the European powers deprived Japan of much-prized territory on the Chinese mainland. Japan deeply resented this intervention, spuriously justified as preventing Japan from disturbing 'the peace of the Far East'. Within a few years of their cynical action these self-same European powers, Germany, France and Russia, were securing for themselves, and without the cost of war, the very Chinese territory which they had earlier denied to Japan. If the Japanese were learning to despise and distrust the Europeans they could hardly have been blamed.

The impressiveness of the Japanese military exploits against China was underscored five years later when the European powers and Japan combined to raise the siege of their legations in Peking at the height of the Chinese Boxer Rebellion. The Japanese detachment of about 10,000 men was the largest allied contingent and its men bore the brunt of the fighting, advancing in their white jackets and in suicidally close order against strongly-held positions with a nerveless steadiness. The Imperial troops had apparently absorbed the *samurai* virtue of bravery unto death to the point where General Fey, the commander of the hopelessly inadequate French contingent, could accuse them of taking a positive pride in accepting casualties and suffering the loss of 'hecatombs of men in order to gain for Japan the leading role in the action'.[3] Of the allies, only the Japanese took no part in the looting which followed the raising of the siege and emerged with a deserved reputation as a brave and disciplined force which none of its allies could match.

Russia used the Boxer Rebellion as a pretext to flood Manchuria with troops, thus threatening the Japanese position in Korea. It was clear that the interests of the two powers were on a collision course. Since both Britain and Japan feared Russia's Asian ambitions and each was without an ally, the Anglo-Japanese alliance, agreed in 1902, provided the limited security which both sought. Britain acquired a counterpoise to Russian power in the area and Japan an ally who might keep France and Germany from joining the Russo-Japanese struggle which grew increasingly more likely. The alliance had these obvious diplomatic benefits for Japan, but of equal importance was the psychological boost which came from the recognition which it conferred of its great power status and equality with the Europeans.

The Russo-Japanese War came two years later; it lasted eighteen months and featured some of the greatest land battles that the world had yet seen. In the five-month siege of Port Arthur, Japan lost 60,000 men, the greatest ordeal that its troops were to suffer until the calamity of Imphal in 1944. The lessons of the battles from Port Arthur to Mukden were many, but a particularly pertinent one for the Japanese was that the *samurai* qualities could still be decisive in an age of mass industrialised warfare. The discipline of the troops during and after the Port Arthur siege was remarkable and impressive, as was the Army's chivalrous treatment of Russian prisoners of war. Russian medical officers confessed themselves astonished at the kindness shown to the sick by the Japanese.[4] It seemed that Britain's alliance with 'the gallant little Jap' was more than vindicated. Japan emerged from the war with the southern part of the island of Sakhalin ceded to it, the concession of the Liaotung Peninsula in mainland China and a clear recognition that Korea was its exclusive sphere of influence.

The First World War gave a great spur to Japanese industrial development (as indeed the Korean and Vietnam wars were to do several decades later). Japan strove willingly to meet the demands from Europe for munitions and shipping and to meet the export orders in Asia which the struggling metropolitan powers could not supply. Britain had seen Japan principally as a naval ally in the Far East, but the Japanese statesmen viewed the alliance in quite different terms; their main ambitions were territorial. Korea had been formally annexed as part of the Japanese Empire in 1910 and Japanese engineers had now built the South Manchurian railway as an instrument for the extension of influence and trade. The fall of the Manchu Dynasty in China in 1911 had brought turmoil and civil war, providing fresh opportunities for the extension of Japan's ascendancy which the European powers and, increasingly, the United States viewed with disapproval and some anxiety. Japan willingly acceded to Britain's request to enter the war against Germany, but refused to accept any limitation to its territorial ambitions in the Far East. Before the end of 1914 the Imperial Navy had taken the German-owned Marshall, Caroline and Mariana Islands, the strategic girdle in the northern Pacific, while the Army had captured the German fortress of Tsingtao and was firmly established in Shantung and Manchuria. However, Japan's subsequent demands upon the weak and divided Chinese government pushed its behaviour beyond what the USA could bear with equanimity. Japan was losing the moral authority gained at such cost in the Russo-Japanese War. Its China policy was to be the cause of all its problems with the Western powers. Furthermore there was now growing concern among them, a concern not without its racial overtones, about increasing emigration from the Japanese islands to Australia, the west coast of the USA and Canada. The Kaiser's warning about the 'Yellow Peril' at the time of the Russo-Japanese War was still fresh in the consciousness of the West.

The impressive achievements of Japan's military forces in their overseas campaigns were accompanied by the developing ascendancy of the military in domestic politics. The Imperial Rescript to Soldiers and Sailors of 1882 formalised the position of the Emperor by which he commanded the unquestioned loyalty of the armed forces, with all superior officers notionally acting on his behalf. In 1900, the growing prestige of the military secured for them the Imperial Ordinance by which only serving generals or admirals could hold the cabinet positions of Minister of War and Navy Minister. Though there were subsequent vicissitudes in the power and prestige of the Services, these two developments gave the military the means to bring down governments if they so chose and the authority of the Emperor to justify their actions if they believed them to be in the Emperor's interests.

As a result of the development of armed nationalism in China and the effects of the world economic depression of 1929–31 which hit hardest those social classes from which the military recruits were drawn, the Army became more politically aware and at the same time more extreme and faction-ridden. National Socialist ideas were spreading, with the younger officers particularly prominent in propagating them. In 1931 a *coup de force* by Kwantung Army staff officers in Manchuria led to the seizure of Mukden and ultimately of all Manchuria, though neither move had the prior sanction of the Cabinet or even the General Staff. In 1935–6 a series of assassinations of senior officers and government ministers by junior army officers continued the factional struggles but put the Army in a position of almost supreme power in the land. Military spending now took the lion's share of the national budget. This was not widely opposed since military orders stimulated industrial expansion and military policy was still successful abroad, bringing power and prestige to the state. In 1937 war with China broke out again; the Japanese Army in north China emulated their Kwantung comrades and turned a local skirmish into general conflict. By this time Manchuria had become the empire of Manchukuo, technically an independent state under the nominal control of Emperor Kwang-teh, the former 'Boy Emperor' of China Pu Yi; but in reality a creation of Japan which had arranged Pu Yi's installation and negotiated protectorate powers for the substantial military forces which the Japanese stationed in the new empire. Whatever the Toyko government might have wanted, nothing short of a puppet Chinese state along the lines of this Manchukuo model would satisfy the military firebrands who now seemed to determine so much of Japan's China policy.

Pressure on Japan to end the war in China grew steadily more intense, particularly from the United States. Partly to counter it Japan joined Italy and Germany in the Tripartite Pact in 1940. In the following year it also concluded a non-aggression pact with the Soviet Union. American opposition to the China war had long since caused Japan to express concern over the security of the oil supplies on which the continuance of its campaigns in China depended. In June 1941 Germany attacked the Soviet Union, rendering Japan's northern frontier totally secure. Japan could now concentrate on events in China and the south and begin to consolidate its position by occupying bases in French-controlled Indo-China. The response from the USA, Britain and Holland was the imposition of a strategic embargo; the freezing of those very assets which kept Japan's war machine turning. This action presented Japan with two stark alternatives: either a humiliating withdrawal from China, which was the price demanded for the unfreezing of the resources, particularly oil, which she so desperately needed, or else an offensive to seize the oil resources of the Dutch East Indies and the other raw materials which she needed to win the struggle in China. The civilian members of the Cabinet might have been prepared to accept the climbdown, but War Minister Tojo and the Army were not. The Prime Minister resigned and Tojo was appointed in his place. Japan had decided to take by force the resources of South East Asia and to make war on the Western Allies there in order to secure them.

Japan's plans for expansion into and beyond South East Asia were not simply a military contingency plan to be put into operation in the event of Western, particularly American oil, embargoes. There was a larger political and ideological justification which saw the countries of the region being brought to independence under Japanese leadership with an industrialised Japan replacing the European colonial powers as the importer of raw materials which the region provided, and the exporter to it of the industrial products which Europe and the USA still largely supplied. Japan already participated extensively in this trade, its merchants and commercial agents were scattered throughout the region and their activity had increased significantly during and after the First World War. Industrial production in Japan increased fivefold in the twenty years to 1938; by all the common indices of industrial production Japan had by then overtaken both France and Italy, themselves colonial powers of some significance. Japan had the third largest merchant marine in the world, an essential instrument for trade. As Japan's economy developed so did its dependence upon captive South East Asian markets and sources of raw materials. The population was increasing rapidly and while it had once been a net exporter of food, Japan now had to import it, mainly from Korea. Every legitimate commercial concern seemed to indicate that Japan would replace the European states and the USA in the trading hierarchy of the region. Furthermore, since Japan had already demonstrated the ability both to defeat the European militarily and to synthesise East and West successfully with rapid modernisation and industrialisation, Japanese superiority over the other cultures of Asia seemed to have been adequately demonstrated. The 'inferior' nations of the region would, therefore, be brought to prosperity under Japanese leadership as part of a Japanese empire for which even modern marketing men could scarcely have dreamed up a more appealing title: The Greater East Asia Co-Prosperity Sphere. This was Japan's political trump card; it proved a propaganda weapon of incalculable initial power, stimulating the indigenous nationalist movements and ensuring that the Japanese forces were generally welcomed by the local people when they arrived in South East Asia. They were Asians liberating fellow Asians from Europeans.

With hindsight it is evident that although Japan picked the wrong century in which to enlarge its empire by the inclusion of much of South East Asia, its choice of the end of 1941 for the operation certainly appeared at the time to have much to commend it. By December of that year the Soviet Union was struggling for its life, with German forces at the gates of Moscow. As for the colonial powers themselves, the great distances which separated them from their South East Asian possessions made the control and management of them a difficult enough operation in peacetime; under the strain of war with Germany it was a task from which France and Holland, already under German occupation, had completely abdicated. Britain's armies had been driven from France and Belgium and were fully extended in dealing with General Rommel in North Africa. The British Isles faced an occupied Europe and the threat of invasion, while the seas around them were so menaced by Axis submarines that their total isolation and subjection was a distinct possibility. In South East Asia, the Japanese had already occupied strategically significant parts of French Indo-China, threatening Thailand, Burma and Malaya. The Dutch garrison forces in the East Indies were modest in size for their large territorial responsibilities. Only the USA at its Pacific base of Pearl Harbor had a navy large enough to interfere with any Japanese plans for aggression. West of it, the Philippines and Malaya were the main centres of Allied strength. The embryonic Philippines Commonwealth was defended by an American-led army of 130,000, three-quarters of it hastily mobilised Filipinos who lacked adequate training and equipment. The Malayan garrison, composed of British, Indian and Australian army units and locally-raised forces was of uneven quality, much of it untried in combat, while the colonial administration itself was slow to adjust to the urgency of the threat of war. The great fortress of Singapore was without a strong navy to put muscle into its impressive naval base and the whole of Malaya Command was woefully lacking in the protection of modern aircraft. Moreover the army was spread throughout Malaya, preparing to defend the bases from which the missing aircraft might operate. Burma was no better prepared to deal with the onslaught about to descend upon it, with two untried divisions being charged with the defence of a country the size of France and Belgium combined, whose security had been the responsibility of five different superior headquarters in the sixteen vital months immediately prior to its invasion by the Japanese.

The account of the Japanese war plans and their execution has been too often told to require detailed repetition here. Suffice to say that the plan's first phase required the neutralisation of the Pacific Fleet at Pearl Harbor, the seizure of the Southern Regions and the establishment of a defensive perimeter around them and the Japanese homeland. Its second involved the strengthening of this perimeter with a string of fortified bases, while the final phase covered the interception and destruction of any attempts to break the perimeter until Japan's enemies, operating at the end of long supply lines and lacking well-developed advanced bases, agreed to a compromise peace. If a ridiculously excessive optimism attended the last phase of the plan, the first was attained with surprising ease (though the American carrier force was out of port and escaped destruction), particularly the main drive to seize the Southern Regions, with its two-pronged thrusts against Malaya and the Philippines. In all, the Japanese used only 11 Divisions, less than 200,000 men, for the Pacific and South East Asian operations, compared with the 13 which remained stationed in Manchuria and the 22 involved in the China fighting. This relatively modest force was deployed to conduct many far-flung and disconnected operations, violating the cardinal principle of the concentration of military force. That it should have been so remarkably successful is eloquent of the weakness and ill-preparedness of Japan's opponents, the surprise and disorganisation which so many simultaneous attacks engendered, the superiority of the Japanese forces in the air and at sea and, finally, the remarkable fighting qualities of the Imperial Japanese Army – barely 70 years after its establishment as a modern force. On all sides the European-led armies were beaten and humiliated, the arrogance of the white Europeans' domination of South East Asia was exposed as a hollow pretence and their fighting spirit proved to be, in Japanese eyes, contemptible.

The Japanese Army which achieved these remarkable victories had a superficial similarity to the forces which opposed it. It had been raised initially in accordance with European advice, modelled on the Prussian conscription system and it had been trained and developed under French and then German tutelage, though it managed without a foreign military mission from 1894 onwards except for a spell when the French returned to help the Japanese set up an Army Aviation Corps. By 1941 the Japanese Army was technologically advanced and, though it had gone to some trouble to disguise this from the West, its equipment and armament easily bore comparison with what the Western powers were able to deploy in the Far Eastern Theatre and often outclassed it. To all outward appearances it was a modern, Westernised army. However, the Japanese soldier whom the Western armies were to confront was socially, culturally and in purely military terms a vastly different character from his opponents. He was drawn from a society taught to venerate group responsibility rather than the individual freedom so prized in the West. For him obligations to superiors and to society were the values to be cherished. To these traditional social mores the increasingly fascist Japanese government had added fresh responsibilities which moulded a fighting man whose highest duty was to die an honourable death for the Emperor. 'Death before dishonour' is an ideal which all armies respect though infrequently espouse; for the Japanese soldier it became the permanent operating principle of his tactical behaviour.

The training of the Japanese conscript emphasised the importance of willpower in battlefield success and the attainment of objectives. It made 'a fetish of self-discipline and the cultivation of willpower' and institutionalised the popular belief 'that sufficient willpower can overcome any obstacle if one tries hard enough'.[5] Thus the soldier who had time to eat, had time to clean his rifle; if he had time to sleep, he had time to care for his boots. Success followed will. The system by which these values were inculcated into the Japanese soldier was one of brutality and harshness reminiscent of the early days of the Prussian Army. A failure to learn a tactical lesson or to attain an appropriate standard might result in the recruit being ordered to stand to attention all day. If, after several hours, he collapsed, he would be beaten for disobeying orders. These were routine rather than exceptional punishments and NCOs would regularly beat their subordinates for the slightest infraction. One European observer reported that in an open space in Tokyo alongside a school at which he taught, on several occasions he saw artillery recruits 'knocked unconscious' by NCOs, and this in public view and in the presence of senior ranks, thus testifying to its customariness.[6] Graduations in rank and seniority were also acutely observed in the disciplinary system; all soldiers were required to salute anyone who was their senior including private soldiers of a grade superior to their own. Second-year privates would often establish their own 'kangaroo courts' to try and then punish recruits whose poor performance in training was letting down the platoon, so adding a fresh system of informal sanctions to those officially prescribed. Such punishments would range from slappings and beatings to gang assaults. Clearly NCOs did most of the beatings and the privates generally received them and the practice was most evident in recruit training units, but it was by no means limited to these categories. Physical punishment was customary in operational units and in fighting areas, and officers themselves featured as inflictors and recipients of it. Yet for all the harshness of the military régime, many recruits from peasant families found it a far easier life than the long hours of backbreaking toil in the farming communities from which they came. As late as 1935 when 50 per cent of the Japanese lived in towns, 80 per cent of the Army's recruits still came from the rural peasantry. At the very bottom of the military hierarchy in the Imperial Army came its Korean soldiers. Korea, the cockpit of Asia, had been in the Japanese sphere of influence since the 1890s and was formally incorporated into the empire, as was noted earlier, in 1910. By the late 1930s Korea was the line of communication from Japan to China in whose affairs the Japanese were deeply embroiled. With the escalating manpower costs of the China war Japan began recruiting Koreans for its army in 1938. Conscription was later extended to Korea and the colony ultimately contributed about 187,000 men to the Imperial Army.[7] The Koreans never acquired any status in the army, generally carried out menial, labouring duties and, of course, suffered the same harsh disciplinary system. They did not have the honour of serving as front-line fighting soldiers, but worked in rear areas as porters, guards and communication troops. Besides being at the bottom of the military hierarchy the Koreans were often the subject of verbal abuse and racial slurs. Many of their women were also recruited as 'comfort girls', the mobilised prostitutes who operated in the war theatres for the Japanese troops.

Another factor made the Japanese Army particularly distinctive. This was a combination of those traits called in Japanese *dukudan senko* and *gekokujo*.[8] In military doctrine *dokundan senko* implied the use of 'initiative and originality in emergencies', it did not thereby recommend or condone unauthorised or unilateral action, but the distinction is a nice one. The second term, *gekokujo* signified the 'domination of seniors by juniors' and is close in meaning to the English 'insubordination'. It had been a prominent feature of the behaviour of middle–ranking Japanese officers particularly since the early 1930s and the Kwantung Army in Manchuria had been especially prone to it. Both traits gave to officers in difficult situations and in distant commands a justification for independent action and often frankly insubordinate behaviour which would have scarcely been tolerated in a Western army. When coupled with the Japanese belief in the importance of 'sincerity' in motivation – the belief that an individual acting sincerely for (what he perceives as) justifiable purposes could not be held culpable – a receipe for excesses in military behaviour was well established, particularly in commands like the Burma Area Army which were remote from Imperial General Headquarters and unconstrained by public scrutiny.

Thus, although the Japanese Army which swept through Malaya, Singapore, Java, Sumatra and Burma with such consummate ease, was one which had adopted Western rank structures, forms of organisation, uniforms, weapons and military technology, it was in essence a totally different force. Its *samurai* origins and adherence to some aspects of *bushido*, 'the way of the warrior', account only in part for its distinctive martial and social mores. They were as much a reflection of attitudes and values in the larger Japanese society, conditioned over centuries to operate as a hierarchial structure, to emphasise duty and obligation rather than individual rights and, in the case of the soldier, to see death in battle for the Emperor's cause and at the behest of his local military representatives, as the supreme military virtue. Furthermore, although much Japanese military technology was very advanced, the technological awareness of the peasant-turned-soldier, his general education and his standard of living, were all comparatively low. The conscript's pay was poor, scarcely sufficient to feed him outside barracks, let alone pay for lodging and clothes.[9] His rice-based meals were simple, lacking the meat protein customary in the West but nevertheless often better than his civilian counterparts enjoyed. It has to be remembered that there had been some food rationing in Japan for a considerable time. All in all the military life, particularly after recruit training, was not bad. On the battlefield soldiers of Japanese and Western armies would have had considerable understanding of each other's tactical functions. However if they were ever to meet away from the battle-ground itself, the gap in comprehension between them would be immense.

2

The Western Bastion

It is easier to gain a victory than to secure its advantages
Chinese proverb

WHEN THE dust finally settled at the end of the Japanese offensive in May 1942 a totally transformed political situation in South East Asia and the Pacific was displayed. Within the six months that they had allotted the Japanese had achieved all their objectives at minimum cost to themselves. They had isolated China and had not only devastated the armed forces of the Allies in the process, but had also shattered the myth of the European's invincibility and the permanence of his imperial presence in Asia. The Philippines, despite the protection of the mighty USA, were now firmly in Japanese hands. Malaya, though British for more than a century, was added to the possessions of Japan and Singapore, the port city founded by Stamford Raffles in 1824 and turned into a British fortress in the inter-war years, surrendered after only a fortnight's investment and was now renamed Syonan and serving as a major Japanese military base. The Dutch East Indies had been wrested with relative ease from the feeble grip of the large but unreliable Dutch-led Indonesian forces; Holland, of course, was already in bondage. Even Burma, 4,000 miles away from the Japanese capital and sharing a border with the still powerful British base of India, was firmly under the Imperial Army's control. Away to the east all the island groups in the western Pacific were in Japanese hands and Hawaii, the lynch-pin of American Pacific defence, its battleships disabled and port installations battered, was temporarily impotent. The Japanese had sunk every sizeable British, American or Dutch ship that had ventured into the East Indian Seas or the Western Pacific. Never before had such a large area been conquered in such a short time. It was the greatest ever

14

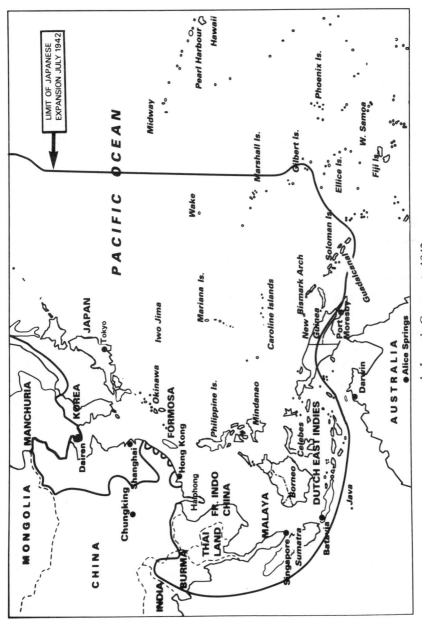

1. Japan's Conquests 1942

victory of Asian over European and had given the Japanese the over-
lordship of 110 million people.

So traumatised were the Allies by these defeats, so profound was
the psychological shock, that the perceived threat from the remarkable Japanese military machine grew to enormous proportions. It
was feared that Australia might be next for invasion, that the
Japanese army might intend to march through India and the navy to
cross the Indian Ocean to link up with the Axis forces in the Middle
East, even that North America itself would be a target with the local
population of Japanese extraction acting as fifth column for their
brethren in Japan. Substance was given to these concerns by the
devastating air attack on the Darwin naval base in February 1942
when 11 ships were sunk, installations were damaged, and the town
was evacuated by nightfall. 500 casualties were caused by the foray
into the Indian Ocean of Admiral Nagumo's Carrier Striking Force
whose attack on Colombo and Trincomalee spread alarm and panic
and gave a severe mauling to the British naval forces based there.
Admiral Somerville was forced hastily to withdraw his main fleet two
thousand miles westward to East Africa. Churchill later noted
ruefully that there had developed 'one of those waves of alarm which
sometimes spread through High Commands'. So far as the threat to
North America was concerned, so great was the concern of the
Government and so intense the suspicion of the Japanese race as a
whole that Canada rapidly uprooted 20,000 Canadians of Japanese
extraction from the apparently threatened coastal regions of British
Colombia and interned them elsewhere, while further south five times
that number of Japanese Americans were hastily removed from the
West Coast by the US Army and put into camps in the centre of the
country. It is noteworthy that similar treatment had not been
accorded to North Americans of German or Italian extraction.
Meanwhile the US coastline itself became part of an operational
command.

In fact the dramatic character of these remarkable Japanese victories masked serious weakenesses in the power base from which they
were launched, in the military force structure and strategy which had
produced them and in the larger plans for the development of the
Southern Resources Area as part of the Japanese-sponsored Greater
East Asia Co-Prosperity Sphere. Although these Southern Regions
contained the raw materials so vital for the prosecution of the China
war, the forces which occupied them never received the priority in the
allocation of military resources which would have helped them to

survive, or at least stave off, the inevitable Allied counter-offensives. Japan retained well over three times as many divisions pursuing the continental strategy in China as she deployed for the invasion, initial control and subsequent defence of the vital resources area including its crucial western defensive bastion – Burma.

The new empire was truly vast, stretching almost 4,000 miles in each direction, its scattered territories occupying five different time zones, though the Japanese imposed Tokyo time throughout the captured lands for all formal purposes. The major island groups of the occupied Southern Regions were separated from each other by great expanses of ocean. From Singapore to Saigon was a distance of 630 miles, and Manila was more than twice as far away. Beyond Manila lay a long journey through the South and East China seas before metropolitan Japan, the centre of Imperial power, was finally reached. Critical for the defence of such an extensive, sea-girt empire would be the ability to move naval forces freely from one area to another, and vital for their fighting effectiveness would be the regular supply to the scattered garrisons of war *matériel*, food and reinforcements. Crucial too for the development of the Co-Prosperity Sphere would be Japan's ability to import the oil and primary products of the region and supply it in return with manufactured goods, bringing the erstwhile colonies to independence and prosperity under Japanese industrial and political leadership. In 1942 the Imperial Cabinet had established a Greater Asian Ministry with the task of putting this national purpose into operation.

For these strategic purposes Japan needed a powerful merchant marine and freedom of the seas. Here lay its Achilles' heel. By the start of the Pacific War Japan had developed the world's third largest merchant fleet totalling over six million tons and consisting of 700 ocean-going freighters, 132 passenger-cargo vessels and 49 ocean-going tankers. Despite this apparently impressive total which reflected a steady expansion in merchant ship-building in the 1930s, the fleet could still only carry 65 per cent of Japan's peacetime imports by the time the southern offensive was launched. For this huge enterprise, the greater part of the merchant fleet was quickly requisitioned for service use, the Army taking 1.2 million and the Navy 1.4 million tons – much of it to be squandered in the operations in the Solomon Islands. The Navy and Army operated their fleets quite independently and the tonnage that was left for civilian and industrial requirements was totally inadequate. Furthermore, the urgent demands of the Imperial Navy now began to take the lion's share of ship-building capacity, often for prestigious battleship projects of dubious value. Nothing was done to increase the capability of the industry until well after the war against the Allies had begun. The result was that at the very time that routine maintenance of the merchant marine was desperately needed, the shipyards were unable to provide it. The amount of shipping laid up increased progressively. An additional grave weakness in the Japanese maritime situation developed from the fact that its naval planners had given little thought before the war to developing measures to protect the merchant marine. They had not planned convoy systems (which were introduced belatedly in late 1943), developed anti-submarine techniques, or provided escorts for aircraft carriers and the like. By contrast, the USA, equally dependent for success on command of the seas, built for itself and Britain 110 escort carriers during the course of the war. The irony for Japan, therefore, was that although by May 1942 it had captured an area which represented one of the richest economic units in the world containing all the raw materials needed for the prosecution of the war, she was going to have the greatest imaginable difficulty in getting these materials back to Japan. In 1940 Japan had imported three million tons of iron ore from the colonial Philippines and Malaya; by 1942 when occupying these territories, the merchant marine managed to transport only 100,000 tons of iron ore back to the homeland. By 1943, the dwindling merchant fleet, under incessant attack from air and sea, was being replaced by wooden ships, vulnerable and very slow.

In Burma the security of sea communications was critical to the strength and stability of Japan's position. As the most distant of the new possessions, control of Burma was essential for its western frontier formed the final defensive perimeter on the landward side. Beyond Burma lay India, the base of the British Indian Army and an advanced base for American forces supporting China. During the Malayan campaign the Japanese 25th Army had already defeated two Indian divisions with relative ease, but other Indian troops were fighting with great resolution in the Middle East. The sub-continent continued to provide an apparently inexhaustible source of military manpower particularly since, forsaking its peacetime exclusiveness under wartime necessity, and the Indian Army was now recruiting widely from all regions and classes. In the first half of 1940 alone 53,000 men joined up. Altogether in 1939 and 1940 a total of eight new Indian divisions were created and more were promised. Although the Middle East, Iraq and China claimed all but three of the new formations, reinforcements had still been available for Malaya, as they would surely be for a campaign to retake Burma, if the Japanese perimeter defences were not held in strength. Burma was also a major food supplier for the eastern states of India and with the Burmese rice bowl firmly in the hands of the Japanese, the discomfort of the British administration in India would be compounded. Parts of the vast sub-continent, particularly eastern India, were already in political ferment with the Congress Party conducting an active campaign against military recruitment, and scores of battalions were deployed on internal security duties alone. Nevertheless, Burma would need to be strongly held by the Japanese lest the British in India, supported by the American forces based there to help the beleaguered Chinese, should push open this back door to the Southern Resources Area. Excellent staging posts were available to help them to this at Akyab and Victoria Point on Burma's west coast.

Possession of Burma also served a second important purpose for the Japanese: it kept isolated the Chinese armies against whom they had been battling without decision since 1937. By 1941 Japan had taken possession of a great swathe of Chinese territory stretching from the Mongolian/Manchurian border down to Shanghai, and held every port of any significance which lay further south. Japan was also in occupation of part of French Indo-China, dominating the French authorities there, and also had a friendly régime in neighbouring Thailand. At this stage the only significant land route over which American supplies could be ferried to the embattled Chinese was the famous Burma Road. This remarkable artery through the mountains had been completed as recently as 1938 by a labour force of 200,000 coolies. It linked Kunming, the provincial captial of mountainous Yunnan with Lashio in Burma, 350 miles to the south west; there it joined the Burmese road system running down to Rangoon. Much of the road was impassable to motor vehicles in the monsoon season (when pack mules took sixty days to cover the route from Rangoon to Kunming) and it was a formidable journey even in the dry. But it was a lifeline to the Chinese and although under Japanese pressure the British had agreed to close it for three months (during the rainy season) in 1940, Japan had been determined to seal off this final breathing hole for an exasperatingly durable Chinese adversary. It is not surprising, therefore, that after omitting Burma from initial plans for an offensive to take the Southern Regions, these plans were rapidly revised as the consequences of leaving this back-door open became clear. Besides, Burma was not without its stock of resources of which Japan could make good use. The abundant food supplies in the rice-growing delta have already been mentioned; but there were also the oilfields of Yenangyaung and at Mawchi 'some of the most valuable wolfram mines in the world' as General Slim ruefully noted when he was describing the relative ease with which the Japanese swept aside the 55th Chinese division and the newly-raised Karen Levies who attempted to defend them. Wolfram is the raw ore of that indispensable armaments metal, tungsten. In addition, Japan found in Burma a ready-made nationalist movement, with the people eager to be free of political domination by the British and commercial exploitation by the Indians who made up more than half the population of the capital city, Rangoon. The political situation in Burma was more suited to Japanese intervention than that in almost any other of the invaded states, and Japanese agents had spent years on intelligence work within the country reconnoitering routes and communications and recruiting nationalists, notably the famous 'Thirty Thakins' whom the Japanese trained abroad as the nucleus of a Burma Independence Army.

To say that Thailand provided the springboard for the Japanese invasion of Burma is to employ an easy analogy for a particularly arduous undertaking, since getting from one to the other by land was a matter of considerable difficulty. Nevertheless it was immensely helpful to the Japanese to have a complaisant if not entirely compliant regime in power in Thailand at the time of the great offensive. Thailand (called Siam until retitled in 1939 by the Phibun government which had taken power seven years earlier) was unique in South East Asia as the only state never to have been formally colonised during the three centuries of European influence. This signal achievement was not accomplished without considerable circumspection on the part of Thailand's rulers and an acute sensitivity to the realities of power in the area. Although Western advisers had been employed to modernise the country's administration and commerce, Thailand managed to preserve its independence often by playing off the interests of the French, based in Indo-China, against those of the British located in Malaya and Burma. Success in this balancing act was at the expense of significant territorial concessions made to both imperial powers.

In 1941 Thailand initially proved very amenable to the diplomatic pressure of Japan, the new influence in South East Asia, particularly since the Japanese proposals to the military government in Bangkok included promises of support for the return of the provinces surrendered to the Europeans at the turn of the century. Besides, Prime Minister Phibun believed that totalitarianism was the ideological force of the future and was more than willing to accept Japan's friendship. However, when on 7 December 1941, the Japanese asked for rights of passage for their troops through Thailand, the Thai Cabinet refused. The following day the Japanese invaded, 5th Division landing at Pattani, Songkhla (Singora) and Ko Samui, the Imperial Guards Division at the mouth of the Chao Phraya river. The Thai forces in the south made some token resistance but were easily beaten off. The Thais soon signed a treaty with the Japanese which permitted the transit through and stationing of military forces in the country; but Thailand formally retained her political sovereignty and a largely autonomous government throughout the war years which followed.

In January 1942 Thailand declared war on the Allies. The United States chose to regard the declaration as unconstitutional and invalid since the country was under occupation. In fact the Thai ambassador in Washington was sufficiently anti-Japanese to refuse to pass on the war declaration to the Americans and immediately set about creating a *Seri Thai* (Free Thai) organisation with rapid US support. In fact Phibun was in reality more traditionally 'Thai' in his attitude to the Japanese than some critics have appreciated. His famous remark to an aide in June 1942 when the Japanese were apparently at the height of their power should be remembered: 'Which side do you think will lose this war? That side is our enemy.'[1] The British, on the other hand, took the Thai declaration rather more seriously, the Foreign Office believing that the Siamese should have done more to resist occupation and that they would have 'to work their passage home'. This was a pity since the indigenous pro-Allied Free Thai movement developed within days of the arrival of the Japanese and the population in general remained largely opposed to the invader and became increasingly so. In view of the events which were to take place in western Thailand in 1942 and 1943, early contact with an organised resistance could have been of considerable benefit to the Allied cause.[2] How easy it might have been to create a militarily effective resistance is, however, another matter.

The Japanese must have been well pleased with what they were able to achieve by diplomacy and with a little brute force. At governmental level at least, Thailand was an ally, a vital consideration if the Burma stategy was to prove successful. Intelligence also played an important role, in particular the intelligence carried out by the large number of Japanese resident in Thailand before the war began, many operating as clandestine agents. With the initial Japanese landings at Pattani and elsewhere, hundreds of Japanese agents appeared in uniform throughout the country, guiding the invaders to designated objectives and routes of advance. Nevertheless, the invasion of Burma from Thailand proved particularly difficult. The motorised units of the Japanese 55th Division had to switch to mules and oxen for the approach march and the heavy artillery had to be left behind in Bangkok to follow later by sea with the reinforcing troops. The march across the hills of western Thailand began gently enough but soon turned into a gruelling climb as ridge after mountain ridge, some with peaks of over 4,000 feet, loomed like a succession of walls, all to be scaled before the division reached the Burmese border at Mae Sot. By the time it arrived there two thirds of its pack animals had been lost.

Rangoon was the key to Burma, and once the Japanese had taken the city the whole country was unlocked. The British were separated from their natural line of communication to the port and fell back to the mountainous north in a fighting withdrawal up the valleys, ultimately to Imphal in north western India where their 900-mile retreat came to an end. The great difficulty of the last phase of this retreat across the grain of the country of upper Burma was that it lay through country with communications which were primitive in the extreme. As the Japanese advanced, the Burma Independence Army (BIA) advanced behind them, the ranks of the original nucleus of Japanese-trained nationalists having been rapidly swelled by thousands of less disciplined recruits who appeared to have joined more for the opportunity of plunder, pillage and the settling of old scores than out of support for Burmese nationalism. By the time Rangoon fell they numbered 5,000 and they began to spread a reign of terror behind the Japanese advance. The hated Indians of Rangoon took to their heels and half a million refugees fled across the Indian border, perhaps as many again dying of disease or starvation before the frontier was reached. The BIA also sought to impose its domination over the other minorities, the Karens and Kachins, who differed from them racially, in religion and in culture. However these groups were strongly based in their hill regions and fought back. Civil war began to develop. The Japanese had little genuine sympathy for these extremes of Burmese nationalism and the chaos they were causing, and once the British had been driven from the country they turned their attention to restoring a semblance of stable government. Unwilling as yet to proclaim

Burmese independence, they established a provisional administration based on the orthodox political parties and the existing civil service, native Burmese being promoted to take the place of the absent British department heads and officials.

Burma's central land mass is cut by the Irrawaddy and Chindwin rivers which provide the main communication arteries of the land, but where these cease to be navigable, in upper Burma, most communication ends as the mountains with which the country is girdled take over. By holding Rangoon the Japanese held the trump card. The trouble was that holding Rangoon meant controlling the Andaman Sea, having sufficient shipping to make the sea journey to the port and enough oil to power the ships that made the journey. Unless the country could be held in strength and supplied with the requisite war *matériel* there was little chance of the western bastion of Japan's defensive perimeter being proof against counter-attack. Admittedly Japan's merchant shipping predicament was eased somewhat by the 800,000 tons which it captured in the early months of the war. One of the first Japanese actions on entering Burma was to commandeer all native vessels and to set about the local construction of wooden coasters about 100 feet long. This hasty action was more indicative of the scale of shipping difficulties than it was a realistic measure to end them; for while Japan was frantically attempting to augment its maritime strength the Allies were already starting to reduce it. By May 1942 when the first Burma campaign came to an end Japan had lost 314,000 tons of shipping of all types, a total of 67 craft. Viewed from this perspective, supply by sea to Rangoon was a costly use of a valuable resource. The sea journey from the main base and headquarters of Southern Army in Singapore involved a round trip of 2,270 miles. The sea time and transport costs were important considerations in themselves; but there were also the opportunity costs to other elements of the overall Japanese strategy for which additional shipping was urgently needed: operations in New Guinea and other parts of the South Pacific. In their search for ways of reducing the cost to their merchant marine of supplying the distant Burma theatre, the Japanese decided to investigate an overland supply route to Rangoon, one that might follow the general direction that their invading divisions had taken in January when they struggled across the Dawna hills to attack Moulmein.

The distance from Bangkok to Rangoon by sea is a little less than 2,000 miles; overland it would be about 350. The saving in time and distance is potentially so great that it is a little surprising that the advantage of a land link between the two had never been exploited earlier. However, arguments against such an enterprise lie in the basic geography of the two states of which these ports are the capitals. Burma and Thailand are the Siamese twins of South East Asia sharing a mountain spine which runs for 1,500 miles from the Shan plateau in the north, down through the Tanen and Dawna ranges to the narrow Tenasserim peninsula where the two states entwine their territorial legs. Yet despite this close proximity there had for centuries before the Second World War been little landward communication between the two. Lying back to back they faced in different directions, and being essentially river basin states ringed by mountains, their human activity was concentrated on their central plains. At the base of these lay the great port cities of Rangoon and Bangkok which were the focus of the economic, political and social activities of each state. Both looked to these major ports and to the seas beyond them for their major trading links with the outside world. To the south of them both lay the Malayan peninsula, the last 500 miles of territorial spine completing the barrier between the two countries. The fact of the matter was that neither Burma nor Thailand saw their lack of common communications as any sort of handicap since the orientation of their trade was in opposite directions. It required external powers who saw communications in hemispheric or at least in regional terms to perceive a need for such a landward link, as the Japanese now did and as the British had done before them.

In the effort to dominate Chinese trade and save the cost of the immense detour around Malaya, the British government in India had investigated the possibility of a canal and then a railway across the Kra isthmus at the southern boundary of Burma and Siam, but Kra was no Suez and neither project seemed a viable proposition. As early as 1883 a railway alternative much further north was mooted, where it would link Rangoon directly with Bangkok, but this seemed to have no strategic significance until it became part of a larger proposal to link both capitals with the Chinese city of Yunnan. However few British investors were attracted to the scheme which posed serious engineering difficulties and would never have operated as economically as the slower ocean shipping route. The absence of any great economic incentive and the likely human cost of constructing a railway in such an inhospitable environment were sufficient reasons for the project to be shelved. Its only potential benefit over sea traffic, speed, also ceased to be a valid argument when air transport began to be developed.[3] It required the Pacific war to transform these economic arguments. The Imperial Japanese Army had swiftly overwhelmed the Allied garrisons of South East Asia but the government soon realised that the real test would be in the ability to hold the newly-won territories against the counter-attack which would assuredly follow. Japan's sea power was hardly adequate to take the strain of reinforcing the scattered conquests, so the only chance of success was to integrate by land what had been conquered by sea. Filling in the important gaps in the land communications of South East Asia became a strategic imperative and top of the list for completion was the linking of Bangkok with Rangoon. A connection by land would give a more protected line of communication and it would give speed of movement. A road link was one possibility but in the monsoon conditions of the region roads were impassable for months on end, besides which motor transport was at a premium both in the Japanese homeland and in the occupied territories. Railway rolling stock however was available in large quantities locally as was the ancillary equipment needed. Furthermore there was already a good railway link between Singapore and Bangkok. A new line linking that stretch with the Burmese railway system would provide a permanent way almost to the forward positions of the divisions occupying Burma. When such a line had been mooted at the turn of the century it had been supposed that Siamese labourers would never have consented to work on such a project, while the government of India would scarcely have approved the importation of large numbers of Chinese coolies to do the labouring. In 1942 however the labour problem was already solved; in camps throughout the region the Japanese had more prisoners of war than they knew what to do with. Furthermore in the governments of Burma and Thailand Japan had local allies who could be relied upon to help.

3

The Labour Forces

Do not be taken prisoner alive
Hideki Tojo, Army Minister 1941 Japanese Field Service Code

IN FEBRUARY 1941 when General O'Connor had completed a spectacular rout of the Italian Army in North Africa after a brilliant campaign, it is said that he was contacted by his superior headquarters and asked how many prisoners he had taken. 'Oh, several acres of them', O'Connor is reported to have replied. If, a little over a year later, the same question had been put to General Yamashita, in command of the Japanese 25th Army which conquered Malaya so rapidly, he would have needed a much larger area measure than an acre to answer satisfactorily, if indeed he could have answered accurately at all. The Japanese were clearly surprised by the large numbers of POWs they had captured and in the early days of the occupation appeared to have no very clear idea of what to do with them. The irony is that most of the prisoners in Malaya and Singapore had been under the overall command of the same General Wavell whose subordinate, O'Connor, had had such a remarkable victory over the Italians the previous year. At the surrender parley in Singapore which concluded the Japanese forces' lightning campaign, Yamashita asked the defeated Allied Commander General Percival, whether his troops had captured any Japanese soldiers. 'No', replied General Percival, 'not a single one'.[1] It was an astonishing contrast if a little less than the whole truth since at that time there were at least five wounded prisoners reposing in Alexandra Hospital who were later murdered by rampaging Japanese troops, along with Allied wounded, following Percival's surrender. Nevertheless the numerical disparities were remarkable.

For their attack on Singapore the Japanese employed a force of

26

about 35,000 men, leaving a similar number in occupation of Malaya. The defending troops amounted to about 85,000 out of a total original strength of some 139,000 men. In the entire campaign up to the capture of Singapore the Japanese lost 3,507 killed and 6,050 wounded; a handful were captured alive but injured. British Commonwealth Land Forces casualties were rather fewer; but the total taken prisoner numbered some 127,000 men.[2] To these must be added the many survivors from Allied ships sunk in the various naval actions around the region, those aircrew who had survived the shooting down of their planes over Japanese-held territory and their ground crew and ground defence units taken prisoner during the Japanese advance. In addition there were the large numbers of Dutch prisoners taken in Java and Sumatra who also have an important place in the story. There were also significant numbers of Americans, both soldiers and sailors, who ultimately joined the Dutch and British Commonwealth forces in imprisonment. Of course many of the troops captured in Malaya and in the associated Java and Sumatra operations were native Asians, the Indian, Indonesian and Malayan forces who made up such a large part of the colonial armies; but the totals also included an Australian division, a complete British division, numerous British regiments serving in the 3rd Indian Corps and a substantial US contingent in Java. Commonwealth prisoners in Java and Sumatra added about 8,500 to the totals mentioned earlier.

The POWs also represented a wide assortment of backgrounds, military training and operational experience against the Japanese. On the British side there was on the one hand a regular unit like the 2nd Battalion The Argyll and Sutherland Highlanders. The Argylls had arrived in Malaya from India just before the outbreak of war with Germany; they had trained for two years for mobile jungle warfare and against the Japanese they fought with great distinction all the way down the peninsula until Malaya was finally surrendered, when they were the last unit to withdraw to Singapore island. By the time of the surrender on 15 February 1942 this proud but battered regiment of battle-weary Scots had sustained 42 per cent casualties. 'Into the bag' with it went the men of 18th British Division which had been in action for but a few days before the ceasefire came. The 18th (Eastern) Division had originally been one of the New Army divisions raised by Kitchener during the First World War. Disbanded at the war's end, it was reformed in 1939 when the Territorial Army was doubled in size as one of the emergency responses to the threat of war in Europe. Raised largely in East Anglia the division was mobilised in 1940 ready to move overseas. The plan was for its training to be completed in Egypt; but as a preliminary it went to Scotland, some of its units training in nine inches of snow. Several battalions returned to East Anglia to help with the harvest before the whole division boarded ship in late October 1941 for a sea journey which took its convoy across the North Atlantic to Canada, down east coast USA to Venezuela, back across the South Atlantic to Cape Town and on across the Indian Ocean to Bombay, where its eager and impatient volunteers at last had a couple of weeks on land for some much needed exercise and training after a journey of 17,000 miles. It finally sailed on to Singapore, one brigade sailing ahead in a fast liner but its main body at the end of January when the retreat to the island was almost complete. The division then occupied part of the island's defences until 8 February when the Japanese attacked. A week later came the surrender. The division never fought as a complete formation; some units saw little action at all. If the Argylls had the satisfaction of having fought bravely, skilfully and almost to a standstill, now incarcerated alongside them was a frustrated and bitterly disappointed 18th Division; two years' training and a 20,000 mile journey across three oceans to end up as POWs with scarcely a fight.

The experience of other groups of prisoners was similarly varied. 44th Indian Infantry Brigade had arrived with 7,000 Indian reinforcements on 22 January just over three weeks before the surrender. They were all poorly trained and played no significant part in the fighting on the island. Even less battle-ready in some respects were the 1,900 Australian reinforcements who arrived in a convoy two days later. Some had sailed to the war within a couple of weeks of enlistment; they had learnt no weapon handling skills and only the most rudimentary military discipline. On the other hand these raw recruits had sailed with 2/4 Machine Gun Battalion, a well-trained and valuable reinforcement. However, the South Johore battle was unsuited to the battalion's special skills and on the island it was re-armed and employed as standard infantry; but to little avail. The main formation of Australians who were now prisoner in Singapore were the men of 8th Division Australian Imperial Forces. Some of their men had, in fact, been captured in the earlier fighting in Malaya and were now held in Kuala Lumpur's Pudu Jail. They were an experienced formation with a lot of fighting in Malaya behind them, including some of the bitterest struggles for the control of the peninsula. It was the Australian section of the defences of Singapore island that the Japanese had penetrated on 8 February, the 8th Division having been given a frontage vastly disproportionate to its numbers. It too, two brigades and supporting troops, was now captive.

Over in Java, the Dutch Governor General and his Commander-in-Chief General ter Poorten had surrendered their forces, numbering 25,000 plus a 40,000-strong Home Guard of doubtful quality, at 9.00 a.m. on 8 March. Their British and Australian allies on Java had perforce to follow suit; their food was short, medical facilities were limited and they could expect no help from the local population and received little from the Dutch. Further resistance could not alter the fate of Java which was already largely in Japanese hands. The core of the Commonwealth forces there were the two well-trained Australian battalions, veterans of the Middle East Syrian campaign and only recently arrived in Java with a squadron of British light armour of 3rd Hussars which had originally disembarked its light tanks on Sumatra but rapidly got them to sea again when it was realised that the Japanese had advanced quicker than expected; but there were many other troops in addition. Some were unable to fulfil their proper role, like the five anti-aircraft artillery regiments most of whose equipment had already been lost, a Texas National Guard artillery regiment defending an airfield from which the planes had already departed and a large number of unarmed RAF personnel whose precarious position with the already-surrendered Dutch was a further factor which decided the Allied Commanders, Air Marshal Maltby and General Stilwell, that they should surrender. Also now captive in Java were the survivors of the American cruiser *Houston* and the Australian cruiser *Perth* which had unexpectedly run into the large Japanese invasion convoy in Bantam Bay off the island's north west coast. Hopelessly outnumbered and outgunned, both ships fought heroically and to good effect, but were ultimately sunk. *Perth* lost half her complement, many trapped below in engine rooms and magazines, but 320 finally got ashore and became prisoners. *Houston* sank 20 minutes after *Perth* and over 600 of her crew went down with her but 368 survived to join their Australian comrades in captivity. Hundreds of survivors were picked up by a Japanese destroyer and were later handed over to army guards ashore. Others struggled to land themselves only to be captured by Javanese and passed on to the Japanese invaders.

Yet more of the Allied forces became prisoners on Sumatra. The small British garrison at Palembang and Oosthaven at Sumatra's southern tip had been evacuated to Java rather prematurely when the Japanese parachute troops were first put in. However, much further north escapees from the Singapore *débâcle* had made off by sea for the nearby east coast of Sumatra using whatever small craft they could find, some staging across the islands which lie scattered between Singapore and the mouth of Sumatra's Kempar and Inderagiri rivers. On Sumatra an escape organisation had been set up to ferry people across to the west coast port of Padang in the hope that from there they could make the 1,600 mile passage across the Indian Ocean to the safety of the British base at Colombo. Many did so, including women and children from the Padang base, others were torpedoed by Japanese submarines just when they thought their ordeal was over; still more could not find a boat, or else lost the race against the Japanese who were advancing steadily from the south. The Japanese finally reached Padang on 17 March and herded the would-be escapers into the Dutch barracks. The British prisoners there totalled some 1,200 and in addition to men from the erstwhile Malaya Command and the Singapore garrison forces there were even some survivors from *The Prince of Wales* and *Repulse* which had been sunk over three months earlier at the start of the Malayan campaign. Now captive with them were men from 18th Division who had been enjoying the hospitality of the citizens of Cape Town, half-way through their ocean odyssey, when they had first heard that disaster had struck *The Prince of Wales* and her sister ship. Ill-fortune and accidents of timing now made them all bedfellows in the grossly overcrowded though reasonably appointed Dutch barracks. Large numbers of Dutch troops were also captured at Padang and elsewhere in Sumatra and there were, in addition, Australians among those taken there. There were also numerous New Zealanders among the prisoners: civil servants, engineers, surveyors and miners who had joined the Federated Malay States Volunteer Force (FMSVF) as well as men who were serving with regular British regiments. About 50 of them were among the great concentration of men in Singapore. Others were among the captives at Padang. They were mainly naval personnel, survivors from ships sunk during the evacuation from Singapore, or else members of air squadrons whom the authorities had been unable to evacuate to Java before the Japanese invasion of Sumatra took place. Among this huge international force of captives were some who already knew their captors quite well from battlefield encounters, had seen their tactics in action and developed a grudging admiration for their fighting qualities. Others knew them scarcely at all, their information on the enemy being limited to the document they had been given on the voyage east, telling them how to differentiate Japanese, Chinese and Malays: the Japanese it appeared always walked with their toes turned in.

It was perhaps symptomatic of the Japanese surprise at finding themselves the masters of such a huge number of prisoners that they should have left them, in the very early stages of captivity, largely to their own devices, merely making rudimentary arrangements to feed them and prevent their escape. The prisoners themselves were no less disconcerted by their new status, or more accurately the absence of any status at all. No doubt each man among them experienced a confusing mixture of emotions and each reacted slightly differently to the circumstances in which he found himself; but there were nonetheless common threads of self-perception and emotion which stirred in the brain and breast of all who were now captive. One emotion perhaps was the almost instinctive sense of disgrace at being a prisoner, of being somehow dishonoured by the act of surrender: out of the fighting and away from the war when in other theatres and on other fronts their comrades were risking death and fighting on. It mattered little to the prisoners that technological advances in warfare had removed many of the reasons for this stigma; for just as the development of the fragmentation shell had long since erased the disgrace of the shot in the back, so the development of strategic and tactical mobility through the mechanisation of warfare had transformed the fact of capture from being something of a personal dishonour to an incidental consequence of the increasingly technological arms race between nations.

There was also the desire to find someone to blame for the distressing events; officers perhaps for their tactical errors, indifferent leadership or lack of aggressiveness; allies for their failure to cooperate or to hold out for longer; governments for their tardiness in reacting to the Japanese threat and in misreading its extent, its power and direction. Those captured in Java and Sumatra could have been excused from apportioning some of the blame to the native Indonesians themselves, for they were actively hostile to their erstwhile Dutch overlords and their allies, deeply imbued with nationalist sentiments and Japanese manufactured anti-colonial propaganda and were frequently active in capturing isolated groups of Allied troops. This was much less the case in Malaya and generally untrue of the attitude of the Chinese population both there and in the mainly Chinese-populated Singapore, where they often took great risks to help Allied POWs and had their own nationalist quarrels with the Japanese. But even more significant was the prisoners' humiliation at being so comprehensively defeated by an Asiatic race. Over the years the colonial powers had taught themselves to believe that they were invincible in the Far East and they had taught their subject races to believe it too. Each accepted without question that the unchallenged prestige of an omnipotent ruling race was the birthright of almost every white person. This illusion was now totally shattered and the debasement of the Allied prisoners was now completed by their being paraded by their captors in front of those who had shared the illusion and believed and trusted in the ability of their white masters to protect them. Attitudes were much more deeply racial in the 1940s than they are today and though the war against Japan was fought over political and economic issues, racial stereotypes and the belief among the Allies generally in the utter superiority of Western civilisation were an important factor in the conflict. Allied propaganda about the Axis powers in Europe presented the dictators Hitler, Mussolini and their henchmen as the main targets: in the case of Japan, however, it was the Japanese race as a whole which was identified as the enemy – hence the attitudes mentioned earlier of the USA and Canada to their *nisei* populations. Thus, when after some days of relative freedom, the various groups of POWs in Malaya, Singapore, Java and Sumatra began to be concentrated in fewer compounds, their journeys to these prison camps emphasised their humiliation. Carrying their few possessions and many with incomplete uniforms, they were marched to them by their Japanese captors, generally junior NCOs, before crowds of native Asians who previously had been their subject races and had seldom thought to question the Europeans' privileged position and right to rule. Harsh treatment by their Japanese captors in front of these erstwhile Asian subjects hurt the Allied prisoners in prestige terms much more than the physical abuse itself, the Australian General Thomas Blamey was later to aver.[3]

The Japanese themselves contributed to this sense of dishonour and debasement in several ways. One of their first acts after the surrender was to separate the Asian soldiers in the Allied armies from the Europeans. While the Allied POWs in Singapore were marched off to the various Changi barracks, the Indian officers and troops were housed separately at Nee Soon and at Farrer Park. There they were subjected to the exhortations of Captain Mohan Singh to join the Indian National Army. Of the 45,000 Indian captives some 5,000 stoutly refused to do so; for the rest, among them many raw recruits imperfectly trained and dispirited and bewildered by their new circumstances, many did break their oath of allegiance and change sides to become the guards of the camps in which their erstwhile comrades in the Allied armies were now imprisoned, and later, to serve against the British in Burma. In guarding the six areas of the Changi compound some of them behaved with particular harshness to those held there. The Japanese also propagandised their 'Asia for the Asians' policy widely among the other captured Asian troops and did all they could to remove the trappings of European rule; bonfires were made of English language books and documents and traditional British observances were replaced with Japanese ones, particularly ceremonies of reverence to the Emperor in which prisoners and citizens alike had to take part. General Yamashita, the 'Tiger of Malaya', was once moved to tears when Chinese children in Singapore sang the Imperial national anthem on the Emperor's birthday. 'Just like Japanese children aren't they', he remarked to a colleague.[4] At the POWs' daily *tenko* parades counting in Japanese became *de rigeur*.

In the war in Europe the English-speaking Allied soldier's humiliation at surrender and imprisonment was mitigated to some extent by the fact that POWs were usually treated with a certain amount of respect. It was generally accepted, outside Soviet military police circles, that becoming a prisoner was a misfortune that might befall anyone. By and large prisoners were treated in accordance with the terms of the Geneva Prisoner of War Convention. In the war against Japan the situation was entirely different. Japan had indeed signed the Convention (and military officers were among her delegation's signatories) and though she never formally ratified it, the official policy of the Imperial government was that the Convention's terms would be respected. However the reality of the situation had little to do with international treaties and conventions. What determined the Japanese military attitudes to their POWs more profoundly than anything else was General Tojo's injunction which heads this chapter and the military belief system which lay behind it. The Japanese solider had been taught that the greatest honour he could aspire to was to die in battle fighting for his Emperor. Nor was this some abstract principle more honoured in the breach than the observance; for the Japanese Army fighting to the last man and the last round meant precisely that, when the tactical situation demanded it. The converse, not fighting to the death despite circumstances which required it, was vigorously condemned. As early as 1908 the Army Criminal Code had declared, 'A commander who allows his unit to surrender to the enemy without fighting to the last man ... shall be punishable by death.[5] Surrender was the ultimate disgrace for the

Japanese men-at-arms. Even if they should fall into enemy hands as a result of being wounded and unconscious they were enjoined to 'quickly commit suicide' the moment consciousness was regained.[6] For the Japanese every battle was to be a Masada – death would be preferred to defeat. It was not surprising, therefore, that the soldiers of Japan should have been conditioned to regard their prisoners with contempt as dishonoured men who had forfeited the right to live. As Japanese railway engineer Futamatsu Yoshihiko, not himself a soldier, explained it, all military men believed that to become a prisoner was 'a most shameful thing' and that to become one voluntarily was 'to put oneself beyond the pale'. Japanese soldiers therefore had 'nothing but contempt for men whose disgraceful cowardice obeyed an order to become captive and still live'.[7] With such attitudes prevailing it is perhaps not surprising that the Japanese should have completed the humiliation of their prisoners by requiring certain of their camp administrative staff to wear armbands bearing the Japanese inscription 'One who has been captured in battle and is to be beheaded or castrated at the will of the Emperor', that all rank badges should have been removed and replaced by a single star worn on the left breast by all officers irrespective of rank, or that they should have insisted that all prisoners of whatever rank salute all Japanese soliders however junior. So although the Allied POWs were, in a sense, 'out of the war', they were in reality fighting another war within the formal struggle. This infinitely sterner conflict was not limited to hours or days of heady action, but was to be a continuous battle for survival against a régime which set no great store by its prisoners' continued existence and in a physical environment which presented many threats to it. Furthermore it was to be a struggle for mental stability, wholeness of spirit and human dignity in circum-stances in which these qualitites were to be under daily siege from the war within the war.

From the Japanese military viewpoint the use of the prisoners as a labour force provided a rationale, a productive purpose, for their continued existence; it also conveniently emphasised the superiority of the Japanese race by having working for them a labour force of Europeans (*White Coolies* was the title used by one ex-POW for an account of his experiences), which was no doubt a particularly satisfy-ing arrangement after all the political and diplomatic slights which the Japanese had suffered at the hands of the Europeans since their country's forcible 'opening up' in 1854. This racial dimension of the struggle had been emphasised in a pamphlet issued to Japanese officers and soldiers immediately after embarkation for the Southern Regions. It had spoken of the Westerners having treated the Japanese 'as an inferior race' and enjoined the troops that they 'must at the very least, here in Asia, beat these Westerners into submission, that they may change their arrogant and ill-mannered attitude'.[8] Most important of all, however, were the imperious demands of the war itself.

Logistics may not be the most exciting aspect of military operations but the Japanese strategists were beginning to realise their significance. It was now patently clear that the integration of the landward communications of the new Empire was to be as critical to Japan's final success, as were the spiritual qualities – as the Japanese viewed them – of their fighting men. Throughout South East Asia prisoners were soon to be labouring on road, railway and airfield projects: repairing and developing the chain of airfields in the Tenasserim Peninsula, constructing the Pekan Baru to Palembang railway on Sumatra, building a new airfield at Changi in Singapore, developing a new road from Thailand to Burma or, as 60,000 prisoners finally were, building its big brother the Burma–Thailand railway, the largest and most formidable engineering project that the Japanese were to undertake throughout their newly-won Empire. It was fortunate that the prisoners were available in such large numbers for manual labourers were already scarce in metropolitan Japan, while at the farthest reaches of the Empire not only was Japanese manpower for logistical projects in short supply, the products of modern technology which lightened human toil in all industrial societies were at a premium there as well. It rapidly became clear that the new railway would have to be built by labour intensive methods rather than modern technological techniques.

However, their military prisoners were not the only potential labour force available to the Japanese. Burma was now under occupation and although its leaders were Burmese nationalists looking for complete independence now the British had been ousted, they were very much under Japanese control, required to participate fully in the anti-colonial war effort before the luxury of full political sovereignty could be accorded them. U Hla Pe, Director of Press and Publicity during the Japanese occupation, later spoke of his fellow nationalist political leaders as being merely an 'executive commission' for the Japanese military government in Burma.[9] The provision of labour forces, in particular for Japanese communication projects, was one of the major demands to be made of the Burmese leadership. Equally important for the viability of the railway project

was the state of the Burmese economy in 1942. Nearly all essential
labour in Burma prior to the Japanese occupation was Indian, the
Burman himself having exhibited little enthusiasm for industrial
manual labour. As we have seen, much of this Indian labour force
(perhaps half or more) had disappeared to India, or died on the way,
at the time of the original invasion. The Japanese rapidly set about
employing the remainder, offering them the inducement of free railway passes to their workplaces. Indians caught near the frontier were
stopped from crossing over and paid in cash and in rice to induce them
to stay in Burma and work. But logistical projects as labour intensive
as those which the Japanese were planning required the recruitment
of a much more substantial labour force than the despairing and
desperate Indian community could provide.

Two factors combined to give the railway planners at least short
term help in furnishing it. The first was the perilous state of Burma's
rice economy, the second the persuasive skills of the 'deeply
dedicated' Japanese Colonel Sasaki, as Dr Ba Maw, the head of the
Burmese Administration later described him. By 1941 Burma had
become comprehensively integrated into the world economy; lower
Burma, Tenasserim and the Arakan formed a huge single-crop area
producing about 40 per cent of the rice entering world trade. India was
Burma's chief rice buyer and together with Britain, the rest of Europe
and Ceylon it took 85–90 per cent of Burma's overall export trade,
leaving only the small remainder for the countries of South and East
Asia with which Japan was now trying desparately to integrate the
Burmese economy. The trade dislocation which Burma suffered when
the Japanese occupied the country was therefore greater than in any
other part of the Co-Prosperity Sphere. The rice growers were left with
a huge unexportable surplus on their hands, the price fell disastrously, future sowings were much reduced and many agricultural
labourers migrated to the towns in search of work. This was fortunate
for the Japanese whose demands for labour were considerable in this
most disrupted and distant of all their overseas possessions. They
enlisted the Burmese into *Heiho Tat*, a Labour Corps which was
actually part of the Japanese Army and provided coolies, pioneers
and occasionally transport drivers. Similar to it was the *Hle Tat* or
Cart Corps for which each village had to supply carts on demand for
use as Army transport.[10]

Besides these there were the efforts of Colonel Sasakai, the officer
appointed to recruit local labour for the projected Burmese–
Thailand railway and who had the task of gaining Burmese support

for it. He explained to Ba Maw that the railway was to be part of a wider communications project designed to bring the region's countries closer together in collaborative commercial harmony. His words, Ba Maw recalled, 'gave me a glimpse of the Asian future we were fighting for'.[11] The railway would also wipe out the 'deep historical wrong' according to which the European colonial powers had kept Burma and Thailand separated in order to preserve imperial spheres of influence. Ba Maw was 'immediately captured' by Sasaki's scheme which had the additional virtue, he noted almost as an afterthought, of providing wartime necessities quickly and safely. 'All the members of the government were won over' by Sasaki's vision, he noted, and the terms of the first recruitment of 30,000 labourers for the railway project were quickly negotiated and confirmed. The workers were to be paid by the Japanese and advances of pay were agreeed; they were to receive a travelling allowance and food; accommodation and health care were to be arranged by the Japanese railway administration. Ba Maw noted that provision was also to be made for the families of the labourers to join them after an interval and that Colonel Sasaki willingly accepted these conditions.

A strong labour bureau was set up and the Burmese government's own political organisation took an active part in the drive for labourers. The greatest publicity was given to the recruitment campaign, some of it the Director of Press and Publicity admitted, painting 'the rosiest of wage terms and tempting pictures of commodities coming in by way of Thailand' in all the newspapers.[12] In addition ministers toured the populous southern districts of Burma 'to whip up recruitment'. Everything proceeded, according to Ba Maw, in 'complete harmony and understanding'. Not surprisingly the first 30,000 quota was filled in rapid time*, the government being pleased that it was able to show the Japanese that it could work efficiently and keep its promises. The only disquieting feature at this early stage in the recruitment process was the discovery by some of the Burmese officials that the Japanese had already begun recruiting directly in the Moulmein and Thaton Districts before the discussions with the government had been completed. If the Burmese ministers ever heard of this cavalier behaviour it appears not to have destroyed their confidence in Colonel Sasaki, whom the Deputy Prime Minister later described at a banquet to celebrate the success of the first phase of the

---

* This was U Hla Pe's judgment. Actually only 26,000 appear to have arrived at their place of work.

railway project as 'a great, good and generous man' who was breaking down an age-old barrier between Asian peoples. In Ba Maw's subsequent totalitarian organisation of Burmese society in accordance with a Four Army Plan for the fight alongside the Japanese ally to achieve full independence for Burma, the railway labour force, much expanded from these early beginnings, became known as *Let Yon Tat* or 'The Sweat Army'.

With Thailand, the other state over whose territory the railway would be built, the planners of the new line had to proceed with a little more respect for the diplomatic niceties. Although the country had been attacked and practically occupied by Japanese forces, it still remained technically independent throughout the war. In the negotiations following the Japanese invasion, the Thais accepted only the fourth, the least obligating, of the defence pact options which the invading authorities offered to them. This did not include Japanese help for the return of the provinces lost earlier in the century as part of the colonial dispensation; but it also placed least obligation on the Thai government itself.[13] Indeed part of the reason for the delay in starting the railway project at the Thai end was the opposition of local Siamese landowners who had to give up property to make way for the new line. Negotiations were necessary and a series of conferences was held in Bangkok between Thai government representatives, Thai National Railways and the Japanese authorities in the person of Major General Shimoda, in charge of 2nd Railway Control of the Japanese Southern Army. An agreement was finally reached according to which Thailand provided the land for the Japanese right of way and also agreed to undertake some of the work at the south (and much easier) end of the projected line. The Thais were to help with the railway roadbed construction between Ban Pong and Kanchanaburi, where the line was to run parallel with a motor road already in existence, and for the continuation of the motor road from Kanchanaburi to Wanyai which lay some 120 kilometres to the north west of the line's projected start point.[14] With Thailand bearing some of the cost and supplying a portion of the labour and materials, it appeared that the Japanese construction task would be eased considerably.

As early as April 1942, over a month before the Japanese 15th Army in Burma made its final attempt to cut off the withdrawing British forces at Shwegyin in Upper Burma, the occupying armies in Java, Sumatra and Singapore were beginning to marshal their military prisoners northwards for participation in numerous construction and labouring assignments including the monumental railway engineering project of which the POWs were as yet quite unaware. On 4 April 1942 1,125 British POWs from Changi under command of Lieutenant Colonel Hugonin RA were shipped off to Saigon in French Indo-China for labouring duties. A year later when the pressure to get the railroad finished began to mount, over half of this Saigon force would be switched to Thailand to lend extra muscle to the enterprise. The next party to move north was 'A' Force composed of 3,000 Australians under Brigadier Varley, the 49-year-old First World War veteran who had been promoted to command the Australian 22 Brigade at the height of the battle for Singapore. This group was sent from Singapore to southern Burma by sea in two 'small, very dirty steamers', *Celebes Maru* and *Tohohasi Maru*, which began their voyage on 14 May. This was the first of the 'hell ship' journeys which thousands more prisoners were to experience before the full railway labour force was assembled. A Force was to work initially on the airfields of the Tenasserim peninsula at Victoria Point, Mergui and Tavoy before moving to the site of the railway later in the year. Also on the move northwards were many of the prisoners from Padang in Sumatra. On 9 May a force of British POWs (480 soldiers and 18 officers) later known as the British Sumatra Battalion together with two Australian officers and a party of Dutch prisoners about 1,200 strong began their northward journey. They moved by rail and road across the island, past the beautiful Dutch hill resort at lake Toba and down to the little northern port of Belawan Dewi which faced Malaya across the Straits of Malacca. The Sumatra POWs began their voyage on 15 May in a small sloop and two other ships (the British troops travelling ironically in the *England Maru*) joining up with 'A' Force from Singapore and some Japanese troops to form a convoy for the journey up to Burma and similar airfield and construction work before their railway task began. Some of the Dutch and Australian prisoners were landed at Victoria Point but the British and a second Australian battalion sailed on to Mergui for the start of their period as white coolies, while the final group were disembarked with the commander Brigadier Varley at Tavoy at the end of a miserably crowded twelve-day voyage which, as the Brigadier's diary recorded 'will always remain vivid in the minds of all'. Similar experiences were to be etched on the memories of thousands who followed them north to Burma and Thailand.

4

Planning the Impossible

*To use prisoners of war and with their cooperation to complete the task
constituted a unique phenomenon in world railway construction.*
Futamatsu Yoshihiko railway *gunzoku*.

THERE WERE two possible routes which the projected railway could
follow; both traversing ancient but minor and little-used trade
routes. The first ran westwards from Phitsanulok on the existing Thai
railway system, crossing the river Ping at Raheng before rising on to
join the Burmese national railways at Moulmein. A project following this route had been mooted by British engineers as early as 1885,
but it had remained on the drawing board on account of its doubtful
economic viability and the extreme engineering difficulties it would
encounter as it drove head-on across the mountains of the Dawna and
Tanen ranges. The alternative route, of similar length but more
southerly, left the Thai National Railways system near the regional
centre of Kanchanaburi and travelled north west, following river
valleys in the main and crossing the border at the Three Pagodas Pass
before joining the Burma railways at Thanbyuzayat on the line running from Moulmein south to Ye.

This second route had been considered at various times by British,
Japanese and German railway experts and had come under particular
consideration when the Burmese coastal line from Moulmein to Ye
was completed in 1925. Surveys from the Burmese side had considered
possible extensions of the new coastal line up to the Three Pagodas
Pass. Although this southern route would have been about the same
length as the northern Raheng–Moulmein option it appears to have
been favoured by the Japanese because of its somewhat easier topography, the proposed trace running in general with the grain of the
mountains rather than across it. Besides this, it offered a more direct

route from Bangkok and Singapore to Rangoon, using less of the existing Thai railway system and thereby avoiding congestion due to additional military traffic. However, the greatest attraction of the southern route lay in the fact that for about 60 per cent of the way it followed the valleys of the river Maekhlaung, and later its tributary the Kwae Noi which was navigable, as was noted earlier, for a considerable distance.[1] This was a most important factor because in a practically roadless country as much of Thailand was in 1942, as we have noted, rivers were the main means of communication. Furthermore at the junction of the two rivers stood the district town of Kanchanaburi, a major centre for the agriculturally productive lowlands which surrounded it, and a potential supply base for the railway operation. Kanchanaburi was only 50 kilometres north of Nong Pladuk, the town on the Singapore–Bangkok railway from which the new line was to start. A motor road already linked the two towns. The engineering and logistical advantages of the southern route therefore seemed compelling.

Although the formal orders for the construction of the railway were not issued until June 1942, it seems that the railway organisation of Southern Army had already set about the project long before that. Such unauthorised action was not, as we have seen, untypical of the Japanese operational armies; nor was it in this case simply an unplanned reaction to difficult logistical circumstances. The southern railway route to Burma had been the subject of an IGHQ feasibility study as early as 1939, undertaken by a Mr K. Kuwabare of Japan National Railways,[2] and it had been under discussion since the war began. It was this riverine route which Tokyo finally authorised on 20 June. However five months earlier, in January, No. 2 Railway Control of Southern Army had decided to investigate the route and its commander, Major General Fukube, had resolved to make a survey on the ground and begin the preparations for construction. He apparently took this independent initiative because of the 'negative attitude' of Southern Army's main headquarters.[3] It was perhaps a good thing that he did, for the survey, undertaken by a railway staff officer and an attached civilian expert named Shijima, concluded that the project was likely to take two years to complete; a long time in a war which Japan needed to win quickly. There was clearly a need to get things moving. In March a start was made in collecting the necessary materials and the orders went out for the railway construction units to start their preparations. These units were 5th and 9th Railway Regiments and 1st Railway Materials Workshop. The rough plan to which the controlling railway HQ worked was to gather the necessary stores, equipment and labour forces and to do the preliminary planning and survey work during the monsoon season of 1942, so that the actual railway building could begin as the rains lessened towards the end of the year.

Japanese railway regiments were normally 100 per cent military and capable of undertaking the construction and operation of railways under all field service conditions and as far forward as the tactical situation would permit. Civilian specialists known as *gunzoku* could be attached as required to deal with particular technical projects. In peacetime there were two railway regiments in Japan based at Chiba and Tusdanoumea, both near Tokyo, where they acted as the training units. Each took in 600 recruits a year and gave them a full two-year training. Officer cadets generally entered after they had completed their college education and did a year in the ranks followed by six months' officer training and six months of practical leadership training. However the academic requirements were scaled down as the war situation became more urgent. The regiments were less technically equipped than the conventional British railway regiment, but were allocated in Japan, prior to their departure overseas, survey instruments, winches, tackle for bridge building and a range of track tools. An additional interesting item on their establishment was four diesel lorries capable of being converted to operate on metre or standard gauge rails and 16 flat wagons. These proved very valuable in Burma and Thailand. At full war establishment a Japanese railway regiment had 83 officers, 271 non-commissioned officers and 2,196 soldiers covering the range of necessary trades.[4]

The two regiments allocated to the new project had not exactly been inactive in the month since they received the call to arms. 5th Railway Regiment had been raised in early 1938 and after training it had been sent to northern China where it operated various railway lines at Tientsin, Hankow and finally Kowloon. It had also actually built a light railway in China before it was moved to Saigon in French Indo-China in October 1941, to prepare the railways there for the movement of the large numbers of troops and supplies required for the Malayan and Burma campaigns. In December it had moved to Bangkok and then followed General Yamashita's victorious army down to Malaya where it repaired and re-opened the Taiping–Singapore line as the battle for the island progressed. After the conquest of lower Burma it moved north to take over from Burma National Railways the operation of the Rangoon–Mandalay line.

Then came the message that the priority was to be the construction of the new rail link with Thailand. 5th Railway Regiment was given responsibility for the building of the Burma side of the line, and in June 1942 the Kamitani Detachment of its 3rd Battalion began the survey of the section which the regiment was to construct, the 135-kilometre stretch from the northern terminus at Thanbyuzayat down to the junction point with its sister regiment's section at Nikhe in north western Thailand. Repairs were made to the track of the Moulmein–Ye line and a road was started for the transport of supplies beyond the railhead. As the monsoon abated the remainder of the regiment joined the advance party at Thanbyuzayat.

9th Railway Regiment had been founded rather later, in 1940. October 1941 found it at Haiphong in French Indo China and after the start of the offensive into Malaya it too moved south behind the advancing armies, the original intention apparently being that, like its sister regiment, it should re-open and operate part of the Malayan railway system, in its case the east coast line. This branched off the main line which ran up from Singapore at the junction town of Gemas and then ran directly north to the frontier with Thailand just south west of the east coast port of Kota Bharu, where the Japanese had made their early landings. Since there was no east coast highway the British authorities had expected a major Japanese advance along the east coast railway line and had consequently destroyed all the major and some of the minor bridges along it. This action certainly helped to prevent any substantial advance along the eastern flank, but it also presented 9th Railway Regiment with a colossal repair undertaking. It was not long before the decision was taken to abandon the line altogether and use its rails, steel bridging and other materials for the 'Thai Burma Rail Link' as the Japanese officially called it.[5] This may appear a drastic decision, but from the viewpoint of the Japanese military planners it was perfectly sound in the short term. The Malayan west coast line was well developed; it served the more populous side of the country and was quite adequate for the requirements of the Japanese military authorities.

Accordingly the main body of 9th Railway Regiment quit Malaya and was moved up to northern Burma in April 1942 where it set about repairing and operating the line north of Mandalay which the British had done their best to put out of action on their withdrawal to India. However one of its battalions was diverted to Sumatra to restore the railway system there which had also suffered damage during the campaign. It was this battalion which became the regiment's advance

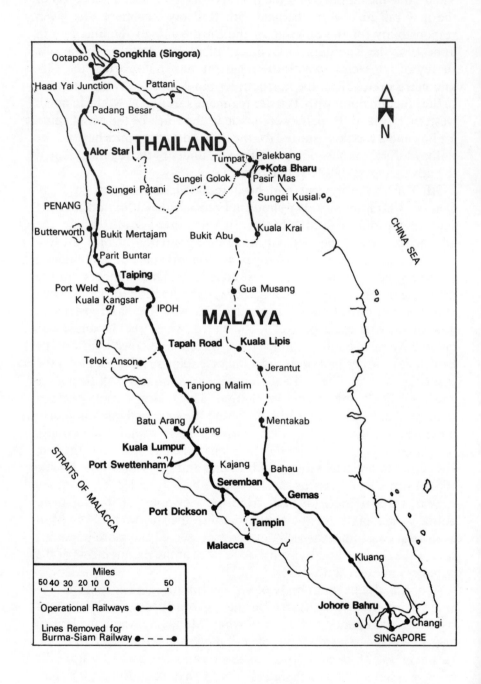

2. Malayan Railways 1942

1. Hut building at Chungkai Camp (*Stanley Gimson*)

2. Building the roadbed (*Jack Chalker*)

3. A Dysentery Ward (*John Mennie*)

4. Chungkai Medical Centre (*Stanley Gimson*)

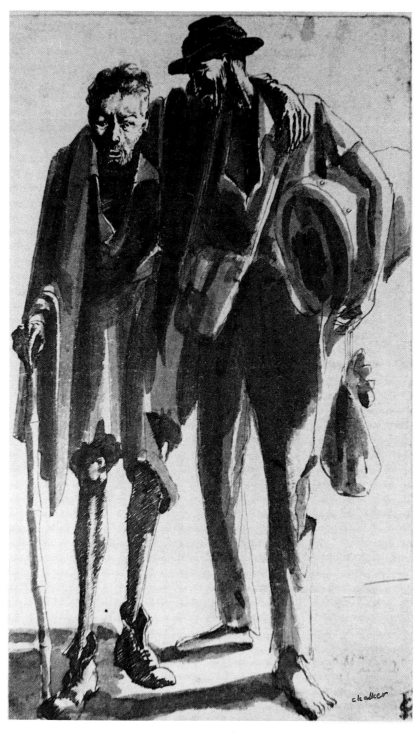

5. 'Working Men' – Prisoners on the Move (*Jack Chalker*)

6. Building the Wampo Viaduct (*William Wilder*)

7. Interior of a flooded hut (*Philip Meninsky*)

8.   Cholera 1943 (*Ronald Searle*)

party in Thailand, sent to carry out the first preparations for the construction work. By May elements were already at Nong Pladuk and in the following weeks the other battalions began to arrive. No. 2 Railway Control set up its HQ in the Bansoe switchyard north of Bangkok, its office walls papered with ten metres of aerial photos giving a complete stereoscopic picture of the proposed railway's trace on a scale of 1:20,000. On 5 June the expert survey unit erected the 0.0 kilometre post at Nong Pladuk station with some ceremony and the battalions of 5 Railway Regiment moved off to set about the survey proper. The formal orders from Tokyo authorising all this activity decreed that the railway was to be completed by the end of 1943, was to carry a daily load of 3,000 tons in each direction and was to be built from materials available in the local area, with any additional needs being supplied from Japan. A sum of 100 million yen was allocated to the project. IGHQ was itself to conduct the inter-ministerial and diplomatic negotiations and Tokyo also took the formal decision, already anticipated by the actions of Southern Army, to employ POWs on the enterprise.[6]

The Japanese railway construction force which was now assembling at both ends of the proposed line was of considerable size. In addition to the two railway regiments, each of four battalions and totalling roughly 5,000 men, there was the Material Workshop of about 1,000 men with its main strength at Nong Pladuk and the remainder at the Burma terminus, Thanbyuzayat. The Nong Pladuk workshop was reputed to be the best-equipped in South East Asia. There were also special bridging units, a signals unit, a labour unit and, of course, a number of attached civilian specialist engineers. Supporting them were medical hygiene units, a water supply unit, a field hospital and a commissariat. The total Japanese involvement in the enterprise amounted to about 13,000 men. Many of the officers in the railway regiments were specialist railway or construction engineers and, together with the civilian engineers serving with them, they certainly had the expertise and the experience to undertake the project. Although Japan's first railway, an 18-mile line between Tokyo and Yokohama, had only been built in 1872 and even then under the guidance of foreign experts, Japan had made rapid strides to technological independence soon thereafter. In 1877 there had been 120 British engineers, drivers, foremen and the like employed by the Railway Administration, but by 1880 only three foreign advisers remained. By 1910 the Japanese were capable of building and operating their own railways, constructing their own engines, carriages and waggons and even manufacturing their own steel rails.[7] By this time the original 18-mile line had become a domestic network of 5,140 miles of track. Many Japanese engineers trained originally at British universities and some went on to gain reputations far beyond the shores of the home islands. One such, Kaichi Watanabe, contributed to the construction of the Glasgow underground, canal and harbour works before returning to Japan where he worked for the Japanese National Railways Bureau designing railways throughout the country. He has even been credited with a role in the design of the old Forth Bridge, the engineering marvel of its time.[8] With such luminaries as Watanabe, Japanese engineers could scarcely be called inexpert, and with the mountainous terrain of the islands to contend with, it is not surprising that they became expert in tunnelling as well as bridging. Many officers in the railway regiments as well as the *gunzoku* working with them were engineering graduates, with civilian experience in building and operating railways in Japan and Korea or in other parts of the original Japanese empire before their mobilisation and transfer to repair and construction work behind the field armies of the Pacific War. Consequently the river Kwai railway was not to be a test of the technical competence of the Japanese engineers but rather of their ability to build quickly, to build without the machines and equipment which would normally have been associated with an enterprise of this kind and, crucially, to build in uniquely inhospitable and uncompromising circumstances. The *canard* of Pierre Boule's *Bridge on the River Kwai*, given global currency in David Lean's film, that the Japanese lacked the technical competence for bridge building has little basis in fact and is resented by the Japanese much more than many other criticisms of the railway episode.

When engineer Futamatsu had his first sight of the photograhic survey in the Railway Control Office he immediately felt uneasy, wondering how the work teams were going to get into the 'impenetrable jungle belt . . . and how it was possible to survive in it'.[9] It was indeed a daunting prospect. The route along the River Kwai may have been the easier of the two possible approaches to the railway enterprise; but the building of it was nevertheless bound to encounter the most formidable obstacles. The first 50 kilometres from Nong Pladuk to Kanchanaburi presented few major challenges – the land was flat, the communications were good, the area was populous and supplies of food and construction materials were plentiful and near at hand. However, beyond Kanchanaburi the difficulties began. Having run alongside the river Maekhlaung hitherto, the railway would have

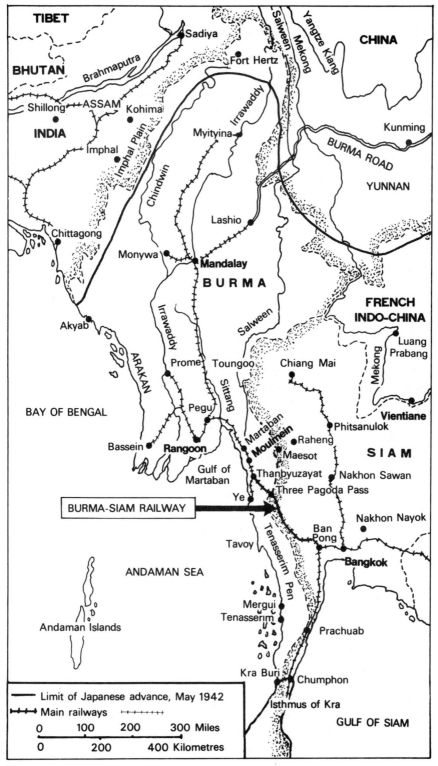

Map labels:

TIBET

BHUTAN

Sadiya

Fort Hertz

CHINA

Brahmaputra

Shillong ASSAM Kohima

Myityina

Irrawaddy

Salween

Yangtze Kiang

Mekong

INDIA

Imphal

Imphal Plain

Kunming

BURMA ROAD

YUNNAN

Chindwin

Lashio

Chittagong

Monywa

Mandalay

BURMA

Akyab

Irrawaddy

ARAKAN

Prome Toungoo

Salween

Chiang Mai

FRENCH
INDO-CHINA

Luang
Prabang

Mekong

Pegu

Sittang

Phitsanulok

Vientiane

BAY OF BENGAL

Bassein Rangoon

Gulf of
Martaban

Martaban

Moulmein

Raheng

Maesot

SIAM

Thanbyuzayat

Nakhon Sawan

Three Pagoda Pass

Ye

BURMA-SIAM RAILWAY

Nakhon Nayok

Tenasserim Pen

Ban
Pong

Tavoy

Bangkok

ANDAMAN SEA

Mergui

Tenasserim

Prachuab

Andaman Islands

Kra Buri

Chumphon

Limit of Japanese advance, May 1942

Main railways

Isthmus of Kra

GULF OF SIAM

0   100   200   300 Miles

0   200   400 Kilometres

3. The Branch Line to Burma

to cross that river at some point so that the valley of its tributary, the Kwai, could be followed. The bridging of the Maekhlaung would in itself be a major undertaking. The river swelled massively during the monsoon and neither the steel bridging nor the equipment for constructing the bridge piers was available locally. From this point on, the route became progressively more difficult as the Kwai, flowing initially south east across the north–south mountain-ridge, cut for itself a narrow valley through the hills with sides which were ravine-like in one particular stretch. The Japanese engineers planned to carry their railway round the edge of this ravine, carving cuttings through the rock in some places and building viaducts into the cliff face in others. The trace was to rise steadily in height as it pushed north, meeting countless smaller ridges which ran at right angles to the river valley, and crossing innumerable gullies which carried fast-flowing streams and small rivers into the main flow. Across all of this a route would have to be gouged out, or bridges erected, to allow the railway track to pass. Beyond Kui Ye, about 190 kilometres from the southern start point, a higher level of plateau was reached and the landscape changed from almost uninterrupted jungle in which bamboo of all kinds predominated, to more open country where thorn scrub and stunted trees were more common. This form of vegetation was to continue until the crest of the route was reached at the Three Pagodas Pass which marked the Thai–Burma border. The pass was a low saddle about 903 feet above sea level and from this feature the line was to descend via the valleys of the Zami and Mezali rivers, across the Sedaung Taung hills and numerous river obstacles down to the coastal plain and Thanbyuzayat at its western edge. As the trace moved down into Burma, so the vegetation thickened again and the problems of cutting the way through jungle reappeared.

To the difficulties of topography and vegetation was added the immense complication of the monsoon. The more cynical of the humourists of the British 14th Army in Burma used to say that Admiral Mountbatten had been made Supreme Commander in South East Asia because his naval training made him better able to fight a war in monsoon conditions. The rains certainly dictated the whole pattern of life in the entire Burma–Thailand coastal belt. So far as the railway area itself was concerned, the monsoon was not equally intense in all parts of the route proposed. However, in general terms and over most of the region, the dry season lasted from November until March and in the latter part of this period the weather became unbearably hot. The rains began in April and rose to their heaviest, in the southern part of the railway area at least, in September and October. In those two months, in Kanchanaburi for example, the already soaked landscape receives about 112 inches of rain out of a total of 280 for the full year, but in the following three months scarcely any at all. However further north in the Nikhe area which is nearer the coast and less protected by the mountains from the full force of the south west monsoon, the contrast was much more dramatic. The annual rainfall here was 620 inches, and while the four months from November to February were practically dry, from April to August 490 inches of water poured onto the countryside, 127 inches in August alone.[10] The effect on the area in which the railway was to be built was dramatic: the existing rivers became hugely distended and where they have flowed between steep banks rises in water level of four or five metres in a single day were not uncommon; dried-up watercourses were turned into raging torrents, dirt tracks became a morass of mud and silt and low-lying areas were under water for months on end. In such conditions the only satisfactory communications were along the rivers themselves; where roads existed they were often washed away. Railways would have to be well-engineered and maintained if they were to survive the monsoon onslaughts in such difficult terrain; so would human beings.

Because the conditions were so difficult, the valleys of the upper Kwai and the Zami and Mezali rivers in Burma were, in 1942, virtually uninhabited. On the navigable lower Kwai traders plied up and down the river regularly, but further north as the conditions grew more difficult and river navigation more hazardous travellers seldom ventured. There were a few cultivated settlements worked by Thai squatters who would till a riverside patch of land for a couple of seasons before moving on. This was basic subsistence agriculture with no surplus to meet the needs of the huge labour force which was soon to occupy the countryside alongside the few peripatetic natives. What is more, this pattern of shifting cultivation led to the development of secondary jungle along the river fringes which was to prove particularly difficult for the railway labour force to penetrate. To complete the picture of local conditions which engineer Futamatsu found so forbidding when he first studied the aerial photographs in the Bansoe office, malaria was endemic in the whole region and the waters of the local rivers provided an ideal medium for the spread of cholera.

The local area did furnish one resource in great abundance – timber. Wood of all kinds from the smallest, thinnest bamboo to the huge hardwoods of the jungle were available in great quantity and could serve every conceivable purpose in railway construction and operation from providing sleepers for the rails to fuel for the engines. The workers' camps were generally built entirely of bamboo and atap and many of the shorter and even some of the larger bridges were to be constructed almost wholly of timber. Stretches of the trackside road were to be 'corduroyed' with logs to make them passable in the monsoon season; bamboo rafts would transport stores up-river and elephants would manoeuvre logs which were floated down the Kwai from up-country for projects in its lower reaches. The ubiquitous bamboo would be put to a thousand uses; it served few purposes in the construction of the railway itself but was able to make life bearable in the camps by being transformed into a score of different utensils and providing the only material for making furniture and beds that the workers were to see throughout their captivity.

Not everything needed for the enterprise was as readily available or as easily accessible as was timber. Nor, since Thailand was still not formally under Japanese occupation, was it possible to requisition the more specialised equipment needed for the railroad, though some Thai diesel engines were later used for journeys up to Thanbyuzayat. The Japanese intended to transport much of the necessary railway material up from Malaya, as was noted earlier. A 200-mile stretch of running line was ripped up from the east coast railway between Mentakab and Kuala Krai, together with several shorter lines linking the less important west coast ports of Malacca, Telok Anson and Port Weld with the external west coast line which ran from Singapore to Kuala Lampur and ultimately Bangkok and which the Japanese did their best to keep serviceable throughout the war. In all, Malaya lost 276 miles of running line and 57 miles of second line, including sidings, most of it going to the Burma–Thailand Railway, but some to the Kra Isthmus line which it was planned to construct between Kra Buri and Chumphon. The Malayan Railways also contributed 30 locomotives, a third of its pre-war stock, and about a half of its inventory of 5,600 waggons, together with a large number of passenger coaches, to the railway projects in the north. This led to a grave shortage in Malaya which the Japanese alleviated by transferring locomotives and rolling stock from Java, in a 'robbing Peter to pay Paul' manoeuvre which was typical of the hand-to-mouth extemporisation to which her logisticians were frequently reduced.[11] In this particular case the transfer led to many operating difficulties since the Javanese rolling stock was in poor condition and had buffers six inches higher than the local type. But even these substantial requisitions proved insufficient for the planners of the new line; more rails were taken from Java and, to provide lines for the Burmese end of the operation, the Japanese pulled up a 170-mile stretch of the double track between Rangoon and Toungoo and used it for the northern section running down from Thanbyuzayat.[12]

Railway fittings were similarly requisitioned from the neighbouring occupied countries; many of the minor bridge spans in east Malaya were dismantled and stacked at wayside stations in north Kedah and southern Thailand in readiness for use. A great deal of the workshop equipment also came from Malaya, extracted from the maintenance depots and workshops of the tin mines with which the country abounded; the rest being from the railway workshops of Kuala Lumpur, Java, Sumatra and, a very small percentage, from Japan itself. Japanese engineers who were interrogated after the war claimed that about 50 per cent of the rails used on the new line had to be imported from Japan. Given the track length required and the quantities requisitioned locally this seems unlikely. Certainly the Malayan Railways could not have withstood the loss of much more of its permanent way and rolling stock and still remained viable. However, quite a lot of the bridging equipment for the new strategic railroad had to be imported from Japan though Sumatra supplied some. For heavy construction equipment and excavating machinery the engineers of the railway regiments were left to their own devices. There was very little available in the local area and so they replaced it with the commodity which they had in almost limitless supply – manpower. In June 1942 the second major group of prisoners was sent north, this time to work straight away on preparing for the railway operation itself.

In many POW compounds which occupied much of the Changi area in the north east of Singapore, rumour had been rife of further possible moves ever since the first party had been transferred to Saigon in early April 1942 and Brigadier Varley's much larger working party had sailed off to lower Burma over a month later. The outside working parties with their wider range of contacts were the usual source of such 'news' and in May they were reporting that a major move north was in the offing. In June the rumour became reality and the British High Command, which still had considerable responsibility for the adminstration and management of the POWs, delegated by the Japanese, (whom those who remained inside the compounds seldom actually saw) received orders to provide these large 'up-country' parties. 'Up-country' was often as precise as the British adminstration could be; all they apparently knew was that the parties were going to Singapore station and could take with them whatever they could carry.[13] A 600-strong party left Changi on 18 June for Singapore city and it was followed by four other groups of similar size travelling at two-day intervals. The groups were mixed since no complete units fitted precisely the movement programme of the Japanese in these early moves. There were regiments drawn from the 3rd Indian Corps, from 18 Division and from the Singapore Fortress garrison, including substantial numbers of medical personnel, some from the Federated Malay States Volunteer Force, local Europeans whose knowledge of the country, the languages and the possibilities and limitations of the rice-based diet which they were all to exist on, proved of great value to the British prisoners who were woefully ignorant in these matters. Some groups travelled by lorry to Singapore station, others had to march there; one early group included the Argylls who had made such a spirited resistance to the Japanese in the fighting in Malaya. The Argylls' group was treated to an inspirational lecture from an English-speaking Japanese officer before they began their march to town. He told them that their journey was to take them to a camp with good food and recreational facilities and a modern well-equipped hospital. The first group to go up-country was B Battalion commanded by Major R. S. Sykes RASC. Its 600 men were drawn mainly from 54 Brigade Group Company RASC, a unit of 18th Division. The succeeding groups came from other camps in the Changi area, from Sime Road, Adam Park and Changi Village.

Waiting for them at the city station was a long train of enclosed steel goods trucks into which, having loaded their non-personal and heavy baggage in a separate waggon, the prisoners and their personal effects were unceremoniously herded, about 30 to a truck. Without the baggage this would have been excessive overcrowding; with it there was not even enough spare room on the floor for everyone to sit and turns were taken in standing and sitting. Some men devised ways of hanging their gear from the sides and roof of the trucks to create a little more floor space. For several hours of the journey north the sliding doors of the waggons were kept closed and in the tropical temperature the interior rapidly became unbearable; discomfort, heat, thirst and fatigue made conditions nightmarish after only 24 hours. Some time after the journey had started the guards allowed the sliding doors to be opened so that fresh air reached those nearest to the opening and, by the agency of the draught stirred up by the slowly moving train, also those at the rear. But at the front of each truck the atmosphere was hot, foetid and airless, while the metal roof and sides became too hot to touch under the effect of the blazing sun. At night the iron sides cooled and 'sweated', chilling the backs which came into contact with them. To make matters worse, drinking water was in short supply and that for washing practically non-existent.

Twice a day the trains made a pre-arranged stop at a station on their slow crawl up the Malayan peninsula and the prisoners received a bowl of rice, some vegetable soup or stew and perhaps some tea. These stops also provided a brief opportunity to use the washplaces or hastily dug latrines. In addition there was the chance to buy local fruit, hard-boiled eggs, coffee or some other nourishment. Although the diet was generally much inferior to what Europeans were used to, deficient particularly in meat protein, in these early days of the railway project it could occasionally be supplemented by some surprising additions. One group's train halted at Prai where they received a dawn breakfast of real bread and almost a third of a tin of salmon each, and when they later stopped in southern Thailand the local stationmaster distributed a free platter of fried eggs around one lucky crowd of prisoners.[14] These highlights apart, it was a tired, unwashed, undernourished and thoroughly dispirited workforce of 3,000 POWs which finally reached the destination station of Ban Pong, close to the point at which the new railway line would diverge from the Singapore–Bangkok line and begin its journey to Burma.

The men chosen for these early work parties were in the main reasonably fit, but the poor, unbalanced diet was already beginning to have an effect and disease was starting to undermine their vitality. Cases of malaria, dengue fever and a range of lesser afflictions were beginning a progressive debilitation; there were also dysentery cases for whom the journey to Thailand of four days and nights with few stops had proved a tormenting trial. Whatever the shortcomings of the Changi area as a POW camp in these early days, it did have the advantage of relatively modern buildings and basic amenities, an established administrative framework for the prisoners' lives and reasonable access (through fair means or foul) to additional provisions and medical supplies. However once the journey to Thailand began, the distance between the prisoners and those facilities generally taken for granted began to lengthen. They all came face to face with taskmasters who were low-ranking Japanese guards or else even less well-regarded Korean military auxiliaries. When the prisoners disembarked at Ban Pong they were marched through the small town and on beyond it to what was to be the main staging camp for the railway labour parties. It was no more than a large clearing where great quantities of bamboo and atap had been assembled for the construction of camp huts. Some had already been expertly built by the local Thais; the remainder the prisoners were to construct themselves. Parties which came up-country a few days later found the huts already completed and the camp area fenced off from the surrounding countryside, a Japanese guardhouse near the entrance and beyond it long lines of bamboo and atap huts ranged closely together.

Many thousands of railway labourers were to pass through this transit camp over the next twelve months. Aside from the few occasions when they were able to occupy conventional buildings or when they lived under canvas awaiting the completion of huts or else survived without any shelter, the kind of atap hut which the POWs built and occupied at Ban Pong became the standard camp building all along the railway trace. It was a variant of the local native dwellings which were all made of bamboo with atap-covered roofs though the locals often took the monsoon-wise precaution of building them on stilts above the ground. The prisoners' huts tended to be built to a common pattern, eight metres wide at ground level and with the roof sides sloping down to within a couple of feet of the ground, making the insides rather murky, for the structures were often very long and the light could only penetrate from openings at each end and in the middle of the hut, apart from the little which was admitted under the low eaves. Within the huts platforms extended along the full length of each side. Constructed again of bamboo and covered with split and flattened bamboo these formed the communal beds. Each man had a section of these platforms perhaps four feet wide, giving him a personal space about eight feet long on which to range his few possessions and his weary limbs at night. Down the centre of each hut, between the bed platforms, ran the common passageway about two metres wide. The hospital hut at Ban Pong was exactly the same, so that to get close to a patient the medical staff had to get onto the sleeping platform itself and crouch or kneel beside him. The huts were spaced only a couple of metres apart and the narrow strip between them was the area in which all ablutions had to be carried out.

The arrangement and construction of huts in other camp areas differed in detail from this description of the situation at Ban Pong; but all shared the characteristic of atap roofs which sheltered swarms of mosquitoes and bamboo bed platforms which provided habitats and feeding grounds for armies of insects and ants. Many camps shared with Ban Pong two other disadvantages: the Japanese sited the latrine pits too near the huts themselves (those at Ban Pong ran initially only a few yards away from them) and they were frequently only shallowly dug. Secondly, the source of water was often some way from the main camp area making its supply difficult and laborious particularly with the inadequate containers which were all that were available. Providing water for cooking and drinking was difficult enough; there was little surplus for washing. These early parties arrived at Ban Pong when the monsoon rains were building to their peak and the flat and open camp-site rapidly became a morass of mud. From the base camp working parties were soon being sent out to clear other areas of vegetation for working camp sites similar to, if smaller in some cases, the one at this southern railhead. These advance parties would live in tents or bivouacs until they had built huts for themselves and their fellow workers from the supplies of long bamboo floated as rafts along the river Kwai by native working parties further up-country. The first Singapore up-country party to arrive was at work by 24 June constructing the base workshop and stores for the Japanese Materials Depot.

Similar activity was taking place at the Burma end of the railway. Brigadier Varley's 'A' Force from Changi and the British and Dutch troops from Sumatra were now completing their separate airfield construction tasks at Victoria Point, Mergui and Tavoy. In August and September they were gradually concentrated at Tavoy where work continued for a while with the much enlarged labour force in conditions which were rather better than at the other locations. At all three sites the work had been reasonable though living conditions and food were poor. The men began to be paid for their work after a while and canteen funds were established for the purchase of extra supplies. At this stage the attitude of the Japanese was relatively lenient and some of the overcrowding, particularly at Tavoy, seemed to be the result of the authorities being totally unprepared for the arrival of such large numbers of prisoners.

By the middle of September the work on the Tavoy airfield was finished and the POWs began to be moved north once more. This time the destination was the Thanbyuzayat railhead. Some travelled by barge down the Tavoy river to the sea where they transferred to small ships for the journey up to Moulmein. After a night in Moulmein jail they were marched to the station for a 30 kilometre journey in cattle trucks to Thanbyuzayat. By 1 October some of them had already been put to work. Lieutenant Colonel Green's 2/4 Machine Gun Battalion

had arrived at Kendau, 4.8 kilometres from the base headquarters and
on the 5th, Lieutenant Colonel Anderson, who had won the VC in his
battalion's action against the Japanese Imperial Guards Division in
the battle of Muar, had his units building an embankment on the
outskirts of Thanbyuzayat. These early arrivals were rapidly
followed by other groups, British, Australian, Dutch and American.
The British Sumatra Battalion of Major Dudley Apthorpe arrived at
the railhead on 23 October to find numerous railway parties, POWs
and native labourers, already at work. They stayed at Thanbyuzayat
for a few days, leaving their sick at the base hospital which had been
established there and then marched off along the railway trace. The
lorries took on the heavy kit and then returned for the POWs whom
they finally deposited at Hlepauk camp 18 kilometres down the trace,
where Colonel Anderson's men, having been moved on from the base,
were already in occupation. The Burma labour force was soon joined
by others from further afield, for the Japanese were now moving up
prisoners from Java, staging them through the camps at Changi.

In early October a party of 1,800 prisoners, in the main Australians,
but with about 200 American and 100 Dutch among them, were concentrated at Tanjong Priok in Java and embarked for a miserably
overcrowded and ill-prepared voyage to Singapore. They landed at
Keppel Harbour and spent a few days in Changi before once again
travelling to the docks for another voyage north, this time to
Rangoon, once again in dreadfully overcrowded conditions – 1,800
men crammed aboard a 7,000 ton Japanese supply ship. At Rangoon
they transferred to smaller vessels, one the *Yamagata Maru* built in
1916, and sailed eastward to Moulmein, finally to pass the night in
Moulmein jail before moving on to the railway trace. These 'hell
ship' journeys, as they were dubbed by some of those who were
crammed into the inadequate and airless holds of the vessels, were as
eloquent of the parlous state of the Japanese shipping resources as
they were of the captors' insensitivity to the needs of their prisoners.
Throughout the southern regions, merchant shipping was in short
supply and all manner of ancient and ill-maintained craft were being
pressed into service for purposes for which they were never designed.
In August 1942 negotiations had been completed for the exchange of
diplomatic staff and civilian internees between the combatant states,
and early that month the British diplomats interned in Thailand left
Bangkok for a voyage to Lourenço Marques and an exchange there.
Only a proportion of the civilian internees were able to accompany
them. The remainder were committed, like the prisoners of war, to

passing a further three years in Japanese hands, because Japanese shipping resources were inadequate and they could not be included in the exchange.[15]

Major movements to Thailand of the Singapore-based prisoners began again on 9 October and over the next month trainloads of them were setting off almost daily for the slow and tormenting journey to Ban Pong. The POWs were drawn from the camps at River Valley Road, Sime Road, Adam Park and Changi Village. The last of these mass transfers of British prisoners was a contingent from the Great World Camp which left the city station on 9 November. It brought the total trainloads in this second batch to 27. There was also one trainload of 400 from Kuala Lumpur composed of the British prisoners from Pudu Jail. This brought the total of POWs sent north to Thailand during the year to more than 20,600.[16] They formed an exclusively British labour force and were soon hard at work with the others in the camps north of Ban Pong. At the Burmese end of the railway the situation was more complex. Further parties of Dutch prisoners had followed the small group which had left Java with the largely Australian force in the early days of October. There was now a heterogeneous group of 9,800 prisoners operating on the line, comprising roughly 4,500 Australians, 4,600 Dutch, the 500 men of the British Sumatra Battalion and almost 200 Americans. Besides these there were the larger numbers of native labourers supplied by the Burmese government to the Japanese. The Deputy Prime Minister Thakin Mya and the Labour Minister Thakin Ba Sein paid a visit to the Thanbyuzayat railhead at the end of 1942 and saw '10,000 men of the "Sweat Army" at work under proper conditions' as part of a labour scheme which they had negotiated earlier with their allies.[17] At the southern end of the line the Thai authorities had workers engaged in developing the road which was to run alongside the railway.

This large and complicated organisation spread across two countries and 420 kilometres of territory under the overall direction of the Japanese railway headquarters with its own very considerable specialist labour force. There was also the separate POW guard force. This was initially a purely Japanese organisation, but soon after the major moves northward began, contingents of Korean auxiliaries arrived to replace and supplement them. This change may have eased the Japanese manning problem somewhat, but it scarcely worked to the benefit of the POWs. In general the Korean guards proved more brutal and less comprehending than their Japanese masters.

Furthermore since they were at the bottom of the military pecking order they were often ill-used by the Japanese and, in the way of these things, were wont to pass on their own ill-treatment to their prisoner charges. They seldom managed to establish any moral authority over them, which led to frequent beatings to establish their physical domination. The POWs might have chosen to explain the situation less dispassionately; in the words of one medical officer the Koreans were 'purely amoral coolie vermin ... brutal by nature as well as by orders'.[18]

The Japanese organised the building of their strategic railway by dividing up the proposed trace into numerous sections, allocating a force of prisoners and other labourers to each of them. The Burmese part of the line was divided into two sections and prisoner groups No. 3 and No. 5 were allocated to them, acting under the direction of 5th Railway Regiment. The other four groups of prisoners, Nos 1, 2, 4 and 6, operated on the Thai side of the line in the territory of 9th Railway Regiment. Within each group several camps would be set up, each responsible for providing the labour force for the engineering tasks to be undertaken on that particular section of the line. The Japanese engineers would be encamped somewhere nearby. They would determine the workforce required for a particular task and it would be the responsibility of the Japanese camp staff to provide it. The labour required would then be notified to the camp's own administration – their British, Australian and Dutch officers – and these in turn would have to find the required number of fit men. The general camp administration was a matter for the prisoners themselves with the Japanese leaving many matters to the prisoner officers to sort out, only providing them with the absolute minimum of materials, medicine and other assistance. Once the general pattern of work and camp duties was established the guards interfered little in the camp routine providing the needs of discipline, security and size of labour force were met. It was often the case that they were not, and the result was lengthy searches, interrogations, inspections and beatings which added substantially to the miseries of incarceration.

In the Burma section, Colonel Nagatomo who commanded No. 3 group met the senior prisoner in his group, Brigadier Varley, in early October and notified him of the headquarters staff he would be allowed to have in order to manage the prisoner labourers of the group on behalf of the Japanese. It consisted of a General Affairs Department of 10, a Foodstuffs Department of 17, a Property Department of 17 and a Medical Department of 12. This considerable delegation of authority by Nagatomo to Varley was a mixed blessing for the Australian Commander and posed him, as it did all other POW commanders for the railway similarly tasked, with an acute moral dilemma: to cooperate with the Japanese in the building of the railway was to aid their war effort, to fail to do so was certain to bring down severe punishment, and possibly worse, on the prisoners themselves. Varley cooperated, as did all the other commanders in varying degrees, and by so doing gained considerable leverage with Nagatomo and his staff. As Apthorpe of the British Sumatra Battalion put it, Varley 'and a small staff virtually ran the whole show. Movement of POWs, working parties, hospitals, pay and a mountain of clerical work, were all organised and Nagatomo was helpless without them'.[19]

5

The Battle Begins

It is a squalid, monotonous, depressing and humiliating existence. How long is it going on?

Dr Robert Hardie
Ban Pong Camp, July 1942

BY THE TIME the south west monsoon abated in November 1942 and the Japanese were able to turn their attention from collecting materials and setting up base camps to starting the railway construction itself, the need for such an overland route to Burma was being underscored by military events throughout the war theatre. The spectacular initial triumphs over the forces of Britain, Holland and the United States had come sooner and far more cheaply than the Japanese had dared to hope. Driven by a conviction in their own invincibility they then decided to expand their defensive perimeter rather than consolidate it. The result was a series of land and naval actions which produced a perceptible change in the fortunes of the Pacific War and accentuated the most significant weakness with which Japan had entered the conflict, the small size and inadequate protection of her merchant marine.

The Japanese first prepared to capture Port Moresby in southern New Guinea and later Tulagi on Guadalcanal Island as bases for the further isolation of Australia and New Zealand by the capture of other island groups which lay to the west of these Allied strongholds. A major expedition was also planned against Midway Island, designed to draw the American fleet into battle and destroy it. However all three operations ended in failure. Forewarned of the impending amphibious assault on Port Moresby, an Allied naval force was assembled to oppose it and for three days in early May 1942 the first carrier-against-carrier battle in history took place, initiating a whole

60

series which were to be a unique characteristic of the Pacific war. Tactically, the fierce action known as the Battle of the Coral Sea was a draw, but strategically it was an Allied victory, for the Japanese amphibious force turned about and abandoned its attempted assault. The overland advance on Port Moresby which took place later in the year proved equally unavailing. The disaster which overtook the Japanese at Midway in June was much more decisive. Forewarned of Japanese intentions as they had been in the Coral Sea, the Americans assembled as large a task force as they could collect in the available time. In a few short hours of an early summer's day, US carrier-borne dive-bombers sank all four of Admiral Nagumo's fleet carriers in what was arguably the decisive engagement of the entire war against Japan. In August 1942 American forces began the reoccupation of Guadalcanal, provoking a violent reaction from the Japanese and a series of naval battles for the control of the island which raged for a full three months while the struggle on land lasted twice as long.

The nearest of these engagements took place nearly four thousand miles from the labour forces toiling at the construction of the Burma–Siam railway, but the naval struggles were not without significance for their task or indeed their plight. From the British strategic viewpoint these Japanese reverses meant that there was no longer any fear of a repetition of the carrier force foray into the Indian Ocean which had caused such anxiety and panic the previous April. From the Japanese perspective, the long journey around the Malaya peninsula to Rangoon was likely to be an increasingly perilous undertaking for the few merchant transports that could be spared to risk its dangers.

The Japanese still depended upon free movement in the Andaman Sea and control of facilities at the Rangoon docks in order to operate the 30,000 or 40,000 tons of shipping which needed to make the trip to the main port of Burma each week if its forces were to be kept supplied. The reverses in the southern and eastern Pacific made this schedule increasingly difficult to maintain, particularly since the three pools of cargo shipping, Army, Navy and civilian, continued to be operated independently with the military demands becoming all the more urgent and insistent as the commander concerned struggled to restore the operational situation. Efforts were made to have vessels in the military pools load strategic materials for the return voyage to home waters but this was generally unsuccessful. The amazing spectacle of Japanese ships moving in ballast in opposite directions at a time of severe shortage of shipping continued virtually throughout the war.[1] Even this inefficiently operated cargo traffic was increasingly exposed to Allied attack as the war progressed. The astonishing Japanese failure to develop plans to convoy and protect their merchant marine has already been remarked upon and these vessels proved easy prey for allied submarines and, as allied air power developed, for aircraft as well. For all these reasons the balance of merchant shipping available to the Japanese began to decline as early as April 1942. By the end of that year losses totalled 214 merchant ships (139 sunk by submarine action), a gross total of over a million tons, one sixth of the total with which Japan had entered the war.[2]

By the end of the year the Allied air forces based around Calcutta were also becoming a little more effective against the Japanese lines of communication to the Burma theatre. They had been at their weakest during the monsoon period when operational flying was in any case very difficult. However this breathing space did give them time to construct new airfields in Assam and bring to combat readiness the fresh squadrons with which they were at last being reinforced. The result was that when the severity of the monsoon lessened in September they were in a much better position to dispute command of the air with the Japanese. Since the heavily wooded nature of much of Burma deprived the bombers of suitable tactical targets, it was on the enemy communications system and the Japanese airfields that they concentrated their attacks. The British bomber squadrons began a systematic offensive against the railways and airbases of Burma, conducting their daylight attacks at targets near enough for the range of their fighter escorts and at night bombing further afield unescorted. By the end of October 1942 their colleagues in 10th United States Army Air Force had been sufficiently reinforced with heavy bombers to undertake major raids on Rangoon, Mandalay and other targets. The Liberators even penetrated as far as Bangkok when on 26 November a force of eight of them made a round trip of 2,760 miles for a surprise attack on the Thai capital's oil refinery and power plant. It was the Rangoon area that was most persistently attacked in this early stage of the Allied fight-back, since it was the focal point of the Japanese supply system and also the one major target that was within regular operational range of the heavy bombers. Although such raids were relatively few during 1942 because of problems over spare parts and repair facilities it was already clear to the Japanese that things were likely to get worse rather than better. Work on the new railway itself was proceeding unmolested; but even at this early stage in its construction there was already, as the air attacks on Bangkok and, especially, Rangoon, were demonstrating, a developing threat to the two railway systems which it was intended to join. If the new line was to serve its strategic purpose, it plainly had to be built quickly. Furthermore every logistical indicator pointed to the Japanese Southern Army in Indo China, Malaya and Burma having to subsist on its own resources and on whatever else could be obtained locally, rather than upon supplies sent from Japan. None of this was good news for the Southern Army railway authorities; it would have been distinctly bad news for their multi-national labour forces if they had been privy to it.

The early signs were that all was not going well with the new railway project. One area in particular which was falling short of expectations was the assistance promised by Japan's allies in the war effort, the government of Thailand and the executive administration which the Japanese had to set up in Burma. It proved difficult for the Thai authorities to recruit the labour for their agreed part of the project. The Thai people did not take kindly to menial non-agricultural labour and working in a mercenary capacity for their new-found friends the Japanese did not come easily to them. Indeed, despite the tardiness of the American Special Operations Executive (SOE) and Force 136 on the British side in coordinating and developing the Thai Resistance Movement *Seri Thai*, at quite an early stage in the formal Thai–Japanese cooperation hostility to the Japanese forces and aims in Thailand was already developed and organised. The first serious and purposeful meeting of anti-Japanese Thai leaders headed by Pridi Panomyong, a member of the Council of Regents, took place as early as 11 December 1941.[3] Against this background it is not surprising that the Thais should have been so dilatory in undertaking the railway work allotted to them. Japanese railway *gunzoku* Futamatsu commented that the plan for cooperation with a Thai workforce 'did not work out', and that the Japanese authorities suspected that some of the POWs were in league with pro-British organisations among the Thais.[4] This was perhaps an unduly fearful interpretation, but there was some truth in it.

As for the Burmese, their performance did not reach Japanese expectations either, but for organisational reasons for which both parties were to blame. Since the main Indian labour force had already fled the country, it was no doubt too much to expect the native Burman suddenly to become an enthusiastic, efficient and hardworking manual labourer, despite the numerous radio broadcasts urging him to do so. In addition it soon became clear that the many inducements offered by the Japanese to encourage recruitment of the labour force had failed to materialise. For large numbers of the railway coolies, even basic pay arrived irregularly. There was widespread discontent concerning poor food, lack of medical attention, the dearth of facilities for writing home and conditions in the railway camps generally. Desertions were common. Even Premier Ba Maw later ruefully admitted that although this early period of cooperation with the Japanese was 'rich in dreams' the Burma labour force soon paid a heavy price for the reality. As he noted later, 'Upon their arrival [at the railway site] the men were rapidly swallowed up by a scrubby, steamy, malaria-infested land inhabitied only by a few wandering jungle-dwellers'.[5] By the end of January 1943 the voluntary recruitment into the 'Sweat Army' totalled 87,000 men but the poor conditions under which the coolies worked meant that work rates were poor, sickness was soon widespread and desertions commonplace. Unlike the POWs, the coolie forces were administered directly by the Japanese railway regiments and as stories of the primitive working arrangements filtered back to the townships and villages whence they came, recruitment became more difficult and desertions more frequent even before the labourers had reached their appointed section of the railway trace.

Desertion was not an option for the thousands of prisoners of war who were now working on the line. Although they suffered from the disadvantage of being entirely in the power of the Japanese, their military organisation, social discipline and medical services helped them to survive the ordeal by labour that their lives were becoming. They had a rudimentary but efficient camp organisation which attempted to ensure that the basic facilities would be available for the workers when they returned from their long day's labour on the line. Cookhouses were set up, stoves and ovens were improvised from a variety of sources, cooking pots were fashioned, water carriers were manufactured, a water supply was arranged, anti-malaria parties were set up, sick bays and camp hospitals were established and the prisoner camp commandants through whom the Japanese conducted the operations did their best to appease their captors and, at the same time, to protect their men from excessive toil, harsh punishment and sickness. In most of these objectives they could claim only a modest success.

The work organisation which the Japanese established for the enterprise was straightforward enough. The engineers would decide on the task for the day, establish a work-norm for each labourer and therefore the total number of workers they would need. The Japanese camp organisation would be told the number required and the prisoners' camp commandant would then be ordered to produce the men. For the management of the prisoner labour forces throughout the conquered territories the Japanese relied heavily on the POWs' own existing rank structure for the transmission of their orders and the organisation of labour gangs. The morning *tenko* or roll call would determine whether the Japanese order had been obeyed. If it had not, then the camp staff would probably have to make up the numbers and camp fatigues would not be completed, or else the camp hospital would be raided by the guards and the healthier-looking of the sick (generally those without any visible symptoms of illness) would be ordered out to work, over the protestations of the medical staff and not infrequently to the accompaniment of a beating for all concerned at the indiscipline and disobedience of orders which the incident exposed. The work parties themselves were called *kumis*, groups of 30 to 50 workers in the charge of one of their own officers, the *kumicho*, who was usually a lieutenant; two *kumis* would make a *han* commanded by a *hancho*, a captain. These officers wore armbands and it was their responsibility to see that the designated work task was completed on schedule, to negotiate over difficulties, to intercede on their men's behalf and to attempt to avert the beatings which the Japanese were wont to inflict on those who failed to obey their orders instantly. Once out at railway trace markers and tapes would be put out by the engineers and the order would be passed to the *kumicho* that so many yards of jungle had to be cleared or so many metres of embankment built. Given the almost universal ignorance of the Japanese language among the POWs and their captors' similar lack of English, misunderstandings were frequent; the frustration of the Japanese and Korean orderlies at the failure of their charges to react appropriately was as likely to vent itself in a beating of the officer who had not transmitted the order correctly as of the men who had ultimately failed to carry it out.

The *kumicho* and *hancho* officers were thus put in a very difficult position. They were technically required to act as the labour gangers of work groups which were soon too undernourished to take on the strenuous tasks allotted to them, work which in any case contravened the international agreements on the treatment of prisoners of war which Japan had agreed to observe. Refusal to carry out the orders frequently resulted in frightful beatings or other punishments and occasionally in death; collective 'go-slows' by prisoners were soon reacted to by the guards with collective punishments, threats, or the withdrawal of privileges. The officers generally took the only course

possible, that of cooperation with the Japanese to the minimum
degree compatible with protecting the men and themselves from the
bashings and ill-treatment which were the only routine inducements
to cooperation which the Japanese employed. It was not an enviable
role; to the men their *kumicho* was a buffer against the brutality of his
captors, to the Japanese he was the ganger, responsible for getting the
task completed on time. The easy time which some of the men com-
plained their officers were having often involved the risk of a beating
for misunderstanding an order, for attempting to save the sick from
labour, or for trying to cover up for mistakes or absences. In fact in the
early stages of the railway work when the labourers were still
reasonably fit, when the diet still sustained them and the work itself
was not too strenuous, many groups found their daily task was achiev-
able without the total exhaustion of those concerned. The Australian
'Black Force', for example, working at Beke Taung camp in Burma
was building the roadbed behind a native labour force which had
cleared the jungle along the track. With the soil relatively soft and
the 'carry' not too far, the man-task of 1.2 cubic metres of soil per day
was not unreasonable; but the rate did not remain constant, nor did
the conditions; while the tools provided for the work were primitive in
the extreme. For moving the large quantities of earth from where it
had been dug out to where the railway roadbed was to be located, the
prisoners had to construct crude bamboo carriers known, at the northern end of the line at least, as 'yo-hos'. These consisted of a stout
bamboo pole about six feet long and two inches thick suspended from
which was a rice sack, held to the pole by baling wire tied to its four
corners and which contained the spoil for the embankment. Two
workers would shoulder an end of the pole each and, taking care to
keep in step, carry their burden to the desired spot, deposit it and
return for more. Those who dug out the spoil for the embankment
would toil all day with spades, picks and heavy native hoes called
chunkels.

At the Burma end of the line the officers generally managed to get
the agreement of the Japanese authorities to their not being used as
coolies; but this was not always possible at the southern Siamese end
where most of the British officers were located. This was because there
was a much higher proportion of officers in these camps; a situation
which resulted from the Japanese policy of separating the British
Indian Army officers from their men immediately after the capitulation in Singapore, leaving them with no soldiers to command. Thus
it was not long before separate officer *kumis* were operating on the

railroad, though not without protests from the officers concerned and frequently only after confrontations with the Japanese authorities and threats of severe punishments, and even death, if they did not comply. Such a confrontation later became one of the central features of *Bridge on the River Kwai* (*Bridge built in the Battle Zone* in the Japanese version). Despite the fictional nature of the film's story-line, it did seem to be the case that the officer *kumis* were often reserved for bridge building tasks, perhaps because the Japanese thought this work was more suitable for the Allied *shokos*, as they called them.

The preliminary work on most of the track, once the agricultural plain around both start areas had been left behind, was jungle clearing, for which the additional tools provided were two-handled saws, axes and rope. Mechanical power was a rarity on the railway and was only used for tasks which were quite beyond execution by human muscle. Clearing stretches of jungle for camps or tracks was back-breaking work, pulling out large clumps of bamboo being one of the worst tasks since the canes clung tenaciously to the earth with a strength-sapping obstinacy. Each stalk had to be removed separately and it took ten or more men pulling on a rope to do it. One *kumi* might spend a whole day shifting a single large clump. Tree-felling too had its problems, beginning with the exertion required to saw through a tropical hardwood trunk with a blunt two-handed saw. This task completed, a severed trunk would remain upright, secured to its near neighbours by a mass of creeper and intertwined branches. Consequently, two or three trees might have to be sawn through before one could be felled. In the up-country camps the task of moving the tree trunks to the railway site and manoeuvring them into position was assisted by trained elephants which arrived from the teak forests with their *mahouts* and worked side by side with the prisoner working parties. These beasts worked with remarkable intelligence and efficiency, pushing over tree stumps so that they could be uprooted, and dragging felled trees to the edge of the trace. They also played a valuable part in the bridge-building itself, manoeuvring the big timbers into position before the human labour force took over again. At the height of the construction activity there were 200 elephants in use in the entire railway area.[6] One prisoner commented that although the beasts worked splendidly and with an understanding that was almost human, maltreatment and starvation gradually took toll of them.

Bridge-building was indeed a major railway task; altogether some 688 bridges were built over the whole course of the railway ranging from the huge 14-span steel bridge over the Maekhlaung at Tamarkan to the scores of wooden structures which spanned the many smaller rivers and streams which crossed the trace in the hillier areas. Most of these were built from locally cut timber and were quite well designed following the standard American Merriman-Wiggin practice for wooden structures. They were most unconventional in being built with human labour alone. Teams of prisoners operated primitive steel-capped wooden piledrivers, while other groups would spend long periods waist-deep in water holding timbers in place while they were fixed to the existing bridge structure. However, in their construction policy the Japanese often sacrificed safety for speed by using softwood for bridge-building when hardwood, more difficult to work but infinitely more durable, was readily available. On the other hand, the knowledge that unlimited labour was at hand for rapid repairs and renewals probably made this a justifiable risk given the urgency of the operation in the rapidly deteriorating strategic situation.[7] Nevertheless the Japanese clearly intended some of their structures to last. Seven of the bridges they regarded as permanent; these were the steel bridges built with concrete piers. Aside from the major Maekhlaung bridge at Tamarkan there were six other bridges which crossed tributaries of the Kwai in Burma called the Zami, Apalon, Mezali, Winyaw, Khonkhan and Myettaw rivers.

In the south the Japanese engineers and their labour force made rapid progress with the railroad. Here the land was flat, communications were comparatively good, food was plentiful and supplies of spares and equipment in 9th Railway Regiment's materials workshop were close at hand. 3rd and 4th Battalions made great strides in building the roadbed with 2nd Battalion following behind laying the track, as Futamatsu put it, 'with textbook efficiency'. They were using 100-type railway tractors and 97-type flatcars for this work. The procedure was simple but effective; a flatcar loaded with sleepers and rails would be pushed along the existing line to its end, the sleepers would be unloaded and put in place at stated regular intervals by the labourers; the rails would then be lifted off the flatcar and fixed to the sleepers. As each new stretch of line was completed, the flatcars would advance along it and the process would be repeated. Empty flatcars would be removed from the track and the ones left behind them, laden with a fresh supply of rails and sleepers would move forward to provide a new section of line.

Steadily the line moved forward parallel with the broad Maekhlaung river until, at the river's junction with the tributary

Kwai, the Japanese were faced with their first difficult engineering decision. Supply considerations dictated that in this roadless land the military railway should run alongside a waterway wherever possible. The River Kwai was to be this logistical artery for the majority of the railway's course. However in order to reach the Kwai the engineers had first to bridge the Maekhlaung; the difficulty was to decide where to make the crossing. If the river was bridged as soon as practicable after the confluence, the Kwai could become the supply route straight away. However for the first 25 kilometres of its independent course the Kwai flowed south west in a long and wide meander before it turned north west, pointing its course in the direction of the Three Pagodas Pass and the Burma frontier which was the interim Japanese objective. If the railway made this early crossing and followed the river valley route it would involve additional effort in building the roadbed and laying the sleepers and rails over the extra mileage which the detour represented. This would waste time when time was at a premium; but more important it would encounter the most formidable engineering difficulties of the entire projected railway course, for in this section hills crowded the river bank, blocking the route. Cuttings would need to be gouged out for the roadbed here while in other areas viaducts would have to be built into the sides of the hills themselves where they ran precipitiously directly into the waters of the Kwai. Neither cuttings nor viaducts would present great difficulties to engineers disposing of the customary range of specialised machinery, but when their only rock and earth moving equipment was human muscle, a sore trial for their prisoners would be the inevitable consequence if this route were chosen.

The alternative was for the railway to follow the course of the main river beyond the confluence with the Kwai and further north until an easier crossing point was reached and then to take a cross-country route over flatter terrain until the logistical security of the Kwai valley could be attained. This solution would have the virtue of a slightly simpler bridging operation for the crossing of the Maekhlanug, since further north the river's flood plain in the monsoon season was not nearly so extensive as it was where the two rivers joined. But the further north one travelled beyond the junction the greater became the distance between the two river valleys and the problems of supplying the labour force over land rather than along water would begin to mount up. There were no roads, only dry weather tracks linking the two valleys and though the engineering of a roadbed would not present the formidable challenges of the alternative possiblity, it was not without its own difficulties. One possible crossing point was near the village of Laddya (Lat Ya) which today stands on the metalled road which runs north to the Burma border. In 1941 the road from Kanchanaburi to Laddya was little more than a track, but the route was nevertheless practicable. Near the point where the railway would have crossed the river stood a hill called Khao Chungkai. Ultimately the Japanese did not choose this northerly crossing but determined to hug the waterways by building their bridge near the confluence, thus inflicting on their prisoners additional labour in extremely difficult terrain on the first stretch of the Kwai. However the need for speed dictated the construction being undertaken simultaneously at many points and the proximity of the river provided the only certain means of moving both supplies and stores to all of them at once rather than as the track itself progressed. The fact that the prisoners called the cutting and the camp alongside it 'Chungkai' despite the fact that no native village or local landmark bore that name, has prompted some commentators to suggest that the Japanese engineers had originally intended to make the crossing further north where the hill Khao Chungkai stands but by mistake had bridged the river earlier and thus encountered the formidable engineering problems and the delays associated with them.[8]

It is an interesting speculation, but one which Futamatsu, for one, does not entirely support. It was he who, in June 1942, had been attached to 1st Battalion 9th Railway Regiment 'as leader in charge of construction plan and survey'. The aerial photographs which he had first seen placed around the walls of the railway control office had certainly not covered any alternative crossing further north along the Maekhlaung and his account makes no mention of the route diverging from what had been previously planned. He was, moreover, the designer of the steel bridge which eventually spanned the river and his account supports the view that a service road to Laddya would hardly have been a satisfactory means of supplying the labour force in the rainy season, particularly in view of the desultory approach to road-building of the Thai contractors. Moreover the 20–25 kilometres of overland traverse between the two river valleys would have been a particularly unreliable supply route during the monsoon. Even with one river or the other close by and serving as a regular supply line, the problems of logistics were to be intense, particularly as the upper reaches of the Kwai near the Burma border were reached. Finally, it has to be added that any geographical conclusions drawn from what the Allied prisoners called particular localities around the railway trace have to be tentative in the extreme. The spelling of Thai names, whether of people or places, presents great difficulty to Europeans whose atonal language and restricted alphabet can do justice neither to the Sanskrit Thai script nor its multi-tonal spoken form. In any case, soldiers have a renowned facility for turning foreign place names into something they find readily pronounceable but which differs significantly from the original. This characteristic applied in Burma and Thailand in the Second World War as it had in France and Belgium in the First; the only difference was that in the area of the notorious railway the names were as often introduced to the POWs by the Japanese who had their own difficulties with both Thai and English. The nomenclature of railway features is therefore not a reliable guide to very much.

However, the bridging of the Maekhlaung was certainly a problematical operation wherever it took place. Near the confluence with the Kwai the river was, though not very deep, some hundreds of metres wide and much silted up; it also widened dramatically in the rainy season, as has been noted. For these reasons the engineers of 9th Railway Regiment planned the crossing two kilometres upstream of the confluence. In fact two bridges were designed for this major crossing. The main structure was to be the steel bridge with concrete piers, capable of coping with all monsoon pressures. The completed structure was to be 300 metres long with 11 spans of 20 metres over the watercourse itself. A wooden bridge was to be built 100 metres downstream to take light rail traffic and for emergency use while the primary construction was being assembled. 9th Regiment's 3rd battalion started work on the substructure of the main bridge in September 1942 with its labour force of largely British prisoners who had formed the early drafts from Singapore. The regiment's 5 Company was in charge of this operation while 6 Company began work on the wooden bridge.

In order to excavate the hard river bottom the necessary seven to eight metres below the surface to take the well cribs for the concrete piers, a specialised piece of equipment called a Gatmel dredger was required. At the time none appeared available in Thailand, so Futamatsu was sent off to search one out in Malaya and Singapore with Sergeant Nagata and Superior Private Yasawa as his assistants. Futamatsu appeared quite taken by the authority thus given him, noting that his escort had 'to cooperate with a *gunzoku* without supervision'.[9] The rivers were still in spate when his journey started and the move merely to Bangkok involved a trip by river steamer since the southern part of the Thai National Railway was still flooded.

Futamatsu spent two months in a fruitless search down the Malayan peninsula, indeed he finally discovered a Gatmel on a dredgeship in Singapore harbour but it proved to be too small for the task at Tamarkan. At this point he received a telegram from his headquarters, 'Gatmel in Bangkok, come'.[10] The required piece of machinery had been discovered in Southern Industries in Bangkok. It needed some modification at the railway workshop but was then hurried to the bridge site and from then on the work was pushed ahead with speed.

Prior to its arrival the work of removing the silt to enable the concrete piers to be bedded in was undertaken by four prisoners using an old-fashioned diving helmet linked to an air supply. It was slow and dangerous work for which they received extra rations.[11] The delay had been almost two months, during which time work on the lighter wooden bridge had progressed rapidly. During September and October heavy squared timbers were floated out into the river, upended by the work parties and then driven into the river bed by the hand-operated pile-drivers. They were then held in place by cross-beams and other sections, similarly constructed, were built above them until the bridge rose to the desired level of the track. During this activity at the bridge site, one Japanese author has written that the construction area 'seemed as if it were on fire with enthusiasm'. The labour force might have expressed it differently; but at least the supply situation at Tamarkan was reasonable by comparison with the camps further up the Kwai, though the work was exhausting and the living conditions and medical arrangements were rudimentary in the extreme. When Futamatsu returned from Singapore at the end of December to celebrate the New Year with his fellow engineers in Thailand, he found the wooden bridge completed and light trains able to carry supplies across to the first stretch of the track beside the Kwai where the labourers were struggling with the most difficult engineering tasks of the entire railway, the Chungkai cutting and the double viaduct at Wampo.

6

Lives on the Line

Nothing kills sooner than hard work with insufficient food under a tropical sun

A. H. Brodrick
Beyond the Burma Road

THE ARRANGEMENTS for the celebration of Christmas 1942 in the railway camps of Burma and Thailand, short and welcome break that this represented from the labours on the line, were as festive as they could be made under the circumstances of captivity. They were inevitably overlaid with melancholy reminders of Christmas as it was normally enjoyed at home. Two elements in particular were absent from the meagre festivities along the Kwai: seasonal food and family company. News of their families had been entirely absent from the lives of the prisoners since the start of their captivity. Indeed the only information of the real world beyond their tropical prison which was generally available in the railway camps was not of a personal kind at all, but dealt with the larger ebb and flow of the world war as it was reported via the numerous wirelesss sets hidden and operated secretly up and down the line. A few days before Christmas, men in some of the camps were given postcards carrying preprinted messages to send home; only the second opportunity they had had since their captivity began to establish a tenuous connection with their loved ones back in East Anglia, Texas, Sydney, Amsterdam or, in the case of many of the locally-enlisted volunteers, in the internment camps in Japanese-occupied South East Asia where thousands of European families were now held. But of return messages from these distant families there had as yet been none.

The other great need in the railway camps was Christmas fare of the kind the men had enjoyed in the years before the Pacific war began;

though in every camp there were spirited efforts to make the most of what was available. The cooks did their best to make something approaching a recognisable festive dish; but in most cases it was merely a matter of a few extra rations – an unexpected pancake, perhaps a taste of chicken in those camps frequented by Thai traders from whom a fowl could be purchased with canteen funds, or merely an extra egg. The irrepressible Argylls at Tamarkan even managed to acquire some Thai whisky for Hogmanay and enlivened the local Christmas celebrations with eightsome reels danced to their own pipe music. At the Thanbyuzayat base camp some Americans captured an immense water buffalo just before Christmas, but the beast broke away as it was about to be slaughtered. However three other cows were shot and the Japanese allowed further animals to be taken from the reserve stock; so that for one day at least the protein ration along one section of the line was adequate.

But aside from these occasional dietary diversions, the offering of the primitive camp kitchens was the same rice-based provender as the prisoners had subsisted on since early in their incarceration. All that was generally added to the basic rice was small quantities of protein in the form of salted fish, buffalo or pork. The rice was of poor quality, generally broken-grained or polished, inferior to that which the Japanese, native Thais and Burmans consumed. The inevitable result was that the men steadily became more and more malnourished. Indeed large numbers had been showing evidence of deficiency diseases even before they left Singapore, Java and Sumatra for their railway destinations. In Pudu Jail, Kuala Lumpur, for example, where in May 1942 there had been just over a thousand Allied prisoners, 25 cases of advanced beriberi had been reported with 180 cases of the disease in not so severe a form and 100 others showing early signs of it. Symptoms of Vitamin B deficiency had appeared fairly generally within three months of the capitulation. Among the unpleasant physical symptoms that bespoke this deficiency were the cracking and peeling with subsequent rawness of the genital skin, known inelegantly but very appropriately by the sufferers as 'rice balls', since it was largely the rice-only diet which caused the complaint; persistent nocturnal tingling and stabbing pains in the feet which the prisoners, with their enduring capacity to joke about their predicament, called 'happy feet', and the distended tissues of the typical wet beriberi sufferer. The weakening diarrhoea and curiously symmetrical skin rashes of the pellagra victim were evidence of a deficiency of another vitamin, niacin, which was available in abundance in a normal Western diet rich in potatoes, meat and fish, but seen only in negligible amounts in the normal diet in the Kwai camps. The most serious consequences, yet to appear in the railway camps, but dreadful afflictions when cases finally occurred, were blindness and dementia. All these various visible symptoms were deeply distressing in themselves; but the poor diet which they signified had other serious consequences for the prisoners. Their debilitating effects made it even more difficult to meet Japanese work requirements and to observe the personal and social discipline, particularly in hygiene matters, which were the vital rules if the crowded and public camp life was to be bearable and the risks of contracting the many tropical diseases endemic in the area were to be minimised. Undernourishment and vitamin deficiency also rendered the men that much more vulnerable to these very tropical diseases which were a chronic curse even for the local native people. Furthermore the slightest scratch from a thorn or bamboo splinter could soon develop into a spreading and deepening ulcer which often defied all available treatment. This was no doubt partly a consequence of the tropical conditions themselves which meant that healing was a somewhat slower process for the European skin, and also the result of the general absence of modern dressings and drugs; but more than anything it was an indication of the lack of resistance to infection resulting from a deficient diet.

Much of the area over which the railway was to be built was endemically malarial and the mosquito-spread disease was to be one of the sorest trials of the railway prisoners throughout their captivity, many of them suffering repeated attacks. By the start of the war sufficient was known of the incidence and spread of the disease for it not to be a particular problem provided anti-malarial drugs were available in sufficient quantity and proper steps were taken to destroy the mosquitoes in their breeding grounds and to stop men being bitten by them. But in all three respects the railway camps were sadly lacking. Quinine was the most important drug used in the treatment of malaria, having a remarkable success rate greater than that of any previous drug used to treat infectious disease. By chance the Japanese occupation of the Dutch East Indies deprived the Allies of their main source of the drug, which is prepared from the bark of the cinchona tree, and which had been so successfully introduced in Java from Latin America in 1865 that the Dutch East Indies had become the prime source of supply by the time the Pacific war started. A desperate and ultimately successful search for alternative drugs began and once these were developed they were administered to the Allied forces with great success. However this was small comfort for those on the railway. Although the Japanese had cornered the main source of quinine they supplied it irregularly and in insufficient quantity to their prisoners. Although the POWs at Kanchanaburi, for example, received no suppressive quinine, the Japanese troops there were taking a three-grain tablet every day. The supply elsewhere was erratic and at times totally absent. Furthermore few prisoners had mosquito nets and the morning and evening *tenko* parades provided the ideal circumstances in which the ever-present mosquitoes could spread the disease-bearing parasite from man to man. It also proved difficult to get the Japanese to sanction regular anti-malarial parties to deal with the mosquitoes' breeding grounds, or to allocate sufficient men or materials to the task when they did.

Dysentery was another curse of the railway camps and one whose control and treatment made great demands on the organisation, discipline and social sense of the POWs. The disease had already been manifest in the first camps to which they had been taken after the surrender and had been a particular curse on the journeys up to Burma and Siam when the men had been confined in the holds of ships or in the steel rice trucks for the journey through Malaya. Contaminated food and water were the cause of its spread and flies the main agent of the infection. All the circumstances of the jungle camps seemed on the side of the fly, none on the side of the prisoner. Latrines had to be dug as far from the food preparation areas as possible; latrine covers had to be made to keep the flies away; cooked food had to be covered until consumed and all water had to be boiled. Many prisoners probably owed their lives to the rigorous observance of these hygiene rules and others certainly died from their failure to follow them. But who could blame the famished worker who declined to throw away his precious rice ration merely because a fly had landed on it, or fail to sympathise with the thirst-crazed emaciate who drank from a nearby stream? There was also a high incidence of scrub typhus in the railway camps; the indigenous people of the region had some resistance to this mite-borne fever but non-native newcomers like the thousands of Allied prisoners were particularly prey to it. Many were prostrated by its crippling headaches, fever and skin rashes; not a few died of it. The ubiquitous mosquito was also responsible for the violent attacks of dengue fever which laid its victims low with a high fever, headaches and disabling pains in the muscles and joints. Dengue was seldom fatal on its own, but victims who were already weak and suffering from other ailments could succumb to it.

Patients recovered slowly from attacks of dengue and remained very weak for some time afterwards, scarcely fit for the work on the railway trace to which they were quickly consigned once they appeared to have recovered.

The challenge which this situation presented to the prisoners' medical officers is described by the author of the British medical history of the Burma campaign who noted that 'there were very few other theatres on earth in which an army would encounter so many and such violent hazards. In Burma all the dread agents of fell disease and foul death lay in wait'.[1] In General Slim's Army, which in 1943 was preparing to contest the ownership of Burma with the Japanese, there were 120 soldiers evacuated sick for each man evacuated with wounds; and in the same year the annual malaria rate was 84 per cent of the total strength of the army. Such were the dimensions of the health problem in a force adequately supplied with food and medicines and fighting for a cause in which it believed, against an enemy it detested. How much greater was the challenge to the railway prisoners' doctors who lacked the drugs and medicines to treat their malnourished patients and were themselves prey to the same sickness and debilitation. Many of them had been unexpectedly diverted to the Far East from their original Mediterranean destination and were as little prepared to be practising medicine in its malarial jungles as were the diverted and reinforcing formations to be fighting in them. Battle casualties and routine temperate-climate diseases they were trained to deal with. The clinical predicament presented by tropical diseases complicated by severe malnutrition with neither the drugs to defeat the former nor the dietary supplements to combat the latter, and in circumstances in which the incidence of both increased steadily, proved as daunting a professional challenge as many were to meet in their entire medical careers. Most rose to it commendably.

It was not as though the Malayan campaign itself had given the doctors much preparation for the ordeal that lay ahead, despite the contrast it provided to the period of peacetime civilian or military medical practice which had been the general experience of most of them before the war began. In common with the other swift military disasters which had preceded it – France, Belgium, Norway, Greece and Crete – the Malayan campaign was over too rapidly for anything new or of real significance for military medicine to emerge from it. The circumstances of a rapid military *débâcle* are not, as the official historian dryly put it 'conducive to the development of advantageous modifications of medical policy or practice'.[2] The contrast with the medical demands in the railway camps was total. To quote the medical historian again, 'It was as though stripped of all modern diagnostic aids and all therapeutic agents they had been flung back into the darkest of the Dark Ages when famine and pestilence stalked through the land to decimate the population and bring to an end all community life.'[3] Moreover, the attitude of the Japanese themselves to the incidence of sickness among their prisoners presented a fresh dimension to the difficulties of the camp doctors. A prevailing assumption of the Japanese appeared to be that sickness resulted from a lack of determination to remain fit. They showed little concern for their own sick who consequently often had surreptitious recourse to the prisoners' medical officers in order to obtain treatment. The camp authorities also reduced or stopped completely the issue of rations to the sick, either as an inducement for them to return to work or else, it has been suggested, because they genuinely believed the sick needed less food. Either way it generally fell to the medical officers to argue the case for their patients: for them to remain in the camp hospital rather than go out with the others to the railway trace; for them to have extra rations rather than none at all; for the Japanese to provide them with the drugs and medicines necessary for their recovery but which the authorities seemed always unwilling or unable to make available. Taking on these moral responsibilities with their attendant personal risks as well as their traditional professional ones demanded qualities of character and leadership in the railway medical officers for which little in their previous training or experience had prepared them; but they were seldom found wanting despite operating in the same circumstances of undernourishment and disease as the majority of their patients and occasionally becoming prey to professional despair. 'The state of health in these camps' noted an Australian medical officer, 'can only be regarded as an everlasting appalling disgrace and a perfectly natural result of the administration and general treatment.'[4] There can be few situations better calculated to drive a medical officer to utter desperation than being able to diagnose the diseases and sicknesses from which the men were suffering, knowing the specifics required for their cure, but being quite unable to provide the drugs, the equipment and the additional nourishment with which to effect speedy cures. It drove one Dutch medical officer to temporary total depression and inaction and others to a bitterness which was never totally to disappear.

In consequence, improvisation became the watchword of the jungle hospitals. Bandages were made from all available strips of cloth, even leaves and raw latex tapped from wild rubber trees being pressed into service on occasions. Dressings were made from the bottoms of old mosquito nets; tin cans and discarded metal junk were beaten into medical bowls and containers and the ever-present and versatile bamboo was shaped to a score of medical uses. Some medicines were purchased clandestinely from Thai or Burmese sources, others were obtained through the agency of Japanese guards in payment for treatment by POW doctors. Those with experience of tropical conditions adapted more readily to the circumstances along the railway trace; prominent among them were medical officers of the Federated Malay States, the Straits Settlements Volunteer Forces and the Dutch colonial forces. These often knew of unusual sources of food supplements, local cures and alternative treatments for some of the tropical complaints which afflicted their patients. One such, a Dr Henri Hekking was a Leiden-qualified doctor who had spent years treating the natives of the Celebes for a range of tropical complaints, adding to his own conventional medical knowledge a familiarity with a range of local herbal cures which he had gained from his grandmother who had been an experienced tropical herbalist. Hekking worked mainly with the 190 Americans who were part of the Burma-based labour force. In the opinion of one of his US marine patients, Hekking was 'light years ahead' of the European doctors in the treatment of tropical complaints and not much approved of by them for his unorthodoxy which involved using tropical plants as dietary supplements and treatments for particular complaints. One particular example from Hekking's herbal remedies was a low growing creeping plant with drooping flowers – *Cephaelis ipecacuanha* – whose dried rhizome and roots proved valuable in the treatment of amoebic dysentery. It is claimed that Hekking's American patients had the lowest death rate in any of the 60-odd camps along the railway.[5] There were many other outstanding contributions by the jungle doctors, among them surgical operations performed very satisfactorily in the most primitive of conditions. One undertook an operation for a perforated peptic ulcer by the fitful glare of hurricane lamps and large fires lit outside the operating tent to give better light for the surgery.

More drastic operations, amputations, were often resorted to as the final treatment for tropical ulcers whose spread had continued until bone was exposed and arteries threatened and, with them, life itself. Many amputations were undertaken successfully in the primitive camp hospitals, the patients surviving to hobble around on bamboo crutches or locally-fashioned artifical limbs.

In the static and reasonably well-equipped base camp in Singapore the early evidence of undernourishment and vitamin deficiency had been combated at least in part by the establishment of unit and group gardens, a practice which the Japanese encouraged and for which they supplied seeds. As early as March 1942 an area of 120 acres outside the camp perimeter at Changi was allocated for this purpose and was soon productive, contributing a valuable addition to the diet. However, similar enterprises were seldom possible on the railway itself during the period of construction; the labour gangs moved location too frequently and the basic business of keeping the camps habitable, hygienic and with facilities for cooking for the workforce took all the energy of the non-labouring camp staff. Edible tropical vegetation was added to the diet when circumstances permitted and the know-how was available, and the troops were urged to eat the normally-discarded rice polishings which were rich in food value. Malnutrition was a never-ending concern and the risk of disease and its spread among the prisoners a constant worry. Enforcing necessary hygiene measures on a dispirited and weary workforce was an endless problem. The attitude of the troops to malaria discipline was often, as one medical officer on the Thai section of the line noted, 'deplorably careless'.

An additional factor which made the spread of disease particularly difficult to control was the close proximity of the locally-recruited native labour forces. At this stage in the construction programme this was a significant factor only at the Burma end of the project where, it will be recalled, there had been an energetic recruitment campaign which, in four separate drives between July 1942 and January 1943, had enrolled 87,000 Burmese labourers for the railway work. In the base camps the disaffected workers who deserted were easily absorbed into the local population. At the up-country sites, however, this was less simple. The coolie labourers often occupied camps adjacent to those of the Allied prisoners, sometimes sharing the same water supply and often making up neighbouring working parties. Unlike Allied troops, the native labourers came under the direct supervision of 5th Railway Regiment whose 2nd Battalion was responsible for providing accommodation for them and running much of their internal camp administration. The engineers clearly gave little thought to these responsibilities and the coolies, disillusioned, leaderless, uneducated and with little understanding of the requirements of hygiene in the primitive conditions rapidly fell prey to all the diseases that were afflicting the Europeans but without any of the latter's understanding of the ways to cure them and certainly with no knowledge of how to prevent their spread. Their camps were consequently a major source of infection. Although these differed little in terms of basic amenities from those of the Allied captives, the conditions in them rapidly deteriorated. While each of the POW-administered camps had its own hospital area, none was set up for the coolies whose only medical assistance came from the Japanese medical officers (MOs) themselves. It was generally inadequate. The hard work, the poor quality of the food and its insufficient quantity, the lack of recreation and the frequent slappings and beatings for the slightest offence induced even more of the Burmese to attempt to return to their now distant homes. But, since the only recognisable route north was the railway trace itself, they were frequently intercepted further up the line and put back to work on another site. As no effective local treatment was available for those who became sick, many did not recover but died on their bamboo bed platforms while others slept alongside them. Their deaths were unrecorded, their graves or funeral pyres unmarked and often unnoted.

Hospitals were finally established for the coolie forces but not for each individual camp for which there was no specific medical cover; only the very serious cases were admitted to the base hospitals and even then they had to walk to them. The hospitals themselves had few medicines and until they were established the coolies relied upon local facilities. There were initially about seven medical officers in each of the two regiments, supported by about four times that number of orderlies. This force was quite inadequate to the task, even if it had regarded the treatment of the Burmese workers as a high priority which it clearly did not. The plain fact was that the coolie forces were left largely to their own devices. 'These men', the Burmese government's Director of Press and Publicity was later to record 'were taken into malarial jungles without sufficient clothes, food or shelter, and made to clear the wonderful road that was to make Burma a Paradise of a terminus of a gigantic Co-prosperity Sphere railway'.[6] By contrast the POWs, whatever they lacked in food, medicines and amenities, were reasonably well supplied with medical personnel. It has to be remembered that when Malaya Command capitulated in February 1942, the trained medical and support staff of five military hospitals, 18 field ambulance units and numerous medical support teams fell into Japanese hands. Many of these specialist units ended up in the camps along the Kwai.

Notwithstanding the serious labour problems which sickness was now causing, the Japanese engineers were pressing on with their assignment with unrelenting determination. At the Thailand end where initial progress had been so rapid in the flat plain up to Kanchanaburi, the most challenging engineering difficulties were now being encountered as the trace hugged the right bank of the Kwai on the second and by far the longest stage of the riverine journey to join the Burmese railway system. The first major obstacle which lay in the projected path of the trace was the rocky hill known by the labour force as Chungkai. In mid-August 1942 Colonel Imai, the commander of 9th Railway Regiment had conducted a personal reconnaissance by boat of the regiment's area of responsibility accompanied by *gunzoku* Futamatsu. As they turned west into the waters of the Kwai, Futamatsu later noted, 'Soon on the right bank appeared a rocky crag sticking out like a bone. It was the crag of Chungkai'. This was the feature through which the engineers of 4 Battalion (Tarumoto Unit) had now to drive the trace with the aid of one of the first parties of prisoners to have been transported up to Thailand. Normally speaking, engineers would have planned a tunnel at this point, but 9 Railway Regiment had no tunnelling experience and little of the specialist equipment needed for it and so a deep cutting was planned instead. The cutting was ultimately 100 metres long and 40 metres deep and required the excavation of 10,000 cubic metres of rock. It was dangerous work with much rock blasting and, Futamatsu noted 'no lack of prisoner victims'.[7] Boreholes for the explosives were made with a crowbar and sledge-hammer, and preparing one of the deeper ones, perhaps a metre in depth, could be a day's work for the prisoner 'hammer and tap' party. But they were not always well prepared: sometimes the charges were laid in shallow boreholes and were not properly tamped so that the explosion went upwards rather than outwards. Beyond the cutting, where the river bank dipped again, the embankment had to be erected. Both tasks were undertaken to the accompaniment of heavy late monsoon rain which caused severe flooding in the camps, submerging the latrine areas in Chungkai and carrying their contents to the lines of hutments, entirely negating the painfully-observed hygiene measures which the camp administration had insisted upon. Such hazards and the tiring work at Chungkai saw both the sick rate and the death rate rise significantly, while the actual railway work progressed quite slowly. This concerned the Japanese engineer in charge who demanded more men on the trace. The sick were consequently impressed for the labout force and their condition inevitably deteriorated. The engineer concerned, the English-speaking

Tarumoto, worked the men hard and at times brutally and sadistically. He instituted officer working parties for bridge building skilled work the engineer claimed; but it turned out to be every bit as strength-sapping as the embankment building on which the other rank prisoners were engaged.

Further north, the river bank which had been sandy and flat in some of the earlier stretches, became rocky and cliff-like with no room between cliff and water sufficient to take the railway trace. In this area too tunnels might have been the conventional engineering solution, but bearing in mind the constraints of resources and expertise, the engineers settled instead for a direct run halfway up the cliff face, limiting the use of explosives by blasting out a narrow ledge along the cliff on which to key the roadbed and supporting it with an immense wooden double viaduct around the long 'S' bend which the rock formation and the confluent river made at this point. Ituka Company of 4 Battalion was responsible for this section of the engineering work and took six months to complete it with the aid of a labour force of about 2,000 prisoners based at the three Wampo camps, north, central and south.

The organisation and pattern of work at the Burmese end of the line, where the Japanese 5th Railway regiment was in charge, proceeded much as at the southern end. The major differences were that in Burma much larger numbers of native labourers were employed and were working directly under the orders of the Japanese. In Thailand the civilian workforce was under the independent control of Siamese contractors and from all accounts was not making a great contribution to the logistical enterprise. A further difference at the Burma end of the operation was the presence of Brigadier Varley, much the most senior allied officer in the railway operation. In the early months of the work Varley managed to visit all the camps of No 3 Group and, in the view of the official Australian historian, seemed to have established better relations with Colonel Nagatomo and other Japanense officials than existed elsewhere in Burma or Thailand. This was partly the result of Varley's prudent policy of keeping the maximum number of men at work, his continual striving to improve conditions, and because Nagatomo and his senior administrators were reasonable to a degree that would have seemed remarkable elsewhere on the line and in the Southern Army area generally. A further factor was, perhaps, the nature of the railway work in Burma. Because the line there did not have to follow a single major river, the trace could follow the natural contours of the land and consequently high embankments were rare and rock work of the kind encounterd in Thailand at Wampo and Chungkai was seldom tackled, though more bridge building was required albeit generally not as substantial as the Tamarkan project. The main work consisted of the clearing of dense undergrowth, the felling of large trees and embankment and cutting work. Dudley Apthorpe, commander of the only substantial British contingent working in the Burma sector, later made the journey south on the completed railway and expressed amazement at the engineering difficulties on the Thailand stretch, noting that of those who made a similar journey south, 'there must have been few POWs who were not thankful that they had worked in Burma'.[8]

Whether prisoners worked north or south of the Three Pagodas Pass, as time went on, the possibility of not surviving the railway ordeal increasingly occupied the private thoughts of them all. The risk of death is, of course, part of the unlimited liability to which all members of the armed forces commit themselves, its possibility is never entirely absent from the mind of the soldier on active service; but death as an incidental consequence of the conditions of captivity was a new factor with which the mind of the POW had to contend. Deaths from disease had occurred in all groups before they began their journey to the railway and since the work had started mortalities had increased. By the time the Argylls attempted to enliven the festivities at Tamarkan at the end of 1942, 169 men had succumbed and the numbers were to rise dramatically as the new year unfolded. In January there were 120 deaths and in February, 160, double the total of only two months previously. In March the number buried rose to 190 and in April 1943 it topped 200. It has to be remembered that these deaths from sickness rather than injury were of young men in the main, in the prime of their manhood, ultimately surrendering their lives in conditions for which nothing in their lives or military training could possibly have prepared them. However youth was not on the side of many of the members of 'A' Force in No 3 Group, the first batch of prisoners to be sent up from Singapore. This contained a large proportion of over-age Australians, in the main members of the 2/3rd Reserve Motor Transport Company to which special enlistment conditions had applied. Brigadier Varley had suggested that these older men, scarcely fit for heavy work, should be employed on vegetable growing or repairing footwear; but nothing more appears to have been heard of this eminently sensible suggestion. By mid-January 1943 the deaths in No 3 Group totalled 73 with a further 600 sick in the base hospital at Thanbyuzayat. 'All casualties were given a military funeral', Major Apthorpe reported, 'with escort, pallbearers and bugler'. Death certificates signed by the senior British Medical Officer were held for all the British casualties, but these were later confiscated by the Japanese. The northern death rate, once having risen above 200 in March would subsequently soar far above it and would not dip down below that figure until a further eleven months had passed.[9]

7

Isolation

This complete separation and sensation of being dead as far as relatives or loved ones are concerned brings a cold fear to my heart sometimes
Lieutenant Colonel E. E. Dunlop
12 December 1941[1]

THE ALMOST total absence of any messages from their families or news from their home countries was, for the prisoners on the railway, among the hardest to bear of all the features of their ordeal. It was reflected in a similar depression and at times despair among their families in the metropolitan centres from which the troops had departed, cheerful and optimistic, so many months previously. These relatives had had no news at all of the fate of their menfolk who had fought the Japanese in South East Asia, except for the lucky ones who had managed to escape in the last few days of that disastrous campaign or the relatively small number whose 'first-capture' cards had got through. The government department in London responsible for looking after the interests of its servicemen in enemy hands was the Prisoners of War Department of the Foreign Office. However it was able to bring little comfort to those waiting anxiously at home. In the First World War the department had been separate from the Foreign Office itself, but despite the experience gained in this earlier conflict and the fact that it was the War Office which had charge of enemy prisoners in the UK and whose personnel were the majority in captivity throughout South East Asia, the POW Department remained firmly a part of the Foreign Office throughout World War Two. In the light of this previous experience, the warning of war and the 'phoney war' itself, it does seem that the Prisoners of War Department had not made adequate preparations for its work before the war began, and the matter of providing information for relatives of those

86

fighting in the Pacific war was a worrying issue throughout the conflict.[2] However, through its subsequent hard work and that of the other international agencies with which it dealt, the lot of the British prisoner in Germany was much better than it had been in the First World War. On the other hand the sad fact is that its efforts did not have much impact on the treatment and well-being of the POWs in the hands of the Japanese, certainly not those on the river Kwai railway.

International agreements on the welfare and protection of prisoners of war are essentially a 20th century development in the law-making of states. At the first Hague Convention in 1899, the major powers agreed that prisoners of war were to be humanely treated and they set down the way in which this undertaking was to be carried out. Japan was a signatory of the convention and throughout the Russo-Japanese war its treatment of Russian prisoners was impeccable. A prisoner of war office was established in Tokyo with a major general in charge. It administered 70,000 prisoners, sent information to the Russian government via the French embassy, handled correspondence to and from the captives and took particular care to return the personal effects of men found dead on the battlefield including cash amounting to 2,249,820 Russian roubles.[3] In the opinion of one Western journalist the Japanese Army provided 'considerate treatment of the Russian prisoners which could not be excelled in point of consideration by any army in the world'.[4] Even the Commissioner of the Russian Red Cross Society confirmed this, noting that, 'Since the surrender the whole attitude of the Japanese Army has been exactly the same as if it were dictated by the fundamental values of European civilisation.'[5] The Hague Convention of 1907 slightly amended the first agreement and became the authority for the treatment of prisoners during the First World War. If the observation of the terms of the convention in that conflict was uneven, it nevertheless held up reasonably well and contributed substantially to the well-being of prisoners generally. However twenty years later, as war clouds began to gather once more, the powers met in Switzerland to review the 1907 Convention and see if any amendment to it was necessary. The result of their deliberations was the Geneva Convention 1929 which was to have a considerable effect upon the lives of the POWs in World War Two. Japan attended these Geneva negotiations, the Emperor being represented by the Minister from the Japanese Embassy in Berne, an Army lieutenant colonel and the Naval Attaché from the Japanese Embassy in Paris. All three appended their signatures to the

Convention along with the representatives of 46 other countries; but it was never formally ratified by the Japanese government.

The Geneva Convention was a considerable advance on its predecessor: its 97 articles covered almost every contingency then thought likely to arise during captivity. Thus, some 15 years before the events described in this volume, an international régime had been established which, theoretically, could have ensured the welfare of prisoners of war from almost every aspect. The Convention declared that POWs were to receive rations equivalent to those of the detaining powers' own depot troops, that they were to be supplied with adequate clothing and although they could be required to work, their labour was not to have any 'direct connection with the conduct of the war'. The prisoners' hours of work were to be regulated, NCOs could not be required to work (though they could volunteer); but they could be ordered to supervise the work of their subordinates. Officers could not be required to work at all. A state neutral in the conflict itself could be accorded the status of Protecting Power, representing the interests of one warring state within the territory of the other, with the right to visit all POW camps regularly to ensure that the terms of the Convention were being observed and to hear any complaints about ill-treatment. The International Red Cross Committee (IRCC) was also accorded a particular status under the Convention and had the function of organising a central agency for the exchange between the belligerent powers of information concerning their respective captives and of arranging the distribution of relief supplies to prisoners, besides being free to engage in other humanitarian activities on their behalf. Furthermore the IRCC was well prepared for these responsibilities when the war began, having made plans in considerable detail as early as September 1938 for the placing of its organisation on a war footing.

In December 1941, a few days after the outbreak of the Pacific war the Imperial Prisoners of War Committee, composed of representatives of the domestic committees of the UK, Canada, Australia and New Zealand, met in London to consider the position of prisoners taken during hostilities with Japan. Shortly afterwards a communication was sent to the Japanese government via a neutral intermediary, informing it that the British dominion states were observing the provisions of the 1929 Convention and asking for an assurance that the Japanese would do the same. It was some time before Japan replied, but in February 1942 came the response that although the Japanese Government was not bound by the convention, it would 'observe its terms *mutatis mutandis* in respect of English, Canadian, Australian, New Zealand and Indian prisoners of war'. In addition it declared that it would take account of national and racial customs when supplying prisoners of war with food and clothing. This assurance, conveyed through diplomatic channels, was also repeated by various Japanese commanders when they received the surrender of Allied troops at the end of the South East Asian campaigns. Air Vice Marshal Maltby and his fellow commanders, for example, had received a written undertaking to that effect from General Muriamo when the forces on Java were surrendered. However the Japanese actions failed entirely to live up to these early assurances. Consequently the work of the Prisoners of War Department, instead of being concerned with negotiating and monitoring Japanese observation of the many clauses of the treaty, was reduced to an unending struggle to achieve two basic purposes: to obtain from the Japanese a comprehensive list of their prisoners of war with their locations and to get the authorities to agree on procedures for accepting relief supplies for them. On both accounts, for the POW in the Southern Regions, it achieved negligible results and neither the IRCC nor Switzerland, the Protecting Power, was any more successful when acting independently.

In May 1942 the British Red Cross Prisoner of War Department and the St John War Organisation, entrusted by the Government with much POW welfare work, began to publish a monthly journal *The Prisoner of War* which it sent free of charge to the next of kin of all prisoners registered with it. The journal featured all the news that could be gathered about POWs and their well-being and also gave advice to their families at home. It was soon a substantial magazine with regular features such as 'News from the Camps' which recorded visits by representatives of the Protecting Power and 'Letters They Write Home' giving extracts from prisoners' letters to their families. Letters were featured from the *Oflags*, *Stalags* and Italian *campi* throughout the European theatre, and before long the journal was featuring photographs of POW football teams and hobbies groups and even lists of successes in public examinations which prisoners were managing to study for and take whilst in captivity. The journal provided enormous comfort and reassurance to relatives at home who learnt that the Red Cross parcels really were getting through and that although conditions were by no means uniformly good, or even in many cases satisfactory, at least their menfolk were alive; they were accounted for. However, the families of prisoners in South East Asia scanned the pages of *The Prisoner of War* in vain for news of their servicemen. Information from the northern sector of Japanese occupation, from Shanghai and Hong Kong, was scant enough with lists of POWs held there still not complete in October 1942; but from the southern regions, from Burma, Thailand, Malaya and Singapore there was nothing. The following month the Foreign Office was assuring anxious relatives that they would pass on information to the next of kin as soon as they had it, however as yet there was no news to give. Eventually, in January 1943, *The Prisoner of War* was able to announce that 1,100 'first capture' cards had been received by relatives of men who had surrendered in Singapore, but of what had happened to them in the ten months which had since elapsed and what fate had befallen the thousands of others who had surrendered with them, nothing at all was known. By April 1943 details of camps in Japan itself had been published and it was confirmed that letters were reaching prisoners there. However as late as July the journal was admitting that 'the exact location of the camps in the Southern Area is not yet known'. The editor could only lamely state that 'the next of kin of prisoners in the Far East have the sympathy of all of us. Theirs has been an anxious time of waiting and news is still scarce and hard to come by'.

The basic difficulty was the attitude of the Japanese government which 'while professing their intention to observe the Conventions, in actual fact did exactly what they thought fit, and in all matters what they thought fit differed entirely either from the letter or the spirit of the Conventions'.[6] The authorities would not allow representatives of neutral powers, or the IRCC, to establish themselves in occupied territories. In these circumstances the only possible British approach was to appeal to Japanese pride as a civilised nation in an effort to get them to consider the welfare of their prisoners. While the Prisoners of War Department was very concerned about the lack of information about the numbers and locations of prisoners, it directed its main effort to attempting to get sufficient supplies to them to ensure that they did not die of starvation and disease; everything else was secondary. Many attempts were made to get the Japanese to agree an exchange of food parcels. Red Cross ships from Australia, for example, could deliver parcels to Hong Kong or Singapore and in return carry supplies for Japanese prisoners in Allied hands. All such proposals were turned down by the Japanese authorities. However the exchange of interned diplomats that had been arranged for summer 1942 via Lourenço Marques, the Portuguese East African port, provided an alternative opportunity. It was finally agreed that the ships used to transfer the diplomats could carry relief supplies as well, although the distribution of these supplies in the Southern Regions would have to be left to the Japanese because of their refusal to accept any role there for the Protecting Power or the IRCC. When the diplomatic exchange took place, 3,500 tons of relief goods from the British Empire and 120 tons from the United States were sent along with the diplomats and trans-shipped on to three Japanese vessels, one of which was destined for Singapore. This was the first of only two shipments of relief supplies which were agreed between the British Empire and Japan during the entire war. It represented less than two pounds weight per head for all the British captives in the Far East, and by no means all of it ever reached them; but it was better than nothing.

A second shipment resulted from the Washington Conference in 1943 when it was arranged to send relief supplies to Vladivostok (the Soviet Union not then being at war with Japan) where they would await collection by the Japanese. 2,000 tons of supplies were des-patched but more than a year elapsed before Japan sent a ship to collect them. The supplies were ultimately distributed throughout the Far East and some did get through to the railway prisoners. Many of the parties which made the rail journey from Singapore to Ban Pong in the late months of 1942 had the benefit of an issue of Red Cross supplies before they departed. They received bully beef, milk, porridge and cocoa among other things and many POWs were able to take some of the supplies north with them. Some of the American-contributed parcels eventually got to the Burma section of the line where in the British Sumatra Battalion for example, a parcel for one man was shared among five. In late 1943 an issue of supplies was made in other camps in Burma; at Aungganaung camp, near the Three Pagodas Pass, '105' as it was known to the prisoners, the issue amoun-ted to three small packets of cigarettes per man, an issue of margarine which went directly to the hospital, and a small tin of condensed milk which was shared between eleven men.[7] The quantities each man received were tiny and their contribution to overall nourishment was minimal; but the psychological impact was considerable, something from the outside world had finally got through to them; they were not totally forgotten. For many it was a year before they received a second issue and a further year before their third and final one.

In view of the meagre amount of relief supplies the Japanese were prepared to sanction and the reports which continued to filter through to the British authorities of the great health danger to which the prisoners were exposed because of the inadequate diet, efforts were made to have supplies purchased locally by representatives of the Protecting Power, the IRCC and their agents. Much help was provided by this means, the majority of it orchestrated by the untiring Swiss consul in Bangkok. It was from this source that the Government received the first news in July 1942 that 3,000 prisoners were engaged in road-making activities in the Ban Pong area. However the Japanese refused to allow the consul to operate formally as a representative of the Protecting Power and so it was as a private individual that he was able to arrange certain limited help in cash and in kind and in addition to pass back to the British government a series of illuminating reports over the next three years about the location and conditions of the prisoners gleaned from his own observation and from various other sources which will be mentioned later. The assistance that the consul was able to provide in supplying local currency, medicines and food for the prisoners, although limited in a country in which most commodities were already in short supply and inflation was rampant, was nevertheless a truly life-saving factor. However this support operated mainly on the Thai side of the railway project for, as the history of the Prisoners of War Department ruefully admits, Burma was one of the Japanese occupied areas 'where no means of helping either prisoners of war or civilians could ever be devised'.[8]

Similar difficulties prevented the establishment of a regular mail service to and from the railway POWs via the IRCC organisation and the Protecting Power. The non-receipt of letters or even of 'first-capture' cards in the home countries in the early months of captivity led to a suggestion for the use of the diplomatic exchange ships for the carriage of mail as well. However, as an alternative proposal the Japanese said that as from 15 May 1942 they intended to organise a mail service from Siberia; but this did not materialise until January 1943. Even so the amount of mail received from POWs was small throughout the war. There were very long delays between mail leaving a camp and its official dispatch from Tokyo, which was largely a result of the serious shortage in Japan of qualified interpreters to act as censors. Eventually in January 1943 came the announcement, mentioned earlier, that 1,100 'first-capture' cards had been received. As to mail sent to POWs in the Southern regions, the major problem was to know exactly where to send it. The information so far available on the location of camps related only to the one tenth of prisoners who were held in Japan itself or in the northern occupied territories. By the end of 1942 the IRCC could state with some satisfaction that 250,000 items of mail had been distributed to POWs and internees in Japan and Japanese-occupied areas, 'but nothing was known about mail destined for prisoners in Siam and Indo-China.'[9] In fact it was generally many months before any of it got through to the railway workers and even then the manner of its release was entirely arbitrary and quite unrelated to the logistical problems involved in getting it to the camps concerned. Similarly the men had no idea whether the postcards which they were permitted infrequently to send would ever reach their families.

The only other element which provided the prisoners with a tenuous link with the world beyond their jungle prison, was the regular news broadcasts received on their secretly-operated wireless sets. Throughout the period of captivity several sets were operated up and down the line and the details of the news bulletins were quickly passed by word of mouth so that major events and developments in the war rapidly became common knowledge within a particular camp and were communicated in time to neighbouring ones. The undercover operation of these sets involved great risk; the Japanese regarded their output as dangerous intelligence, their users as spies and even believed, or pretended to, that sets were transmitters as well as receivers. Death was generally the penalty for operating them. However the 'canaries' continued to sing up and down the line throughout the building of the railway and long after it until the final Japanese capitulation. Sets were brought up from Singapore and Java or else constructed from spares in the working camps themselves. One had been transported to the Burma end of the railway from the 'Bicycle Camp' in Java where it had been removed from a US Kittyhawk fighter and modified for battery operation. Another was built by an RAF technician and operated secretly at Tavoy and later at Thanbyuzayat. A further set was constructed and operated at Tarsao and another, cannibalised from Royal Signals equipment, began operating at Ban Pong. Many sets journeyed from camp to camp concealed in dixies, books or even, in one instance, in a water bottle with a false bottom. Providing fresh batteries for them was a further problem and generally an additional hazard; but the risk was often taken by the men whose skill, ingenuity and cool courage kept the supply of real news circulating through the camps, counterbalancing the many 'bore-hole' rumours to which such isolated and fact-starved groups were continually prey, and to helping to deflate the often laughably incredible propaganda of the Japanese. It is arguable that this clandestine news service, drawn from the bulletins of All-India Radio, the BBC or ABC, did more for morale than anything else during the captivity.

The issue of pay to their working prisoners by the Japanese began in June 1942 and though the rates were very low – a private received about enough to buy a duck egg a day at the Burma end of the line – it nevertheless enabled a small supplement to be added to the basic ration. However, the sick were not paid. This may have achieved the desired immediate psychological impact on the numbers attending sick parades each day, but in June the health of the troops had not deteriorated to the point at which large numbers were seriously ill and inevitably hospitalised. Later on the problem of providing additional nourishment for the unrationed and unpaid sick, not to mention the canteen supplements to enable them to regain their health, became a major concern. Towards the end of the year officers were also paid. The payment was notionally the equivalent of their official salary and they received it whether they worked or not. However the Japanese withheld a substantial proportion for their food and accommodation and 'banked' a further amount on their behalf. Officers also made a contribution, usually varying by rank, to the hospital fund or to supplement the soldiers' rations. Most camps established a canteen which sold locally procured foodstuffs and tobacco and which generally also generated a small profit used to purchase medicines, when these could be bought from local traders, or else additional food. The Japanese usually sanctioned these arrangements though they hedged them about with restrictions which could vary from camp to camp and from time to time. Occasionally camp officers, accompanied by a guard would be allowed out of the camp area into a local village to buy additional produce or to trade with a peasant farmer for a cow or water buffalo. The Thai merchants who traded with the prisoners came often from nearby villages, but further up-country where native settlements were few and the terrain was difficult the produce for sale would be brought by the traders by boat up the Kwai, much as most Japanese supplies had to travel. The additions to the diet which the issue of pay made possible were the difference between life and death for many in the camps.

Although pay provided the wherewithal for some additional nourishment for the prisoners, it could do nothing to ease the terrible sense of isolation in a totally alien environment, of being the slaves of a Japanese military culture which clashed so violently with the values of their own. What was more, it was clear from every news bulletin, whose contents were soon the currency of the camps, that there was to be no early end to the prisoners' tribulations, just as it was clear to every medical officer in the jungle camps that the physical condition of the men was getting progressively worse. The ultimate threat which this situation presented was evidenced by the growing number of crude wooden crosses which fringed each camp along the Kwai. What then sustained the POWs through the dark days of captivity? How did officers and men behave in the circumstances of their incarceration? There are no surprises in the answer. Some officers were shining examples of sustained courage and exemplary leadership throughout their imprisonment and this accolade was earned as often by doctors, chaplains and officers in the support services as it was by the teeth arm commanders and the Allied camp commandants themselves. Sufficient was thought of the qualities of one Australian doctor for him to be given command of a prisoner group for part of their period in Japanese hands. Another Australian, writing some years after the war's end, judged a chaplain and a medical officer from his days on the railway to be the most inspiring men he had ever met.[10] Numerous of the camps commandants distinguished themselves during the railway episode, taking immense personal risks for the welfare and well-being of their men. Indeed most officers did their best for their men in circumstances in which it was difficult to do very much at all.

But just as adversity brought out the very best in some, it equally called forth the worst in others. One Federated Malay States Volunteer Force (FMSVF) officer wrote in his diary of the surprising number of British officers who 'do not show much sense of responsibility, and unless forced to do some job simply lie back and contribute nothing to the general welfare'.[11] Similarly an Australian reflecting after the war on the Kwai experience wrote of 'those who bore the badges of leadership, even men of proven valour in action, who reacted to imprisonment with an irritating inertia reflecting suspension of purpose'.[12] Another officer noted that among his colleagues there were 'a few who did nothing other than prepare lists of other ranks available for work, who appeared to take little part in the administration of the camp, and who did little to conceal their ambition, an ambition that we all shared, to survive'.[13] The fact was that the slow motion ordeal they were facing, so unlike the violent and exciting challenge of battle itself, was something for which little in their previous training and experience had prepared them. Courage, resourcefulness and determination were not qualities needed just for a couple of hours or days of desperate and hectic action; they required to be renewed on a daily basis for no-one knew how long. Furthermore the officers of the railway labour force were not exercising real command; they were only in charge to the extent that their Japanese overlords allowed them to be, and only for purposes which these taskmasters sanctioned. This was as clear to the soldiers being led as to the officers still trying manfully to lead. There was a nice balance to be observed between cooperation with the Japanese for the sake of a quiet if difficult life and evident opposition to their more outrageous demands which risked not only punishment of officers and men alike, but also their own deliberate humiliation by the Japanese. It was not an easy row to hoe. In addition, while most officers in the Burma labour force and a good many at the Thai end of the operation were spared becoming a formal part of the railway work parties, there were nevertheless manifold labouring tasks for them to carry out if the camps were to be kept clean, hygienic and habitable. Some of these, for example, anti-malarial trench digging or latrine pit construction were every bit as 'manual' as was the railway work itself. There were officers who were notably unwilling to get involved. Less understandable was the unwillingness of some to make the agreed contribution to the troops' canteen or hospital fund when they received monthly pay whether they worked or not, while the troops forfeited both pay and rations when they were sick. However the squalor and oppression of the situation did encourage perverse behaviour, arguments over small things and an attitude of *sauve qui peut*. But it was only a small minority among the officers who shed all decency in their concern with self-preservation. Only group cohesion could have ensured group survival and it was a general spirit of cooperation and mutual support which finally pulled the majority through this tormenting episode in their lives. By securing the involvement of the whole of the hapless force in the sharing of meagre resources of money, food, labour and physical support it was possible to ensure that many of the sick and weak were able to survive the ordeal. By their example, their organisation and their encouragement, the officers generally saw to it that they did.

Conventional discipline was not easy to enforce since the authority of the POW officers could never be final in the customary sense; but it held up surprisingly well in the circumstances and was certainly easier to maintain, as was its necessary accompaniment, good morale, when original formed operational units, composed of old friends and battle comrades, were able to remain together. It was always a cause of dismay when units which had survived shot and shell together were split up for their initial railway duties or sent to different camps part-way through the project itself, and a great joy when separated friends were reunited, all too frequently in the huts of the larger base hospitals. Keeping units together became a particular problem as the railway work progressed and labour groups moved further up-country leaving their sick comrades to survive as best they could. Because all material necessities were in such short supply, thieving was a common form of petty crime in virtually every railway camp. Often this occurred less because the thief wanted the article concerned than on account of his need of money to buy food or tobacco, or perhaps canteen items for a friend in the camp hospital. Textiles, among many other goods, were in short supply in the region, particularly in lower Burma, and many prisoners were only too ready to sell any surplus clothing, uniform items or equipment to the local people, or personal possessions like watches and fountain pens to the Japanese and Korean guards. Stealing these to get the cash for food was an understandable, though nevertheless illegal activity. The few possessions of POWs who died on the line often found their way to those engaged in this illegal trading. It is difficult for those who consider the morality of this activity from the contented perspective of a full stomach and an unthreatened future to make a satisfactory judgment. For those who faced starvation and battled daily for their very existence the decision was easier to take. Indeed Brigadier Varley of No 3 Group in Burma officially sanctioned the sale of all but the most personal possessions of prisoners who died, the proceeds being used to buy extra food for the sick.[14]

If the mores of the larger social group were difficult to maintain except in terms of the few basic unwritten rules of mutual help and general good behaviour, the comradeship of small groups of soldiers was unshakeable with many examples of self denial on behalf of friends. What modern armies know as the 'buddy-buddy' principle was commonly in action on the railway, where two comrades-in-arms would look after each other's survival and well-being, the fit man perhaps scrounging a daily duck egg for his sick friend who once recovered might well be, in turn, his own guarantee of survival. The Japanese-created social dynamics of imprisonment, like the immediate effect of their initial victory, also put a great strain on relations between the different allied groups when they were reduced to the basic essentials of life in their railway camps. The initial mild surprise of the Australian Java prisoners after their 'hell ship' journey from Tanjong Priok to Singapore on their way up to the Thailand railway, at seeing such neatly dressed, cane-carrying British officers at Changi camp, was an example of such an early perception. Similar was the reaction of the British who were said to have regarded the Australians as 'Java rabble'. These social impressions gave way to stronger views under the pressure of the conditions of the railway where one Australian was later to write of the relations between the two groups, 'Within two months the Australians were to lose all respect for the Englishmen because of their bludging and complaining ways and lack of personal hygiene.' This same officer had no better an opinion of his country's other ally, the 'greedy, arrogant and impetuous Dutch'. 'At least', he wrote 'you knew which side the Japs were on but you could never be sure about the Dutch.'[15] However those whose daily work brought them in very close contact with individuals from the other national groups often developed a high regard for those they met. The men from USS *Houston* and 131st Field Artillery thought sufficient of their Dutch railway medical officer to invite him to the reunions of their 'lost Battalion' over 30 years after war's end and to have his work recorded in the United States Congressional Record.[16]

Part of the problem was that there was little intellectual escape from the tedium, oppression and squalor that filled the eyes and corroded the mind of every prisoner. There were few books available and these their owners clung to through thick and thin. Many were read and re-read in the up-country work camps which were empty of any form of organised entertainment and filled with tired men with little spirit for more active pursuits as their energy steadily ebbed away. One medical officer noted the great pleasure he derived from an old book of *Times* crossword puzzles; others filled the quiet hours with the careful recording of the events of their captivity, an occupation which the Japanese had banned but which continued nonetheless. Living so close to one's fellows for twenty-four hours a day was trial enough, however considerate and socially well-adjusted the individuals concerned may have been; 'we lived and slept like pigs in a litter' is how one officer put it. Consequently some sought opportunities to escape, not from Japanese imprisonment, but at least from the proximity of their fellow men for a while. It was easy to overlook the beauty of the surroundings amid the pressure of work, the sickness and the constant thoughts of food. Some nevertheless found the time, the inclination and the opportunity to appreciate the wild loveliness of the valley of the Kwai with its towering hills beyond the western Burmese bank, its ever-busy river and its varied wild life. The riverline bird life was particularly interesting for those who could get out of camp alone and in the quiet to observe it. Frequently seen were gaunt grey herons, brilliant-hued Pitta ground thrushes, flashing kingfishers, Java peafowl, chattering parakeets and huge, ungainly, noisy-winged hornbills. Most notable of all perhaps were the great colonies of gregarious butterflies, large and gaudy, which literally carpeted the ground on which they settled like so many multicoloured flowers and then all flew off as one, when disturbed, as if the carpet were being whipped away. It was strange how so much beauty and so much hardship and suffering could be so easily juxtaposed.

8

Speedo – The Plan

A great speed-up seems to have been ordered on the railway, and
everyone is taken out to work, officers as well as sick men
Captain J. T. Barnard
Kinsaiyok Camp, March 1943

IN MID-JANUARY 1943 a Japanese railway staff officer from the control
centre for the Burma–Siam railway was summoned to Imperial
General Headquarters in Tokyo to give a progress report on the construction achieved to date. To his surprise and shock he was ordered to
ensure that the railway was completed by May 1943. The staff officer,
we are told, 'was amazed at this reckless command and explained
what at the time was the volume of work still to be done' and stressed
the difficulties involved.[1] Ultimately a three month postponement
was agreed; the railway was to be operational by the end of August
1943.

Back on the railway site itself the engineer officers wondered if even
a full year of construction work, as originally agreed, would be
sufficient to see the project to a conclusion. At the time of this fateful
interview the progress with the operation was indeed relatively
modest. The embankment head in the south had been pushed on to
Wanyai, 127 kilometres from the start point at Nong Pladuk, but
trains were only running from the terminus there as far north as
Kanchanaburi, beyond which the river Maekhlaung crossed their
path though light trains were just beginning to make a precarious
crossing of the river via the light wooden bridge which had now been
completed, and were running beside the east bank of the Kwai for the
first time. However the roadbed along the bank of the Kwai was
progressing only slowly with major construction work still required
at the Chungkai cutting and on to the two great viaducts at the 103 and

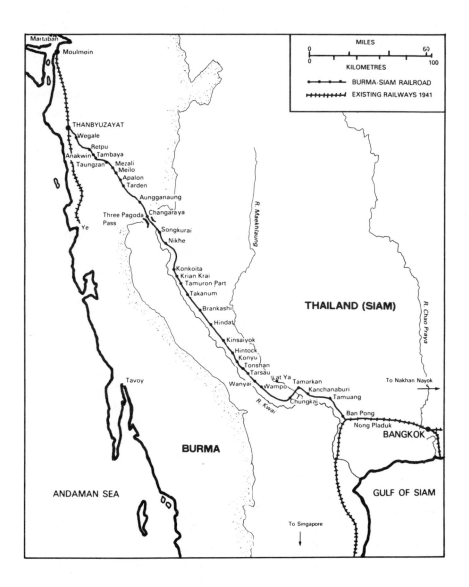

4. The Burma–Siam Railroad

109 kilometre points. As for the main concrete and steel Maekhlaung bridge itself, months of work were required before it could carry the construction materials, sleepers and rails needed for the up-country section of the line. Until then most of these heavy stores would have to make the journey by river. Furthermore the Thai-side survey was still only approaching Kinsaiyok at the 171 kilometre point, with the survey from the Burma end having progressed as far as Nikhe which meant that there was still 100 kilometres of territory between the two which had yet to be closely surveyed. Until that task had been completed the engineers would have no clear idea of the exact construction work to be done or the time that would be required for its completion with a workforce of any given size. As to the rail track itself, in the Burma sector this had hardly moved forward from Thanbyuzayat; work was still going on further north to put a temporary bridge across the river Sittang which would have to be crossed if traffic coming up from Thailand was to get supplies to the operational units in Burma proper. Meanwhile at the railway stores areas at each terminus the rails which had been cannibalised from the Malayan and Burmese railways were being stockpiled with the sleepers, girders, timber and gravel that would be needed as the work progressed. In short, all the materials for the railway's completion were now available, but about two thirds of the roadbed work, including the more difficult and inaccessible up-country sections, remained to be tackled.[2] When he received the revised completion date from Tokyo, Major General Shimoda, the Commander of the Railway Construction Unit, dutifully passed on the orders to his two main subordinates, Lieutenant Colonels Sasaki and Imai who commanded the railway regiments. These officers were as astonished as the emissary to Tokyo had been when first presented with the revised completion date and when they, in turn, passed on the news to their own engineer subordinates, the latter 'one after another stressed how impossible it was'.[3]

This was clearly a critical watershed in the history of the railway project. Important decisions would now have to be taken about fresh reinforcements for the labour force; there were new engineering difficulties to be confronted and additional specialist engineering manpower would be required. It was clear that the labour force would have to work harder and in the more difficult conditions of the up-country sections of the trace. If the revised date was to be met the work would have to continue through the monsoon. This was likely to make transport difficult to maintain along the supply road which was being constructed alongside the railway, but which still awaited completion, though the River Kwai itself, once swollen by the monsoon rains, would be easier to navigate. Besides this, working through the monsoon was bound to exacerbate the sickness problem. A great responsibility rested on the shoulders of General Shimoda whom Tokyo had charged with meeting the revised deadline.

On 26 January 1943 Shimoda and his staff officer Major Irie took off for an aerial inspection of the Burma section of the trace. At about 1400 hours when the general was surveying the area to the west of Nikhe, his plane crashed into a teak forest on the west-facing slope of Khao Mayan Tong. Shimoda and nine other passengers were killed outright, but the navigator, Sakurai, and a war correspondent, Asanaga, survived the impact and struggled out into the jungle. The injured Asanaga lived only for a few days but the navigator managed to survive for a month on water only until discovered by a search party under Lieutenant Nogi sent out from a camp near Songkurai. The weakened navigator was able to confirm the death of the Railway Control commander and his staff. Thus at the very time when the railway project needed the firmest direction from the top, it lost the officer who had guided its planning and execution right from the earliest negotiations with the Thai government the previous year. Shimoda was succeeded at 2 Railway Control by Major General Takasaki from Manchuria, whose own period of command was fated to be limited.[4] The Japanese engineers were understandably uncomprehending when the railway completion date was advanced so dramatically. Yet if they had been in full possession of the facts of Japan's worsening strategic situation they would surely have appreciated the urgency of the task they had been given.

On practically every battlefront in the southern regions the tide was beginning to turn against Japan. The long and costly Guadalcanal campaign was now drawing to a close and though the Japanese garrison continued to fight bitterly, it was gradually being forced into the island's western corner. When the troops were finally withdrawn at the end of January they left behind nearly 15,000 dead. A similar fate had befallen the expeditionary force sent overland to take Port Moresby in Papua New Guinea. By the time the Tokyo meeting about the railway completion date took place, organised Japanese resistance in Papua was almost at an end with the loss of a further 12,000 Imperial soldiers. Similar misfortunes had overtaken Japanese forces in the majority of the naval actions in the South Pacific which were themselves an important determinant of the fortunes on land in these island-hopping campaigns. The persistent efforts of the Japanese to reinforce Guadalcanal led to series of major actions at sea. In the Battles of Cape Esperance and Santa Cruz Japanese naval losses were minimal, though in the latter engagement well over a 100 of her naval aircraft were destroyed; but in the final series of naval engagements in the area, known collectively as the Battle of Guadalcanal, losses were severe: two battleships, a cruiser, three destroyers and eleven transports were sunk and a further three ships were damaged. The assault troops crowded on the transports were drowned. In the last action of all, the Battle of Tassafaronga, fought in the narrow channel south of Savo Island on the night of 30 November the Japanese actually had the best of the engagement in the constricted waters between her destroyers and US cruisers. But the achievement of such a marginal victory whilst sustaining substantial losses in the course of it was of no real service to the Japanese cause. The American production machine was now swinging into action; by the war's end it would be averaging in new production one cruiser and seven destroyers a month, figures which the Japanese had no prospect of matching. The initiative had now been wrested from the Japanese in the South and South West Pacific areas while in the Central and North Pacific Admiral Nimitz's submarine warfare operations continued to erode his opponent's naval strength. Japan's merchant marine was also sustaining further losses which it could ill afford and had little chance of replacing with new vessels. In January 1943 a further 34 merchantmen went down, 158,000 gross tons in all and the second highest monthly total of the war to date; 21 other vessels were to follow them to the bottom the following month. The demands of the bitterly contested southern Pacific campaigns had also meant that those merchant ships which still made the increasingly hazardous voyage around the Malayan peninsula and up the Andaman Sea to the Burmese port of Rangoon, did so without any naval escort to ward off the threat from the British Eastern Fleet as well as from submarines. At the start of 1943 it was estimated that between 30,000 and 40,000 tons of shipping was still passing regularly along the Rangoon river, but developments were soon to put this traffic increasingly at risk.

In the Burma theatre itself the situation was no more encouraging. Having a land frontier with so vast a reservoir of military manpower as the Indian subcontinent represented had always been a concern for the Japanese, though they imagined initially that the difficult nature of the terrain in the Indo-Burmese border area created something of a barrier in itself to any Allied plans for a counter offensive. However, as early as 22 July 1942 Imperial General Headquarters had authorised the study of Operation 21 which was a plan for a follow-through of the Burma campaign with an offensive into Assam in north eastern India. The study called for two divisions to move north west along the Hukawng Valley, two more to take the British base at Imphal and a fifth to capture Chittagong on the coast. The plan was later dropped after opposition from General Mutaguchi, commander of the 18th Division and General Shozo of the 33rd together with their Army Commander General Iida. However, there was sense in the proposal insofar as Imphal was indeed now being developed as a major Allied base. There was much to be feared from this plateau ringed by hills in the north eastern corner of India and now being reinforced with fresh formations. Furthermore, a British offensive was already being launched along Burma's western seaboard before 1942 had actually drawn to a close. This was an advance from the Chittagong area down the 90 miles of the Mayu peninsula to take Akyab Island at its southern extremity. The operation was of modest proportions, but if successful it would have left the British in possession of the northernmost of the string of coastal airfields which fringe the western littoral of Burma, besides giving them their first victory of the Burma war, a fillip to morale which was sorely needed. The advance began in mid-December and initially all went well; the closing days of 1942 saw the British forces in the coastal plain just short of the tip of the peninsula, with Akyab Island almost in sight. However they now came up against Japanese bunker defences for the first time and despite repeated frontal attacks and heavy casualties they failed to dislodge their opponents from them. Ultimately a Japanese counter attack pressed the Allied force back and by May when the monsoon rains began, the Japanese were again in control of the peninsula. However there had been many anxious moments for the occupation forces during the British attack and the situation was not put to rights until reinforcements were marched across from central Burma to assist the coastal garrison. All had ended well but it was clear that once the rainy season was over fresh and stronger Allied efforts directed at the recapture of Burma could be expected.

Within days of the Japanese decision to 'hasten the construction' of the railway came a fresh indication of the British intentions and also of their less orthodox capabilities. On 13 February 3,000 Chindits crossed the Chindwin in seven columns and trekked eastwards two hundred miles into Japanese-held Burma and succeeded in blowing up bridges and cuttings on the Mandalay–Myitkyina railway to the

China front. This was a courageous exploit which took heavy toll of the troops involved, of whom about a third failed to return to base, though the Japanese rapidly repaired the railway and had trains running again in little more than a week. However, the exploits of the Chindits did substantiate the concern of some of those Japanese military planners who averred that the security of north eastern Burma could not be left to the rivers, mountains and jungle which separated it from British India. Reinforcements for the theatre would certainly be required and perhaps a pre-emptive offensive would need to be authorised to take the Imphal base and spread panic and disaffection in the populous provinces of north eastern India with the aid of the Japanese-sponsored Indian independence movement. This would frustrate for a considerable time any counter-offensive intentions by the Allies. Such action from the Indian base was indeed what was now being planned. The Combined Chiefs of Staff had met at Casablanca in January and in addition to taking important strategic decisions for the European theatre, they also recommended the re-establishment of land communications with China, driven through from the tiny strip of northern Burma still in Allied hands, and a major offensive for the recovery of Burma proper (Operation Anakim) to begin in November when the monsoon had subsided. The Americans were already engaged in a massive airlift to the beleaguered Chinese via the 'Hump Route' across the mountains from India, while the rapidly growing complex of air bases in north-eastern India was now supporting an expanding force of long-range bombers.

When the British and American-led Chinese forces had first been driven from Burma there was very little that the Allied air forces could do to help them regain it. At that time Eastern Command India had only a few light bombers available and an unfortunate combination of the defeatist attitude engendered by the long retreat, the poor living conditions and the acute shortage of tools, equipment and spare parts, meant that the serviceability rate of these Blenheims at one stage reached the incredibly low figure of 2 per cent.[5] Although the Americans had some heavy bombers in India these were either birds of passage intended for use in China, or else employed exclusively on the aerial life-line which kept the western Chinese armies supplied and capable of fighting. But as the months went by the situation steadily improved. The first priority was the building of airfields of which north eastern India was woefully short. A programme for the construction of 200 airfields was begun and as this developed so also did the schedule for the build-up of squadrons to occupy them. By the autumn the construction programme and the growing air strength were beginning to show results.

In November 1942 the heavy bomber squadrons of 231 Group RAF began to arrive, in particular 159 Squadron which had been formed earlier in the year and was equipped with B24 Liberators for service in the Middle East. The Liberators were produced in far greater numbers than any other American aircraft during the war, a grand total of some 18,500, and at last the squadrons of Air Headquarters India were beginning to get their share. In the war against Japanese transportation in South East Asia this 'box car' heavy bomber was a most important addition to the Allied armoury. The Liberators did not operate very often before the end of the year for lack of spares and repair facilities; but their remarkable reach was well demonstrated on 26 November by a bombing raid by eight of them on an oil refinery and power plant in Bangkok, a round trip of 2,760 miles. This was a disquieting experience for the Japanese for if Bangkok was within range, all of the projected Burma–Siam railway was vulnerable, and most of it had yet to be built. However, in this early period most strategic raids were directed against Rangoon and the sea traffic which concentrated on the port there. This at least confirmed the Japanese in their belief that an alternative land resupply route to the beleaguered Burmese capital was a vital necessity. This message was being underscored by the US 7th Bombardment Group at about the same time. The Group's 9th Bombardment squadron also began to return from the Middle East in October 1942, bringing with it some B24 Liberator aircraft. While the 9th was returning to India, two new squadrons, 492nd and 493rd were activated at Karachi and similarly began equipping with B24s. A fourth squadron, 436th, was also added to the potential hitting power of this as yet untested force. Two of the squadrons were in action before the end of 1942 and the others by late January the following year. Mandalay and Rangoon were the principal targets for 9 Group but its Liberators also made the long haul to Bangkok for a second attack on the oil refinery two days after the British bombing raid. On Boxing Day 1942 the Thai capital's indus- *? 1943 ?* trial installations were attacked by a force of 12 American Liberators. However the main aim of these early operations was the interdiction of Rangoon as a port and communications centre.

In February 1943 a new phase in this campaign began with the aerial mining of Rangoon, Moulmein and other Burmese ports. This was the first use of aerial mining techniques in the Pacific theatre and it put increasingly at hazard the sea traffic to this, the farthest-flung garrison of the new Japanese empire. With every raid on the Burmese port the significance of the alternative land route to the Burma theatre was brought into sharper focus. The air attacks were growing in strength and frequency though it has to be admitted that they could not be prosecuted with either sufficient strength or regularity in the early months of 1943 for them seriously to threaten the Japanese supplies. It was what these raids portended that gave the Japanese the most serious worries. Such raids were bound to assume more serious proportions when the monsoon ended, when visibility improved and targets could be more readily identified and efficiently attacked. For the Japanese, the monsoon was a breathing space during which it was imperative for them to have the landward supply route to Burma constructed and operational. But the respite of the monsoon for the Japanese logistical planners was to be the curse of those who had to build the railway in the appalling working conditions that the rainy season produced.

It was already clear that the existing labour force of Allied prisoners, Burmese volunteers and contracted Thais would be insufficient for the labouring side of the project. This was despite the fact that further parties of prisoners had been sent north to the railway during the early months of 1943. In January many trainloads of Dutch prisoners had arrived at Ban Pong and begun their laborious trek to their railway camps. These were men who had been captured on Java and transported from there to Changi to await their turn for a major labour detail. Nearly 9,000 of them made the journey in the steel box cars from Singapore to the Thai end of the project and a further 1,600 Australians and over 450 Americans went with them. The trouble was that many of these men were already weak and undernourished and unlikely to be able to withstand the inhospitable and primitive conditions of the jungle camps. The Australian army ration of 1941 was calculated to give a man a daily intake of 4,220 calories; but in Changi they had been subsisting on about 2,000. Many would be patients in the camp hospitals within days or weeks of their arrival. Before the Japanese began planning for additional prisoners to join their workforce to carry out Tokyo's orders for the earlier operation of the line, they had already amassed the impressive total of almost 40,000 Allied prisoners along the railway trace,[6] but it was a figure many thousands short of this total that was fit for work each day.

The slow progress with the more difficult engineering tasks at the southern end of the line made it plain that additional Japanese engineering personnel were urgently required. Colonel Imai travelled down to Malaya to visit the headquarters of No 4 Special Railway Construction Corps which was working there on the restoration of Malayan Railways, now limited to the main west coast line. Imai visited the bridging unit's headquarters at Ipoh where the principal task had been the repair of the bridge over the River Krian. This job was now virtually complete and the unit's engineers were hoping to be repatriated to Japan. However, 'amazed and disappointed' they now heard that repatriation was off and they were to go north to help with the Burma–Siam railway. Colonel Imai explained how badly needed were the unit's special bridging skills, including those of its attached civilian experts. The latter were formed into a special unit under an officer from Railway Control and operated in support of Colonel Imai's regiment with *gunzoku* Futamatsu acting as the Colonel's personal adviser. On March 10 Murahashi unit, as it was called, moved up to Wanyai, 157 kilometres up the new railway from the start point, where Colonel Imai had now established his headquarters. North with it went the three Japanese bridging labour units from Malaya, Nos 1, 3 and 4.[7] The Wanyai base had now been expanded to cope with the 'rush construction'; the service road which now linked it with Kanchanaburi was soon busy with traffic moving up supplies for the construction work still to be tackled in the up-country sections and only recently surveyed. By mid-March the Special Bridging Unit from Malaya had taken over the work on the main Maekhlaung steel bridge from Imai's 3rd Battalion. The concrete bridge piers had now been built and steel girder assembly was the next task. Comb-shaped steel trusses for the girders (curved chord warren-type half-through trusses, for the technically-minded) had been brought north from Java Railways for the project. The bridging unit now began to prepare these to span the 20 metre gaps between the concrete piers. Meanwhile 2 Railway Control, in charge of the entire railway operation, moved up to the neighbouring district capital town Kanchanaburi. In addition, the Imperial Guards Engineer Regiment was brought in to help with the completion of the service road which ran alongside the railway. This was finally finished at the end of March 1943.

On the Burma side of the operation 4 Battalion 5th Railway Regiment which had been stationed further east was brought across to join the main railway project and 2 Labour Unit in Burma was called in to assist with the bridging of the Sittang River. 5 Railway Regiment moved its operational base forward from Thanbyuzayat to Taungzan, about 60 kilometres along the trace from the junction with Burma

Railways. Because of the engineering problems its sister regiment was encountering, 5 Regiment was also apportioned a longer section of the construction work. It had originally been responsible for the 115 kilometres from Thanbyuzayat to Nikhe but now was allocated an extra stretch of almost 40 kilometres, with the new demarcation point being Tamuron Port. Despite the reduction in his regiment's work sector to 245 kilometres, Colonel Imai was under no illusions about the enormity of the task confronting him. In mid March he called his officers together to discuss the period of 'rush construction' which lay ahead. In his pep talk to his staff he emphasised the importance of the job, the difficulties of the season, the need for health care (which he said the Japanese were scrupulous about unlike the POWs and the coolies) and the fact that success would depend upon 'the troops demonstrating their spiritual power in earnest work'. Imai's adviser Futamatsu later questioned his regimental commander about the almost quantifiable impossibility of the task the engineers had been set. Imai, himself an engineering graduate from Tokyo university, answered that it was a soldier's duty to exert himself even to inevitable death and that there was no excuse for thinking about the hardships of subordinate troops.[8]

A further change took place in the wake of the decision to speed up the construction work; this was the decision to put the POW labour camps under the direct command of the railway organisation itself. Previously the engineers had laid down the work quotas and specified the number of workers that were required; the responsibility for providing them had rested with the prison camp authorities. Henceforth the engineers themselves would have the final say concerning who would work and who might be allowed to remain on the sick list. Since the engineers were now under great pressure to push ahead with the work, it is perhaps not surprising that they should have transferred some of that pressure to the workforce. Elsewhere in the Pacific theatre of war the Japanese were being defeated as much by the plenitude of the material resources of their main opponents, the Americans, as by anything else. They were increasingly having to rely on the 'spiritual qualities' of their fighting men – their preparedness to fight to the death – to have any chance of holding on to their expanded empire. This reliance on the spiritual qualities was something they were now increasingly to expect from their workforce as well. Colonel Imai's words expressed the generally-held sentiment among the railway commanders and were to result in the ruthless drive for the completion of the railway whatever consequences this might have for the lives of those labouring on it.

9

Reinforcements

It is sad to see these poor creatures trudging their way up the deep slushy
mud of our road guarded by N troops – a wonderful tribute to the new
order in South East Asia
Lieutenant Colonel Dunlop, Hintock Camp.
22 April 1943[1]

THE RAILWAY surveyors' calculations were that they would have to
move some 20,000 cubic metres of earth and construct 10 metres of
bridging each day if they were to complete the project in the restricted
timeframe now available to them.[2] A significant increase in the size of
the labour force was a clear imperative. To provide it the Japanese
turned to the source from which it could most easily and most
speedily be made available – the government of Burma. This administration was little more than an administrative organ of the Japanese
military government. From the viewpoint of the occupying power the
puppet administration also had the advantage of being highly centralised and, since every Burmese District Officer had his own
Japanese counsellor, the orders for a fresh recruitment could be
readily monitored as well as rapidly transmitted. However this did
not mean that the new recruiting arrangements went smoothly or
according to plan. In fact the recollection of Burma's Director of
Press and Publicity was that it became 'one of the biggest rackets of
the Japanese interlude in Burma'.[3] The basic problem was that by this
time it had become only too obvious that the Japanese promises of
good working conditions, medical facilities and other incentives for
the railway workers were far from being fulfilled. The apparent enthusiasm with which the 1942 recruitment had been undertaken was
certainly not to be observed in the campaign of the following year
when the need for fresh labour forces was even more urgent.

111

The first enrolment into the 'Sweat Army' for the railway work, beginning with an initial draft of 30,000 and followed by several others, had succeeded in engaging and placing on the line about 87,000 workers between July 1942 and January 1943.[4] However once the news of the conditions at the camp sites and the lack of direction and effective management by the Japanese began to filter back to the villages, often via those who had managed to escape from the work parties, enthusiasm for the project began to wane. Furthermore, as time went on, the sites at which the labour was required grew more distant from the base area around Thanbyuzayat at which conditions, if not good, were at least bearable. Up-country the work sites were primitive in the extreme. Thus, by the time plans were being made to acquire the workforce for the 'Speedo' period, 'more than half of the labourers', the Burmese Premier believed, 'had disappeared, having either fled or been killed off like flies by black-water fever'. Against this background, for the new labour campaign to be a practical proposition at all without improved conditions it inevitably degenerated into 'one of the most abominable crimes committed on the people during the war'. But despite the insensitivity and ruthlessness with which it was planned and carried out, it nevertheless proved to be a rather inefficient mechanism for actually getting labourers to work at the railway sites.

The change that was introduced for the 1943 railway recruitment was its removal from the hands of the 'Sweat Army' and transfer to the control of the National Labour Service Corps into which there were 14 separate enlistments between March 1943 and August 1944. This was more than a simple administrative change: the recruitment was no longer on a voluntary basis, the workers were conscripted. Under the centralised adminstrative system the Districts were each allocated a quota of workers which they were obliged to fill. They in turn issued quotas which each village had to meet. This system, which gave the whole power of recruitment to the local officials, with the Japanese labour officers merely saying how many coolies they needed, led to what Premier Ba Maw later acknowledged as a 'colossal racket'. Local officials would see that all their enemies were recruited, rich peasants would buy their way out with large bribes and if the total numbers required were still not obtained, 'the bums and tramps in town would be rounded up, appeased with a small payment', and packed off with instructions to run away at the first opportunity.[5] Reports even filtered back to Allied intelligence agents of ingenious Burmese making a profitable if precarious living by volunteering to go as part of the village quota in place of someone who would pay them from 50 to 100 rupees for their trouble. After leaving the village these fraudsters would defect and then repeat the process. The evidence suggested that the Japanese were taking stern measures against this type of trickery, while the Burmese district officials were reported to be occupied with labour recruiting and little else. One was said to refer to himself as 'head coolie' since the chief use the Japanese had for his services was bringing pressure on village headmen to fill their quotas.[6]

Of course, as time went on the labour supply inevitably dwindled and the opposition to the whole enterprise became overt and widespread. Villages were at times unable to fill their quotas and the Japanese and their agents resorted to brute force and raw compulsion to keep the numbers up. Some men were forcibly dragged away from their homes and packed off to the collection points. It was also reported that some railhead coolies recruited initially by the Burmese government were later on kidnapped by the Japanese and recorded as Japanese-recruited labour, as a means of discrediting the Burmese authorities.[7] These labour conscription methods and the conditions under which the workers operated, their labour potential being largely squandered by their appalling treatment, were such that there was much restiveness among the public officials involved. The British authorities in India certainly believed that the emotive issue of forced labour was a suitable subject for their psychological warfare operations.[8] The first four conscription campaigns under the Labour Service Corps system had quotas varying in size between 15,000 and 30,000 men and totalling 86,000 in all; but in the event only a few more than 50,000 were actually despatched to Thanbyuzayat, as little as 46 per cent of the quota in one particular case. Once at the railhead further desertions occurred, and at the camps themselves, given the primitive conditions which greeted the coolies there, sickness and death soon began to take their toll. As each depressing account of conditions filtered back to the villages of central Burma, so the next campaign to impress yet more villagers would be an even less successful venture. The fifth recruitment for example was for 15,000 labourers, of which the Districts managed to supply only 9,174; 3,135 of these were successful in escaping en route to Moulmein; a further 1,035 disappeared when they finally reached this major southern town and an additional 256 were sent back as unfit. Thus only 4,748 labourers were eventually sent on to Thanbyuzayat, 31 per cent of the number the Japanese had originally specified and 51 per cent of the number the Burmese officials had managed to collect.[9] It was a grossly inefficient system but also, in view of the fate which befell many of those who did get to the railway, a desperately tragic episode.

In the light of the limited success which attended this Burmese operation, it is not surprising that the Japanese turned to a second major pool of available labour which local economic circumstances were to make a very willing addition to the railway labour force: this was the rural Indian population of Malaya now eking out a pitifully inadequate existence throughout the western side of the long peninsula which lay between the Thai border and the main Japanese headquarters in Singapore. Large numbers of Indians had been brought over to Malaya in the nineteenth century to work the lucrative sugar plantations in Province Wellesley. The sugar crop expanded throughout the century until the rubber tree was introduced in 1877 when two cases of seedlings from the Royal Botanic Gardens at Kew were sent to the Botanic Gardens in Singapore. Within a generation their progeny were covering millions of acres throughout Malaya where the cultivated form of the rubber tree, tended by the Indian plantation workers, was producing more latex than was cropped from the entire jungle-grown Brazilian form indigenous to the Amazon valley whence Kew had obtained its original specimens. The phenomenal rise in the demand for rubber led to increased immigration from southern India to supply the plantations' needs. Most of the Indians were Tamils from the Madras Presidency and other southern provinces, though there were considerable numbers of Telegus, a similar racial group who also speak Tamil and often inter-marry with Tamils. By the time of the 1931 census, there were nearly 515,000 Tamils in Malaya and 32,500 Telegus, 83 per cent and 5 per cent respectively of the total Indian population. The proportions would have been roughly the same at the time of the Japanese occupation with the Tamils largely forming the workforce on the rubber estates and the Telegus working on the coconut plantations. The Indian rubber tappers lived on the estates themselves where they were provided with free quarters – long single-storied blocks of hutments known as the 'Tamil lines' – a water supply and often free medical attention. Some also received from their employers sickness and maternity benefits; a dispensary and anti-malarial measures were also generally provided. In some cases the estate workers were permitted to graze their own stock and grow vegetables for domestic consumption. At a rough and ready level it was a comprehensive employment package within a paternalistic but by no means indulgent system.

There was never any lack of prospective immigrants eager to make the journey across the Indian Ocean to enjoy regular employment on the plantations and the reasonable standard of living that went with it.

What made these plantation workers such a ready labour pool for the Japanese was the calamitous deterioration in their economic circumstances between 1940 and 1943. One of the consequences of the huge influx of British, Indian and Australian troops in 1940 and 1941 to defend Malaya was that the cost of living soared for the local residents. For the labourers working on the estates for wages of rather less than £1 per week the effect was disastrous. They asked for more pay and went on strike when they did not get it. The estate managers reacted by cutting off supplies to the 'lines'. The trouble did not finally simmer down until the police were called in and troops given emergency powers: a hard line was taken since rubber was regarded as vital to the war economy, and a wider war was threatening. Beneath the surface serenity which finally returned, a strong Japanese fifth column assiduously fomented the workers' grievances, exploiting the disagreements between the tappers and their European managers. The Indian community was encouraged to oppose British imperialism and work for freedom from European domination. Immediately after the conquest of Malaya, Indian Independence Leagues were fostered by the Japanese authorities in all the Malay states and leading Indian community leaders became the figureheads of the local League organisations. Rash Behari Bose, the Japan-based Indian nationalist leader, was despatched to Malaya in May 1942 to give further impetus to the movement. Support for Japanese enterprises seemed in the interest of Indian nationalism and certainly the self-preservation of the more educated Indian classes. In the light of this appeal to nationalist sentiments it is not surprising that many Tamils joined the Indian National Army. At the same time, once the Japanese occupation took place the rubber and rice economies were thrown into complete disarray and the condition of the estate workers deteriorated still further.

During the Allied withdrawal a 'scorched earth' policy had been adopted so far as the mining industry was concerned and much of the dredging and mining equipment was destroyed. However the rubber and other plantations were left largely unscathed. Nevertheless the departure of the British led to a complete dislocation of estate management; the estate hospitals were closed and the workers were left to fend for themselves. With the European rubber market denied to them, the estates declined; in any case Japan could never have absorbed the Malayan production even if it could have been transported home. Many rubber trees were ultimately chopped down and used for fuel. Furthermore rice, which was the staple food of the people of Malaya, was now in short supply and an extensive black market in it grew up. The British had never encouraged Malaya to be self-sufficient in rice: to the north lay the rich rice-bowls of Burma and Thailand which supplied much of Malaya's requirements in return for rubber and tin. However the ravages of war, Allied bombing and Japanese shipping losses reduced, and were finally to eliminate, the rice trade with Burma. The supply of Thai rice presented a different problem; Thailand was still independent though formally pro-Japanese, but its rice merchants refused to accept the Japanese scrip. The Thai government allocated a fixed quota of rice to the Japanese on a contract system and this was stockpiled in Malaya for military use. They would supply no more unless paid in convertible currency or by other commodities. The Japanese encouraged the wider cultivation of rice, tapioca and other food crops but refused to allow the private enterprise import of rice into Malaya which would threaten their own rice monopolist Mitsubishi Shoji Kaisha.[10] In such short supply did this staple food become that the rice price soon became the yardstick for all payments and charges. Rice control became population control. By the lure of special rice allocations the Japanese got their labour forces for various projects in Malaya and further afield.

For the southern Indians of western Malaya whose estate-managed lives had been thrown into such turmoil, whose livelihood had disappeared with the demise of the rubber industry and who could certainly neither afford the black market prices now being charged for rice, nor manage to subsist on the rice ration issued to them, the Japanese offer of employment in Thailand was not unattractive. Press gang methods of the kind resorted to in Burma were not required. The pay was to be a dollar a day plus 50 cents family allowance and the workers' food and accommodation were to be supplied by the Japanese. However in the railway employment package the rice ration was the critical factor. As one Malayan Chinese observer explained it, 'Thousands of workmen were even lured to service in Burma and Thailand becuase they could not carry on with black-market rice. High wages alone were insufficient. It was high wages plus extra rice – and rice was the infallible draw'.[11] The authorities promised that their Malayan workers would be brought back to their homes on completion of the work which was expected to be in three to six months' time. The recruitment was also helped by the fact that the rubber-growing areas of Malaya in which these impoverished tappers were concentrated – the states of Negri Semblian, Selangor and Perak – were found together on the western side of the peninsula, through which the only railway line to the north now ran.

In the six months beginning in April 1943, 70,000 Malayan Indians were recruited and made the rail journey north to Ban Pong. Some had apparently accepted the offer of work at Padang Besar near the Malayan border and were surprised when their train did not stop until it reached Ban Pong, 750 miles further north.[12] On arrival there they were told that they would be marching to Burma to work, though their clothes were quite inadequate for the early monsoon conditions and their one dollar pay was similarly insufficient for the inflated canteen food prices demanded by the Thai traders along the railway. Many spent their nights in the open and in the wet on the march north to the workplaces where the accommodation prepared for them was primitive in the extreme. One Allied POW described a camp he and some fellow workers built for a party of Tamils who had journeyed up from Malaya. It consisted of about four acres of river bank from which the jungle had been burnt off. Onto this, one-thickness canvas tents with no end or side flaps were pitched high off the ground. Inside these the POWs built two rows of split bamboo sleeping shelves, one above the other, the first a foot from the ground, the second four feet above it. There were no latrines. In each tent 50 Tamils were to live through the height of the monsoon.[13]

The Japanese authorities also continued to exploit the reservoir of POW labour which remained in Singapore. The last major group to move north to the railway had been the 16 trainloads of prisoners, Dutch in the main and originally captured in Java, who had left Singapore station in January and early February. A month later they were followed by the next reinforcement, the 5,000 men who made up 'D' Force. This consisted of 2,780 British prisoners and 2,220 Australians drawn principally from the artillery units of 8th Division which constituted the largest Australian group so far to travel up to the southern end of the line. It was once again, as were all the journeys from Singapore to Ban Pong, made in the steel rice trucks which, in the days of a dwindling rice trade with Thailand, could easily be spared from their principal purpose. Nevertheless the POWs were packed into each truck as tightly as had been the members of the earlier parties for the five days and four nights of the journey north, with one halt a day when the two rations of rice and one pint of water were issued to each prisoner and occasional pauses in sidings while more important traffic rattled past on the main line. Since the track north from Ban Pong along the Maekhlaung plain was now completed, the groups were able to transfer to flat open rail cars for the journey to the ancient walled city of Kanchanaburi which marked the end of the first and easy stretch of railway construction. At this point the Japanese arrangements seemed to have broken down for the men were left to fend for themselves for a week at 'Kanburi' as they called the district capital, trading their personal possessions with the local stall holders and merchants for welcome and much needed additions to their diet. At the end of the week the Japanese and Korean guards arrived, the prisoners were rounded up and the pressure was on again.

Some units of 'D' Force were used first of all on embankment and cutting work and similar tasks where progress had fallen behind schedule, before moving on to the final camps further north from which they would operate during the monsoon on their allocated section of the track. One of the 'D' Force parties was assigned to the camp known as K3 in the Konyu group, about 160 kilometres up the line towards Burma. At this point in its course the river Kwai makes a westerly bend, but the trace of the railway did not follow it and took a much more direct route with the result that it was a considerable distance from the camp to the river, the main communications artery. The only other water was a shallow stream which passed the Japanese camp before it reached the POW compound. The men were given an afternoon and an evening to clear the site and build the camp before they began work on the line itself the following morning. They were to live in tents, one for each 16 men; but each group was given only either the inner tent cover or the outer fly. Since neither was fully waterproof without the other, things did not bode well for the rainy season; the monsoon proper was to break about a month later. The main work for the K3 labourers was the hacking out of a cutting in a hillside, 'Hell Fire Pass' as it later became known. This was in two sections, one about 500 yards long by about 25 feet high and the other about 80 yards long by 80 feet high. For many prisoners it was the 'hammer and tap' routine, drilling out holes in the rocky surface for the gelignite charges to be laid by the Japanese engineers. After the blasting a second group of prisoners would clear away the debris while the 'hammer and tap' men moved on to prepare another section of the rock for the explosives. It was dangerous and exacting work and was performed under increasing pressure as the Japanese engineers struggled to meet their deadlines.

A month later a further increment to the workforce moved up from

Singapore. On five successive days starting on 13 April a train left the city station crammed with 600 more future railway coolies; the great majority of this draft being Dutch but with 150 Australians and a few Americans and Englishmen travelling with them. This was the last major party to be transferred from the Japanese authorities in Singapore to the administrative control of the railway organisation. They were joined in Thailand by 700 prisoners from Saigon, part of the larger group which had been shipped from Medan in Sumatra to the capital of French Indo-China about a year earlier. The Thailand POW Administration had now received almost 50,000 Allied prisoners to support 2 Railway Control's project; roughly 110,000 Burmese workers had been recruited and placed on the line and more were soon to join them. The first groups of Indians from Malaya were making their way north to the jungle camps and numbers of Thai and Burmese contractors were supplying materials at the construction sites. The Japanese engineering and administrative force for the project now totalled some 12,000 men. Equipment for it was being supplied from Burma, Thailand, Malaya, Sumatra, Java and, a very small proportion, from Japan itself.

It was an enormous enterprise, but essentially a labour-intensive one. When the project was at the planning stage it had been estimated that a workforce of 100,000 men would be required. Already this figure had been vastly exceeded but the work was still not proceeding to timetable. The essence of the problem was not that the project was proving more difficult than the Japanese had expected, though there were some formidable engineering complications to contend with given the primitive equipment with which the project was being tackled and the shortage of experienced engineers for the less complex parts of the work. The real difficulty stemmed from defective administrative arrangements and the steady attrition of the labour force caused by desertion, sickness and death. Over 600 prisoners of war had now died and an unknown number of Burmese had also perished. But many times more lay sick in the camp hospital huts, while the remaining proportion of the workforce which was ostensibly fit was being progessively weakened by undernourishment, poor conditions and hard work. It is estimated that only 50 per cent of the camp strengths were working at this stage. The chances of meeting the work schedule and completing the railway on time were decidedly gloomy.

However additional manpower resources were still available from the apparently inexhaustible reservoir in the POW camps of

Singapore. The numbers in the Changi area had been drastically reduced over the months since the bulk of prisoners had been gathered there after the surrender. Work parties had been sent off to Japan and to Borneo as well as to the unknown destination in the north to which it was rumoured that the remainder had been despatched, for this was all that the remaining Changi inmates knew of the railway project. No more than 12,000 or 13,000 men now remained in the Singapore compound of the 60,000 non-Indian troops who were originally imprisoned there, later to be joined by the Allied prisoners from the Dutch East Indies. Conditions in Changi were infinitely better than in most of the camps at the destinations to which the other groups had departed; but the POWs themselves could hardly have known this. The camps were still crowded, the food continued to be the monotonous and inadequate rice diet marginally enriched by the produce of the prisoners' own horticultural efforts in the camp gardens and by a minimal issue of animal or fish protein. Health was universally in decline and sickness a constant worry with medicines in short supply. Nevertheless for the majority of prisoners, actual contact with the Japanese guards was minimal and the work, except for some of the labouring groups who operated outside Changi, was not too arduous. When the rumour passed around the prisoners in early April that the Japanese planned to move a large party of them out of Singapore where it was difficult to provide food for so large a body, to a new location to the north, many of the captives believed that this could only be a change for the better. A move north would be a journey away from the year-round equatorial heat and introduce a little seasonal change; it would, furthermore bring them nearer to the rice bowl of Asia where at least the basic food item should be in good supply. The city of Singapore was short of food for reasons which most of the POWs could readily understand.

This news was the prelude to the formation by the Japanese of two further major reinforcements for the railway. 'F' and 'H' Forces ('G' Force being a labour party destined for Japan). It was in large measure the ordeal suffered by the 10,000 men who made up these two parties which gave the Burma-Siam railway its notoriety as the 'railway of death'. The two groups were also different from all the other large parties sent north in that they remained under Singaporean administration throughout their time in Thailand and were returned to Changi as soon as the railway project was completed.

The first group to form up and move off was 'F' Force, a party 7,000 strong made up of 3,666 Australians and 3,334 British prisoners. The

Australians consisted basically of the 27th Brigade Australian Imperial Force (AIF) supplemented from other units. This brigade had been kept relatively intact since the capitulation and the party it formed was commanded by Lieutenant Colonel Kappe. The British element consisted of the remainder of the 18th Division under the command of Lieutenant Colonel Harris who, with the concurrence of the AIF, was also in overall administrative command of the whole force, using the 18th Division Area HQ as his staff. In their briefing for the operation the Japanese explained that this was not a working party detail but one whose formation and despatch had been dictated by the difficult food situation in Singapore. As there were not 7,000 fit combatants left in Changi, 30 per cent of the party could be composed of men unfit to march or work. They would have a much better chance of recovery, it was explained, in the camp to which they were going. The Australians accepted this order with some reservations and included no more than about 125 unfit men in their group. The British were more credulous and nominated about 1,000 unfit with consequences that were disastrous, but which of course could not have been foreseen. The Japanese briefing also explained that there would be little marching except from the train to a nearby camp and that transport would be provided for baggage and those men unfit to march. All tools and cooking gear were to be taken as well as a transformer to provide power; regimental bands were also to go with the force. At their destination gramophones, blankets, clothing and mosquito nets would be provided as well as a good canteen after the first three weeks, for which reasons three weeks' canteen supplies were to be purchased in advance and taken with the party. 'F' Force would also include a medical party of about 350 with equipment for a central hospital of 400 patients and medical supplies for three months.

The force left Singapore in the now familiar steel rice trucks, about 600 men per train with the first departing on 18 April 1943. The first six trains carried the Australians, the next seven the British and the main Japanese party, together with some stores. The conditions endured during the thousand mile journey to Ban Pong were much as described for earlier parties except that many in 'F' Force received no food or water at all during the last 24 hours of the journey. Some Tamil coolies, also bound for the railway, were squeezed into at least one of the trains when it made a stop at Ipoh in north Malaya.

The great gap between what the prisoners had been led to expect and the conditions which actually awaited them became starkly apparent when the trains deposited them at Ban Pong. They then marched a mile to the transit camp of atap huts erected by Thai contractors and the first parties which had moved north a year previously. The camp, whose entrance bore a sign 'Camp Orders for Coolies and Prisoners of War', was now a squalid mess from overuse, poor sanitation facilities and previous occupancy by native labour gangs from Malaya. It was presided over by a Lieutenant Fukuda assisted by some Korean auxiliaries whose dragooning of the prisoners was accompanied by frequent blows and beatings. At Ban Pong the 'F' Force parties were also shocked to discover that the rest of their journey was to be made on foot. The heavy stores which they had brought with them, the band instruments (piano included), medical stores, tools and much other valuable equipment had to be left behind. There was a great deal of trading between the prisoners and the local Thais, the opportunities for extra food proving irresistible, but the knowledge that the only alternative to selling their kit for whatever price they could get at Ban Pong, was to carry it themselves for no-one knew how far, no doubt played some part in the prisoners' willingness to make the many transactions that now took place.

By the time Lieutenant Colonel Harris and Force HQ arrived on the seventh train there was a considerable dump of stores left in an unfenced open space at the side of the road in Ban Pong, with no guard on it allowed; consequently much of it was pilfered. As each trainload of prisoners arrived and learnt that the rest of the journey was to be made on foot, the party's commander would protest to Lieutenant Fukuda whose response was invariably that the march was unavoidable. For transport the Japanese had available 12 Marmom lorries and one ambulance. On their first run north these vehicles carried the Japanese stores; but few completed a second trip and none a third, since by then the monsoon rains had destroyed long stretches of the service road. The net result of the misinformation and poor organisation of the move was that when 'F' Force marched north towards the Burma frontier it did so without most of its heavy stores and three-quarters of its vital medical supplies; the men were also without their surplus clothing which they had either sold to the Thai traders or jettisoned as the exhausting marches began. Two weeks after Lieutenant Colonel Harris and the main HQ party had left Ban Pong by truck, the rear party completed the job of supervising the remaining trainloads of prisoners arriving from Singapore and left the town in another truck loaded with large wicker trunks containing the only substantial medical stores ever to reach the 'F' group camps near the Burma border. Colonel Banno, the Japanese officer commanding 'F' Force, promised that the remaining stores, stacked unprotected at the roadside, would be sent on later. He was, in the view of one prisoner, 'decent and ineffectual' and was perhaps unaware of the havoc that would be caused to road communications once the monsoon broke in earnest.

From Ban Pong 'F' Force marched north for roughly 300 kilometres, travelling by night and resting by day for a period of 17 days. After the first two stages the road became a rough track, motorable in dry weather only; long stretches of it were 'corduroyed' and the bumps and holes in this uneven surface made the night journey both difficult and dangerous. Once the rains started, it also became slippery and treacherous; sections of it were entirely swept away, other parts were totally submerged. As the conditions worsened with frequent thunderstorms heralding the monsoon proper, the night marches lasted 14 or 15 hours instead of the expected 12 and during the day's rest the exhausted men had nowhere to shelter except on sodden ground under trees and bushes. A march of this length and in these conditions would have been arduous even for fit and healthy infantrymen; but 'F' Force was certainly not that. Among the British were the 1,000 or more unfit men including convalescents whose sole reason for inclusion was the Japanese suggestion that they should be, the authority's promise of transport for them and the attraction of the expected good camp conditions at the destination. Even the relatively fit were weakened by twelve months of inadequate diet; but their tribulations were as nothing compared with those of the beriberi sufferers, those with post-diptheric hearts and other ailments whose fate was effectively sealed from the moment the march started from Ban Pong. It was a further misfortune that the British party with its larger proportion of sick men arrived at Ban Pong on the last of the 'F' Force trains and suffered the worst of the marching conditions when the road surface was deteriorating rapidly as the rains became more frequent. The staging camps were mere jungle clearings at the side of the road and accommodation consisted solely of a cookhouse and open trench latrines. There was shelter in only two of the 15 staging camps and this took the form of tents which could accommodate about 100 men only. Furthermore water was often in short supply and even during the rest periods fatigue parties were required by the Japanese and for water-carrying duties.[14]

The march put a particular strain on the medical officers in the party. They had to attend to casualties on the line of march, hold sick parades during the rest periods and then bear the brunt of the Japanese guards' anger when they tried to arrange for sick men to be left behind at staging camps until they were sufficiently recovered to rejoin the main groups. The arguments generally ended in beatings and with most of the sick being forced to continue the march. At Tarsau, for example, an Australian medical officer got the agreement of his Japanese opposite number that 37 of his men were unfit to travel; but the corporal of the guard would consent to only 10 remaining. When the Australian doctor refused to accept this ruling he was beaten to the ground by the corporal and two other guards and set about with bamboo sticks. The majority of the sick men were then forced to march with the rest of the troops.[15] The guards at these staging camps were not part of the Malayan POW organisation but seemed to be under orders merely to move the marchers on to their workstations as quickly as they could. There were nevertheless increasing numbers of sick at each staging camp left behind by previous parties travelling through. These too became a concern of the medical officers of the marching groups since no-one else was available to care for them. An interpreter with the rear party which was the last group to pass through Kanchanaburi recorded that over a hundred sick men from 'F' Force had had to be abandoned there, sleeping in the open and without medicines.[16] Scenes of this kind were repeated at many of the staging camps along the way until the exhausted men of the much-reduced 'F' Force reached their destinations near the Burma border. By the end of May they would be distributed among five main camps just south of the Three Pagodas Pass: Lower Songkurai with about 1,800 Australians, Songkurai with 1,600 British; Upper Songkurai with roughly 400 Australians, and Changaraya with 700 British prisoners. Changaraya was the camp nearest to the Burma border, 345 kilometres from the start of the march at Ban Pong. There was also a headquarters camp and hospital at Lower Nikhe with 400 more of the prisoners. But 1,350 members of 'F' Force had yet to reach their appointed camps – some had died, some were sick at other camps, while two parties of Australians totalling 700 had been halted at Konkoita, 30 kilometres to the south, and were working directly for a detachment of Japanese engineers. They moved north to rejoin the main force at the end of the year.

As the last groups of 'F' Force were making their journey north from Singapore station, 'G' Force was being got ready to be shipped off to Japan. Immediately afterwards the first parties of 'H' Force were assembled and began their journey to Ban Pong prior to playing their assigned part in the railway drama. 'H' Force was not destined to travel so far north as its predecessor; instead it was to reinforce the labour gangs on the middle reaches of the line where progress had fallen far behind schedule. The railway authorities had asked for an additional reinforcement of 3,270 men and the Japanese in Singapore put these together from the prisoners who remained. The Force Commander was Lieutenant Colonel Humphries and with him went almost 2,000 British prisoners, over 700 Australians, about 600 Dutch and 26 Americans. Second-in-command and leading the Australian section was Lieutenant Colonel Oakes. The first train from Singapore bearing this last major POW reinforcement left on 5 May and five others followed it between then and 17 May when the final party H6, composed entirely of officers, many of them quite senior, departed. At Ban Pong the prisoners got their first sight of the transit camp whose huts were now 'littered with excrement, seething with flies and in that condition of unspeakable filth which only Asiatics can attain', as one Australian POW bluntly put it. Then, like all the previous parties, they were searched, ordered to fill their water bottles and began their first 20-mile march in the darkness to the initial staging camp. The total possessions of one prisoner at this stage were one water bottle, one mess tin, one spoon, a toothbrush and a razor; the complete works of Shaw, *Mein Kampf* and the *Oxford Book of English Verse*. The book of poetry and the Shaw were confiscated at the next search leaving only the acceptable delights of the *Führer*.[17] Once arrived at Kanchanaburi, the men were inoculated, vaccinated and 'glass-rodded' – a dignity-destroying test for dysentery performed by the Japanese – and the march began again.

It may seem surprising that 'H' Force, the last of so many parties to be despatched from Singapore to the site of the new railway, could have remained entirely ignorant of the true purposes of the move and of the conditions that would be encountered during its course and more particularly at its conclusion. This ignorance was a measure of the isolation of the prisoners from all knowledge of the Japanese administrative purposes and plans, and of the routine practice of the Japanese commanders themselves of passing down to their subordinates only the scantiest of information. Aside from the general 'spymania' which seemed to afflict all Japanese units and which ensured that only necessary orders were transmitted to the lower levels, the propaganda services shrouded all major events in a cloud of disinformation. Thus, as late as May 1943 when the railway operations were beginning their second year and 60,000 prisoners had already been sent north to Burma and Thailand, a British lieutenant colonel in command of H5 party could note of his journey up from Singapore, 'I was not informed of our destination and was told very little of the conditions of travel. Until I had spent some hours in the train I was under the impression that we were to travel by day only and sleep on railway platforms at night'.[18] The same officer had no mess tin and many were, like him, forced to try and eat all their issued food at one go and then go without for the next 24 or 36 hours when the next rations would be given out. Again, many men had no water bottle and could only take opportunist drinks at engine filling points or taps at Malayan railway stations at which their train chanced to stop. For the men of 'H' Force who were sustained in such a haphazard way as this, the food and tea arrangements at Ban Pong appeared good, but, inexplicably, many parties in this last group were forced to march north to Kanchanaburi although the railway line from there to the river junction had now been completed, thus bringing further and unnecessary debilitation to an already tired and sickening labour force. After Kanchanaburi came the river Maekhlaung which was now spanned by the wooden bridge, 'nerve-rackingly unstable' as one POW reported it, but of the main bridge only the concrete buttresses were in place, though the metal superstructure was now almost ready for erection. Beyond the river many parties travelled by rail again as far as Wanyai.

The final party of 'H' Force reinforcements from Singapore, the H6 party, had many older officers in its ranks, some in their late forties and early fifties. H6 was about 100-strong, drawn from the remaining officers of 18th British Division with the addition of some from the 3rd Indian Corps and from the AIF with even a few American naval officers from ships torpedoed by the Japanese. The mature years of some of its members appeared to be of no consequence one of them later recorded, since the men were going to a 'five-star rest camp' further north. Like its predecessor H5, the H6 party was bound initially for the camp at Tonchan South, 139 kilometres north of Ban Pong. However this last group was able to travel by rail across the modern steel bridge which had now been completed across the Maekhlaung, making their journey north after a large force of Malayan coolies had already passed through. Further evidence of progress in the engineering work came when this last group reached those difficult areas of the track where it was planned that the line would be built hard up against the rock face which rose sheer from the now-swelling waters of the Kwai. Here the huge Wampo viaduct had finally been completed and was taking traffic.

The arrival of H6 at Tonchan South camp, already occupied by H5, was a cause of consternation rather than pleasure to the British commanding officer of the earlier group. On H5's arrival at Tonchan after the series of exhausting night marches Lieutenant Colonel Newey had been issued with a pile of tools, shown a small area of bamboo jungle and told to clear it and pitch a number of tents for the camp. On his first evening at Tonchan Newey had an interview with the Japanese engineer in charge, Captain Kuwabara. The engineer proposed to take about 60 per cent of Newey's men daily for railway work, leaving the remainder to rest, do camp fatigues, hospital work and so on. The situation so far appeared almost reasonable; there were enough tents to give all the men cover, while the work allocations ensured that for a while at least there would be sufficient camp staff to maintain passable living conditions for those who were toiling on the line. However with the arrival of H6 the situation was transformed; Newey discovered that the new party was to share the tents that were barely adequate for his own men some of whom now had to go without. Furthermore a dispute developed with the Japanese who demanded that the new party should also provide its quota to work on the line. This requirement shocked the newcomers, unaccustomed as officers to manual labour, and though Newey argued the legal point on their behalf it rapidly came clear that the Japanese would insist on these officers doing their share of railway labour as was happening elsewhere on the Thai end of the line. Some were clearly too old for manual labour in these severe conditions, irrespective of their status and seniority as officers; the consequence was that Newey's soldiers had to bear a larger share of the toil to make up the prescribed quota, just as they had also to surrender shelter for their hours of rest. These factors, together with the diet which was atrocious for the first three weeks of their stay at Tonchan, the lack of adequate medical facilities and the Japanese demand for harder work and longer hours, soon began to work its deadly attrition even on this newest and freshest group of railway reinforcements.

10

'Speedo–Worko'

The Japanese are prepared to work – you must work. The Japanese are prepared to eat less – you must eat less. The Japanese are prepared to die – you must be prepared to die.

Lieutenant Usuki, Commandant Konyu 2 Camp

IN MID-MAY 1943, as the last reinforcements of 'H' Force were arriving at Ban Pong for the second stage of their journey to the worksites, the monsoon finally broke over south east Burma and north west Thailand. Its arrival had been heralded by several weeks of heavy showers, growing in intensity; now with the railway force almost complete, the rains arrived in earnest to add their fury to the list of handicaps that stood between the Japanese engineers and their dream of the completed line and between the prisoners and their hope of survival and freedom. The monsoon strikes this area with a particular intensity, pouring 76 inches of water upon it in the space of four months. From May until well into September the rain is incessant and heavy day and night. It is a rarity for more than four hours to pass without a downpour. The River Kwai, shallow and sluggish during the dry season, rises in spate and spreads over a wide flood plain where terrain permits, becoming navigable for a much greater distance. On land, however, movement becomes increasingly difficult. The supply road, built at such cost by the Japanese and their workforce, was soon put at hazard; stretches of it became impassable to motor transport and some sections were entirely washed away.

The monsoon added immeasurably to the tribulations of the railway workers; some had no real shelter at all and were continually wet. Those with places in the atap huts often found them leaky and inadequate. The prisoners were seldom dry and while washing clothes was a simple matter, drying them was a virtual impossibility. Furthermore the appalling transport probems meant that some of the camps, particularly those near the Burma border, were almost cut off from all communication with the outside world. Since no adequate reserve stocks of food had been laid in before the rains came, and as it was uncertain how long it would be before fresh supplies would get through, rations were cut drastically. At Nikhe, for example, one of the camps to which 'F' Force had been sent, in the middle of June each man received as a daily ration 270 grams of white rice, 24 grams of dried lima beans, 15 of dried greens and 50 milligrams of fresh meat. This ration had an energy value of 1,200 calories and was, an 'F' Force nutrition expert's report noted dryly, 'less than that required for basal metabolism'.[1] Yet on this diet men were required not only to cope with the rigours of the climate and the environment, but to do heavy manual work at the orders of the increasingly demanding Japanese engineers. The period of monsoon 'speedo' was to be the sorest trial of the long and arduous captivity. Its effects were felt on every section of the track and by each member of the multinational workforce.

In the north the British Sumatra Battalion seemed perpetually on the move. It had been joined by a group of Americans under a Captain Fitzsimmons and was now employed as a kind of mobile force at the railhead, loading and unloading rails and sleepers. Late April had found them at Hlepauk, 18 kilometres from Thanbyuzayat, unloading atap, rails and rations from steam trains and transferring them to diesel trucks for the journey down the line. Work was going on continuously in three eight-hour shifts, but as the strain increased and fewer men were available for each shift, the Japanese instituted two twelve-hour shifts instead. In May the force moved to Retpu, 19 kilometres further down the line, travelling through continuous rain. The sick rates were now alarmingly high and it was difficult to find work parties of the size the Japanese demanded. The British commanding officer's diary noted that 'loading and unloading went on throughout the twenty-four hours and the drumming of the rain, the croak of the bullfrogs and the curious clang as the rails slid off the trucks, made an unforgettable sound'.[2] Food continued to be a major worry with the supply of meat being particularly meagre and consisting of a few thin cattle which some Australian prisoners drove from the base area along the muddy supply route.

Further down the line at Meilo Camp, about 40 kilometres from the Burma–Thai border, Black, Green and Ramsay Forces of No 3 Group, all known by the names of their Australian commanders, were at work on the track; but conditions were not better here. The whole force had been consistently undersupplied with rations. Workers were leaving camp at 9 a.m. and not returning until 4 a.m. the following day. As the month of May wore on the Japanese pressure and the pace of work intensified. Even light duty men, those still sick or just recovering, worked from 9 a.m. to 10 p.m; while prisoners who had previously been excused work entirely because of their condition, joined them for a shift from 2 p.m. to 2 a.m. Brigadier Varley, the Allied force commander, became increasingly concerned at the reports which filtered back from these up-country camps but could do little to alleviate the situation during the appalling weather. The Japanese seemed to be working to an inflexible programme which required the various sections of the track to be completed to a prescribed schedule from which nothing, certainly not the sickness and death of prisoners, would deflect them.[3]

Even worse placed than the POWs to survive this Japanese pressure were the thousands of native workers who were now crowded into the camps along the line. The Burmese and Thai workers were just as badly treated but they, at least, had the option of deserting the camps and returning to their homes if they could. The Tamils from Malaya had no such choice, nor did the Malays and Chinese who, in smaller numbers had been induced to make the journey north with them. Some had brought their wives and children to the camps, into which they had shambled at the end of the approach marches, drenched, weary and woe-begone and, as one European fellow worker put it 'with their enormous eyes so filled with amazement and despair, that we could hardly bear the sight'. The lack of administrative and medical support for the coolie forces has already been noted. The fact that they were thrown together for the enterprise without any arrangements for the segregation of their races and creeds and the special requirements that these produced meant that all traces of internal organisation soon disappeared from their camps and despair and resignation quickly set in. 'Little has been said of the fate of these men', one rubber planter prisoner at Tonchan (139 kilometre camp) later noted bitterly, 'all of whom enjoyed, or thought they enjoyed, British protection in Malaya ... We had the protection of our officers and doctors; they had nothing but the tender mercies of the Nipponese.'[4]

It was at this point in the railway story, with the Japanese pressure at its height, the men's resistance at its lowest and the monsoon in full spate, that cholera struck the work camps. The mere word 'cholera' brought a frisson of terror to those who knew of the speed with which the disease could spread and the rapidity with which it could carry off its victims, as they remembered, perhaps, the three great epidemics of the 19th century which raced across Europe from their source in the Far East taking hundreds of thousands to a rapid death. In fact the bacillus which causes cholera, *Vibrio cholerae*, is a rather weakly, if mobile, organism; it dies at a temperature above 60 degrees centigrade, is easily killed by drying and it cannot live in the presence of any acid. But when conditions are right it thrives alarmingly and can be a deadly infection; in epidemic conditions up to 50 per cent of those afflicted by it can die. In May 1943 the conditions in the River Kwai camps were ideal for its spread. The camps lay, first of all, quite near to the global seat of cholera at the junction of the great rivers of what are now north east India and Bangladesh from which it easily spreads southwards in the monsoon conditions which at that time affected the whole region. Furthermore the river Kwai proved the perfect medium for its spread, being heavily alkaline and containing much calcium leached by the rains from the limestone catchment area.[5] Finally, the crowded and insanitary conditions of the camps, the poor latrine arrangements, the primitive cooking facilities and the debilitation and disorganisation of the coolie labour forces in particular, provided the optimum conditions for the dissemination of the bacillus, it being found in the faeces of those suffering from it and spread in contaminated water and by flies which now swarmed in clouds about the camps. However it was, above all, the speed with which cholera could kill its victims which proved its most appalling characteristic: a sufferer discovered in the morning with its characteristic symptoms of violent diarrhoea, vomiting, agonising cramps and abdominal pains, could be dead by evening, the body dehydrated, wrinkled, cyanosed and a fraction of its normal weight and the victim's last words being uttered in a hoarse whisper, the typical *vox cholerica*.

It is uncertain exactly where on the Kwai the cholera epidemic began, though the 'F' Force camp around Nikhe was certainly among the first POW areas to be struck by it. Lieutenant Colonel Harris, the 'F' Force commander, noted that all parties of his force staged through Konkoita where they were quartered close to hundreds of native labourers who were suffering from 'an intestinal complaint' from which numbers were dying each day. The whole area was heavily fouled and infested with a plague of flies. It seems certain that cholera was raging in this camp. On 15 May five cases of cholera were diagnosed among a party of Australians which had moved into Lower

Nikhe from Konkoita the previous day. Fresh cases arrived with each party from Konkoita and as infected troops moved on to the other 'F' Force camps, so an outbreak of cholera occurred in each one of them.[6]

Cases were also occurring separately at about the same time on other sections of the river; for example at a trading village on the west bank of the Kwai opposite the camp at Takanum one POW had observed a Tamil dying, as he was told, of cholera on 14 May. By 23 May a British POW doctor at Takanum was noting that 'It looks as though we are in for a disastrous epidemic'. Three days later his worst fears were confirmed as he wrote, 'This is cholera all right. There have been 10 deaths already, death supervening within thirty-six hours of the onset of serious symptoms'.[7] The Commander of 'F' Force reacted quickly to the emergency demanding of Colonel Banno that the Japanese should make immediate local arrangements for an isolation hospital, provide anti-cholera vaccine, prevent all movement into Konkoita and Lower Nikhe camps, or from them to other camps in the area and finally that the senior medical officer and medical stores of 'F' Force should be sent forward immediately to the striken area. An isolation hospital of sorts was set up and vaccine later made available, but movement continued in and out of the infected camps, while a Japanese private soldier at the Konyu base camp refused to allow the stores and medical officer to go forward. As infected troops moved on to the other 'F' Force camps, epidemic cholera broke out in each place. It was six weeks before the senior medical officer arrived, on foot and without his medical stores.

The prisoners' authorities made valiant efforts to halt the spread of the epidemic and achieved remarkable successes given the conditions. The strictest hygiene measures were imposed, all water was boiled, bathing was forbidden, the cholera patients were isolated and care was taken to burn soiled materials and disinfect hospital areas. For the patients themselves only limited treatment was possible. Cholera is relatively easy to treat with modern hospital facilities; but with already weakened patients as most of the railway prisoners now were and only basic medical equipment available, not a great deal could be done. Men already weakened by beriberi or suffering from malaria attacks were in no state to resist the cholera bacillus. However where intravenous saline injections could be prepared and administered they proved a life saver for many. At Nikhe and Lower Nikhe, both mixed camps under the direct control of Force HQ, the situation was quickly controlled and deaths totalled only 24 out of a strength of 1,300. But at other 'F' Force camps, the physical state of the men and the camp conditions meant that medical intervention was less effective and the losses were much more severe. Upper Songkurai lost 59 of its 700 men, Shimo Songkurai 103, Changaraya 160 and Songkurai itself 232 of its 1,600 men, over 14 per cent of its strength. The epidemic in 'F' Force was at its height in May and June when 517 men died and its course was not completed until September, by which time 637 prisoners had perished, 193 of them Australian and 444 British, nearly 10 per cent of the whole force.[8]

By the start of June cases of cholera were being reported from other sections of the line. Outbreaks were also occuring among the coolie forces at the Burma end of the railway, at the 60 kilometre camp, for example, which was occupied soon afterwards by Australians, amongst whom before long the first cases were also being notified. At this camp 34 of the 600 men had succumbed to the epidemic before its spread was halted. The disease also struck Black Force, Ramsay Force and Green Force encamped in the Meilo area before their move up-country and it caught them again during their monsoon trek to the Aungganaung area near the Burma–Thailand border when they staged at another camp where cholera had raged and from which they consequently took the infection on with them to their destination camps. By 14 June the rumours of cholera which coolies fleeing from the north had brought earlier to Hintock camp in Thailand were confirmed by the local Japanese commandant who said that a major outbreak had occurred in one of the native labour camps at Konyu, about 15 miles downstream. This soon spread to the prisoners' camps nearby with the first cases being reported at Konyu on 16 June and at Hintock Mountain camp three days later. The first Hintock case was a typical victim, 'extremely sick on arrival', wrote the medical officer, 'with the most terrible dehydration and no perceptible pulse'. The patient had died before dawn the following morning, the first of 66 cholera deaths at Hintock of the 150 there who contracted the disease.

In another of the 'Hell Fire Pass' camps, Konyu 2, in one spell of 9 days, 72 men died from the disease. The epidemic was soon putting the camp doctors under immense strain. 'These days', wrote one medical officer as the epidemic intensified, 'I spend 14–16 hours a day in the hospital area. This cholera is the last straw.'[9] 'H' Force was hit particularly hard by the epidemic which struck only weeks after the prisoners' arrival in the work area and before sufficient huts had been constructed for the men, let alone satisfactory facilities organised for the sick. The fact that 'H' Force remained under Malayan administration was probably what prevented the sick from the force's Tonchan and Hintock camps being evacuated to 4 Group's hospital at Tarsao only a few kilometres away. The local Japanese medical officer was sympathetic enough and issued three small tents for use as a hospital; but there were few medical supplies and the tents were soon too small for the numbers allocated to them. 'Under these conditions, to develop any sort of sickness meant almost certain death', the commander of H5 Battalion noted grimly. Cholera struck a sub-camp first and within a few days it was rife at Tonchan itself; out of some 25 cases about 10 finally died. However hygiene precautions were rapidly enforced and served to keep the outbreak within bounds. Other elements of 'H' Force were less fortunate; by July 200 of the 400 patients at Malayan Hamlet camp hospital were suffering from the disease. At least 111 Australians and 106 British prisoners in 'H' Force died during the epidemic.[10]

Life on the railway had now resolved itself into two competing struggles; the grim and unrelenting determination of the railway engineers to have the line completed and operational at the designated time, and the dogged and at times despairing efforts of the POW camp commanders and medical officers to win their battle against sickness, malnutrition and ill-treatment. In this latter struggle cholera proved the severest complication. Its occurrence meant that fewer men were available for railway work and so the demand for fixed numbers of labourers meant that those suffering from a variety of other illnesses were forced to join the work parties however unfit they were. The doctors too were drawn into increasingly bitter battles with the Japanese authorities as to which men and how many should be allowed to remain on the sick list. Cholera also meant much more work on camp hygiene, fly protection for camp kitchens where it could be devised, new improvisations to keep latrines covered and disinfected and a sustained effort to produce distilled water for the life sustaining intravenous drips for the cholera patients. Stills were improvised in camps up and down the line, additional firewood parties were detailed and the stills operated day and night to keep the supply of water always available. They were constructed from all manner of unlikely materials but with the remarkably useful 4-gallon petrol can and the omnipresent and versatile bamboo generally featuring somewhere in the apparatus. At the height of the epidemic Hintock Mountain camp had three stills working flat out with officers servicing them in shifts over the entire 24 hours and maintaining an output of over 100 pints a day. Nursing the cholera sick placed an additional strain on the medical orderlies, both in terms of extra patient workload as well as additional hygiene drills and aseptic disciplines, but also by virtue of the fresh blows to their already frail morale which the frequent failures to save their cholera patients now caused. Moreover there were the additional meal-time hygiene precautions which were vital when the risk from fly contamination was at its height. At Takanum all food served was covered over with leaves and men were specially appointed at each meal to fan banana leaves to keep the flies away. Then there was the lugubrious, spirit-sapping task of dealing with the bodies of the dead and finally interring or burning them.

While cholera cut swathes through the ranks of the Allied prisoners, its effects were even more devastating in the coolie camps. Without any understanding of the role of flies and water in the spread of the infection and lacking the support of a medical organisation such as the POWs had, the natives died in their thousands and often lay unburied where they expired. At Tarsao, for instance, in a coolie camp next to the Australian officers' battalion it was reported that 240 died in two days. At Tonchan South camp a party of officers was sent into a neighbouring coolie camp to deal with the sick and dead from the disease. Over 130 dead and dying coolies, mostly Tamils, were collected and buried in a collective grave for which a large hole had been dug by prisoners from adjacent camps.[11] A medical orderly from Konyu 2 camp later wrote, 'when we reached Tamil coolie camp we could see that it was strewn with dead bodies. We were ordered to dig pits and bury the dead, while the Japs stayed at some distance outside the camp. The Tamils had succumbed to cholera.'[12]

As a result of the crisis in the coolie camps and the general health threat that it presented, Lieutenant Colonel Newey of 'F' Force offered to send officers and men from his own camp who knew the coolies and spoke Tamil to organise sanitation and hygiene measures. This was apparently at first agreed to and then countermanded by higher Japanese authority. Eventually a joint 'H' Force and 2 Group cholera hospital was established at which all cholera cases, whether POW or coolie, were treated. At other camps, cholera-striken Tamils were unceremoniously dumped at nearby POW isolation huts where the medical resources were already outstripped by the scale of the epidemic. There were even reports of Tamil cholera sufferers being buried alive on Japanese orders, or finished off with a handtool before joining those who had already expired in a communal grave. Others were taken to makeshift shelters in the jungle and left there. If they had friends to look after them these did what they could; if not they had to fend for themselves. 'When one hears of these widespread barbarities, one can only feel that we prisoners of war', wrote one prisoner medical officer, 'in spite of all the deaths and permanent disabilities which result, are being treated with comparative consideration.'[13]

The Japanese seemed to have a particular horror of cholera and appeared as one prisoner remarked, to be in 'a flat-tailed spin' about it, some even walking about camp wearing masks, an incongruously civilised precaution in the primitive jungle setting. They invariably kept their distance from the cholera patients and took care to see that the infection did not reach their camps. Prisoners who visited their lines had to disinfect themselves before approaching. Anti-cholera measures had been taken before the epidemic broke out; many prisoners had been vaccinated against it before their journey into the Thai interior and rectal swabs had been taken to check on infection. When the outbreak was confirmed fresh vaccinations were arranged and quantities of disinfectant produced. However, a combination of logistical difficulties, poor administration and the low rank level at which critical decisions were taken prevented anti-cholera measures from being uniform, thorough or adequate. The critical Japanese concern was to see that the infection did not spread, though even in this regard their countermeasures were inadequate, with poor isolation policies and the never-ending demand for fresh workers at many sections of the line producing fresh infections as reinforcements moved into cholera-ridden areas. However they showed little concern for workers once they were infected, reacting to the entreaties of the camp commandants and doctors rather than making a positive effort to see those striken returned to health. As to their treatment of their coolie forces, this brought particularly angry reactions from the FMSVF personnel, some of whom had been administrators on the rubber estates from which the majority of the Tamils had been drawn. 'Many ex-planters spoke of instances of loyal kindness and generosity from old Tamil estate workers whom they met on the line', wrote one ex-planter later,[14] but there was little they could do to help them.

So great was the depletion of the coolie forces by sickness in general and cholera in particular, and so chaotic were the medical arrangements made for them, that the Japanese did finally decide to institute measures to redress the situation. In late June 1943, and again in August, the authorities in Singapore assembled medical units of prisoners which they sent up to Thailand to minister to the coolies.

The first to go, designated 'K' Force, was a party of 30 medical officers and 200 orderlies drawn from the remaining British and Australian medical specialists at Changi, with a few Dutch included as well. 'K' Force left Singapore on June 25, being informed before the departure from Changi that since they were going to well-equipped hospitals in the north, it would not be necessary for them to take medical equipment with them. Only on arrival at Kanchanaburi did they discover that they would be treating the coolie forces. The force was split up into parties of one medical officer and four other ranks and distributed among the various coolie camps along the railroad. The earlier misleading information meant that they could do very little for their pitiful charges. One Australian MO with 'K' Force was later reported to be burying about 30 Tamils a day.[15] Another reported that the gravedigging was always done by the medical personnel and owing to the increased death rate and lack of staff there were at one time 500 coolies buried in the one grave at Nikhe. Coolie hospitals were finally established at Kanchanaburi in the south, at Wanyai, Kinsaiyok, Konkoita and near the border at Nikhe where it is thought that as many as 1,750 coolie patients died.[16]

The cholera outbreak, for all its devasting impact on the workforce, brought no respite from the pressures of the 'speedo–worko' timetable. On every section of the line the work continued with the same intensity, many labourers now noticing that it was the engineers who were adopting the harder line in demanding work party strengths to be kept up and quotas of work to be met and often exceeded. The British Sumatra Battalion was now based at Taungzan in lower Burma to which station the railhead had now advanced; but their camp was two kilometres away from the site and approaching it involved the crossing of a wooden railway bridge over the river Winyaw situated 500 yards downstream of a second wooden river bridge carrying the service road. Under the enormous pressure of the monsoon waters the road bridge collapsed and its debris brought the unsteady rail bridge down as well. This caused another interruption to the engineers' completion timetable and resulted in a further twist to the ratchet of pressure being applied to the workforce as activity continued throughout the night to 'corduroy' the camp road, which was now thigh deep in mud, and to repair the vital railway bridge. Generators were brought up to power lights for the night work as prisoners carried bridging materials across a swaying catwalk which the engineers had slung across the raging waters. The rebuilding of the bridge took ten days of continuous effort; but the new structure lasted only 12 hours before it collapsed again and the labour to repair it began once more.

Elsewhere in the Burma sector of the line where Nos 3 and 5 Groups were operating, similar scenes were being enacted; twenty-four hour working was commonplace, the night shifts operating by arc lamps; each day there would be the *tenko* confrontation between the Japanese guards and the camp staff to determine how many of the sick were fit to work, the blitz often being conducted on the Japanese side by a junior NCO. Similar scenes were being played out in all the camps. The daily task of selecting the last few men to go out from a number of convalescents who were really all unfit was heartbreaking, the commander of 'F' Force noted, and a great strain on those to whose lot it fell. In 'F' Force's camps on the border reveille and breakfast began in darkness to the accompaniment of the incessant rain. The work parties would then march off to draw tools and begin the march (often between 5 and 10 kilometres) to work; by this stage in their captivity only about 20 per cent had usable boots. The day's work would then proceed.

For those working on the big bridge at Songkurai much of the day might be passed working up to the waist in swift-flowing cold water. A short interval, perhaps only a few minutes, would be allowed for the mid-day meal – a pint of rice and a few beans – and the work would then continue until long after dark when the tools would be collected and the march back to the camp would begin: a nightmare performance in the mud, rain and darkness. The workers might return to camp at 10 p.m. or even later for the inevitable *tenko* and after dismissal, for their evening meal – rice again and perhaps some vegetable stew. They would then retire to their two-foot by six-foot sleeping space to get what rest they could before the next day's work began. Those who were sick had to be examined by firelight. In these working conditions, with such an inadequate diet and with the prevalence of disease, especially cholera, it is not surprising that by the end of June 1943 only 700 men of the original 7,000 were fit to work in the outside camps.[17] One particular party of 20 men which had set out as the advance party to set up the camp at Nikhe was taken off the line of march by the engineers and spent 14 days pile-driving from first light to 10 p.m. up to their armpits in cold water with half an hour's break for lunch. The entire party finally died.[18] By this stage of the monsoon season all land communication between the 'F' Force camps and the south had been severed, preventing the evacuation of the sick by road to the base hospitals at Tarsao and Ban Pong. It was some time before alternative arrangements were agreed by the Japanese.

Nowhere else along the railway did the work, the conditions, the food and the treatment by the Japanese take such a toll on the workforce as it did in these 'F' Force camps near the border, with the severest of the cholera outbreaks lending a macabre grimness to the circumstances. However, in many other stretches of the track the work was as hard and the pressure equally unrelenting. At Hintock Mountain camp the senior medical officer had noted in March that the 'Australian resilience is startling; the men are extremely cheerful and emphatic that the Ns will never get them down . . .' but by May he was writing of 'men being progressively broken into emaciated pitiful wrecks' and in August he was recording that some men had then worked for 80 days without a break, and later that the monsoon had done more to break the men's spirit than almost any other factor.[19]

The 'Hell Fire Pass' cutting proved a sore trial for all the camps in the Hintock area which were allocated to it. By June 1943 the rail-laying parties had reached the cutting which was still being hacked out and the Japanese intensified the pressure to ensure its completion. The equipment for the cutting was augmented by an air compressor and a dozen Cambodian jack hammers and the labour force was increased. Elephants were brought up and additional men from 'D' and 'H' Forces were moved to the site. The hours of work were lengthened until they reached 18 a day and this pace continued for about six weeks until the cutting was finished. The monsoon conditions hampered all aspects of the work, including the ignition of the explosive charges; as a member of one explosive party put it, 'There were occasions when I had to blow furiously on cigarette and fuze together to effect ignition on a damp fuse while all around me other fuzes were sizzling merrily'.[20]

A second major project in the Hintock area was the 'Pack of Cards Bridge' so called because it fell down three times during its hasty construction. The bridge was 400 yards long, 80 feet high and built of green timber fastened with wooden wedges, spikes, bamboo ties, rattan or cane ropes and wooden dowels. It is recorded that 31 men were killed in falls from the bridge during its construction and 29 beaten to death at the site.[21] Further south at Tamarkan where the construction of the bridges over the Maekhlaung had been the main preoccupation, conditions were much better. During the 'speedo' period the work went on for 18 hours out of the 24; but the camp was at least near the worksite, the food was adequate, the local Japanese commander was not too unreasonable and medical supplies were available. During the period October 1942–May 1943 there were only 9 deaths out of a workforce of 3,500 at the camp. But in May, with the bridges and the embankment completed, Tamarkan became a base hospital and the full horror of the conditions further north became apparent. 'Parties of approximately 100 arrived nightly', wrote the camp commandant, 'and the camp reached its maximum strength by July. The sick were in appalling condition, approximately 75 per cent of the parties were stretcher cases and men frequently arrived dead.'

The full cost of the 'speedo' effort which was at last bringing the results which the Japanese demanded was now being seen in Tamarkan and in the base hospitals being established elsewhere along the line. 'During this time', the Tamarkan commander's report notes, 'we saw scenes of misery that will live for ever in the memories of all of us.'[22]

9. Burning the cholera dead (*Charles Thrale*)

10. Speedo – The journey back to camp (*Leo Rawlings*)

11.   Work on a railway cutting 1943 (*Ronald Searle*)

12.   Japanese guard hut and look-out post (*Stanley Gimson*)

13. Taking rations to Konyu (*John Mennie*)

14. Dysentery Ward (*Stanley Gimson*)

15.   After the surrender: officers' hut at Nakhon Nayok (*Stanley Gimson*)

16. Punishment: the container held water or stones (*Jack Chalker*)

11

Ending the Torment

If there is one foolish man who is trying to escape, he shall see big jungles towards the East which are absolutely impossible for communication, towards the West he shall see boundless ocean and above all in the main points of South and North, our Nippon Army is staying and guarding
Lieutenant Colonel Y. Nagatomo, 15 September 1942

ALLIED SERVICEMEN who became prisoners of Germany during the Second World War soon became familiar with the complex apparatus of incarceration: roll calls, barbed wire, searchlights, guard dogs and, of course, escape committees and escape attempts. It was the prime duty of POWs to try to escape and much energy and ingenuity was devoted to planning escape attempts, digging tunnels, forging identity papers, creating disguises, acquiring maps and so on. Some escapers were lucky and their bid for freedom was successful. For those who were not, punishment inevitably followed recapture: privileges were withdrawn, men were put into solitary confinement, their rations were reduced to bread and water, they were (illegally) deprived of Red Cross parcels and, inevitably, fresh measures of confinement were introduced to ensure that they did not make the attempt again. Generally, the risks involved in efforts to escape and the punishment that came with capture were not such as to deter the many fit young men who were held captive from making fresh bids for freedom. There was, of course, the notorious outcome of what became known as the 'Great Escape' in which 80 RAF officer prisoners made their break-out via the tunnel codenamed 'Harry', at 350 feet the longest escape tunnel ever dug by POWs. Only three of the escapees gained freedom; the majority of those who were recaptured were shot by the Gestapo. This action became one of the notorious horror stories of the war in the West which German authorities attempted to justify after the event with the claim that having so many escapees at large represented a major risk to public security. However the fact that even the Head of Reich Security should have referred to the episode as a 'dirty affair' testifies to the exceptional nature of the punitive consequence of this mass breakout.

The position of the Kwai prisoners in relation to escape was entirely different. From the very start of their captivity in Singapore, Java and Sumatra the physical barriers to freedom had been minimal. In the early days this had been rather more the result of the enormity of the administrative problem of containing so large a number of captives than a deliberate policy, and though the Japanese did manage after some weeks to get their prisoners enclosed and guarded, the relative absence of real physical barriers to escape reappeared once they were transferred to the Kwai camps. The main Japanese weapon for ensuring that their POW labour force did not escape was the crudest form of deterrence – they executed all those who tried and were caught. There was, in any event, a world of difference from making an escape attempt in the European theatre where, uniforms apart, a soldier from one of the Allied armies could look much like a man from the other side. In South East Asia a European was immediately recognisable and had little chance of passing himself off as one of the locals. In addition the Thai and Burmese populations were generally disinclined to help European fugitives. However ill-treated they themselves were by the Japanese, the impoverished and social disorganisation they were suffering were as much the consequence of the Allies' failure to defend their territories in the region as the result of Japanese actions. Certainly this is what the occupiers' propaganda claimed; the Japanese were, after all, freeing the locals from European domination. What was more, there was generally a cash reward for the capture of Allied POWs, and with inflation and shortages gripping most of the occupied territories, the price on the head of a prisoner was always worth receiving. Moreover, months of undernourishment had drained most prisoners of the will to consider anything more than personal survival and perhaps the succour of their comrades who had fallen ill.

However the potential escaper had two other considerations of which to take account, the need for food supplies and the possibility of sickness. Away from the camps he would have no ready source of food and dared not risk visiting a village to get fresh supplies for fear of betrayal and capture. Nor would he have any means of dealing with the army of tropical diseases to which he might fall prey; drugs were in short supply within the camps and were desperately needed for those who were already sick. If these problems were not sufficient to deter escape, there was the knowledge that the nearest Allied lines were 1,000 kilometres away across malarial jungles and with only primitive communications traversing the intervening terrain through which several mighty rivers flowed as additional barriers to passage. It was a prospect to daunt even the most reckless and desperate potential escaper. Finally, in addition to all these hazards was the knowledge that if caught by the Japanese he would surely be killed.

In the early days of 'A' Force's time on the Burma coast the apparent laxity of the Japanese authorities and the friendliness of the local Burmese encouraged some men to attempt escape. On 30 May 1942 a group of eight Australians at Tavoy made such a bid but they were soon recaptured and executed without trial despite the protests of their leaders, Brigadier Varley being compelled to witness the execution. A few days later at Mergui two more were executed after being found outside the wire and on 30 July a prisoner who had gone outside the camp merely to trade with the local Burmese was also shot. A similar policy had soon been in evidence in Singapore, although it was clear that the Japanese had initially been unprepared to cope with the guarding and disciplining of so large a body of prisoners at their own main base. However, in August 1942 Major General Fukuye and a considerable POW administrative staff arrived at Changi and the official attitude to escape soon became evident. The Japanese announced that each prisoner was to sign a statement which read: 'I, the undersigned, hereby solemnly swear on my honour that I will not, under any circumstances, attempt escape.' All refused to sign. Three days later the Japanese executed four men, two Australians and two Englishmen, who had been recaptured after an escape attempt which had got them two miles away from Singapore in a small boat. Once again the authorities insisted upon the senior Allied commanders witnessing the executions. The same day the Japanese concentrated the 15,400 Allied troops then at Changi into the eight acres of Selarang Barracks square as a reprisal. The barracks which flanked the square now had to accommodate 17 to 18 times the number for which they had been designed and consequently many hundreds of prisoners had to sleep without shelter on the barrack square itself. There were only two water taps available and the authorities reduced the rations to one-third of normal. After three days the Japanese threatened to move all the hospital patients into the Selarang area as well. The Allied commanders negotiated for either an amendment of the original no-escape declaration, or its conversion into an order rather than a request. The Japanese finally issued such an order and the Allied commanders were able to agree to their men signing, in the belief that the duress involved rendered their oath invalid. Their aim apparently achieved, the Japanese subsequently dispersed the troops back to their original compounds.

Despite the executions and this crude pressure to force compliance, which was repeated in various forms and at different times in the railway compounds to the north as well, escape bids continued from time to time, though on the railway trace itself the increased difficulty of the terrain and the remoteness from civilisation placed a further damper on ideas of an easy bid for freedom. But on numerous sections of the line and even in some of the remotest camps there were still POWs who were prepared to make the attempt. There was one escape from Tamarkan in Thailand by two officers who were at large for three weeks in the jungle. They were finally recaptured, brought back to camp, interrogated briefly and then bayonetted. In December 1942 three Dutchmen were shot for attempting escape in the Burma sector, and a short while later an Australian who had escaped from Wegale camp and marched the eight kilometres to Thanbyuzayat in a futile bid to reach Rangoon, gave himself up at the Japanese base. He too was executed. This last example was the tragic case of a man who was not entirely normal and there were similar instances. Escapers were occasionally people whom sickness had driven to delirium or whose sanity had been unseated by the circumstances of their lives as coolie captives; but there were also prisoners of sound mind who regarded incarceration in the Kwai labour camps either as an unbearable affront, or else an extended horror which they could no longer stomach. In two remarkable cases they got clean away from the Japanese in the local area and remained at liberty for a surprisingly long time. These efforts both ended in ultimate recapture but, unusually, those who survived the gruelling conditions of their freedom, also endured the interrogation which followed recapture and were not executed but lived to tell their tale.

Perhaps the most noteworthy attempt was that of Private Ras Pagani, orginally of the Reconnaissance Battalion (5th Loyals) of 18th Division who became a member of the British Sumatra Battalion working at the 18 kilometre camp of Hlepauk at the Burma end of the line. On 14 November 1942 he had his breakfast, attended the *tenko* parade and then walked to freedom instead of going to the line. His commanding officer believed that Pagani's decision to escape was the result of a punishment inflicted for a minor breach of camp discipline and that 'he did not know the country, was badly equipped, and left at short notice'.[1] He was wrong on all counts. This was Pagani's fourth attempt to escape the enemy's clutches, the earlier efforts having been at Dunkirk, Singapore and Padang on Sumatra from which he had tried to escape on a steam tug with some survivors from *The Prince of Wales*, only to be fired on by Sumatrans and forced to turn back and give himself up. He had apparently been planning another escape from the moment of his arrival in the Burma coastal area where his party and the rest of 'A' Force were put to work on the airfields, but since on each occasion there was the rumour of a Japanese move north, which was the direction Pagani himself intended to take, he postponed his attempt until his party had finished its movements.

Pagani was clearly something of a free spirit who had earlier refused to work on Japanese military installations as a matter of principle and been assigned instead to hospital duties. His own recollections certainly bespeak considerable premeditation; he walked out of camp dressed as a local with a good growth of beard, a *pugri* round his head and a loincloth around his waist. 'During my stay in the East', he recalled later, 'I found that a European would always be detected, no matter how good his disguise, due to the lack of sway in his posterior. So of course this I had perfected whilst a POW, and I had hardened my feet by never wearing any footwear, as bad feet were the escaper's downfall.'[2] He walked first to the coast and then north to Thanbyuzayat and was befriended by local Indians who saw him across the Salween, past Moulmein and Martaban. From then on he came into the hands of the pro-British Karen Christian community, initially of Saw Po Thin, a timber merchant who had been contracted by the Japanese to provide sleepers for the railway and who used this position to obtain intelligence for the British-led Karen resistance of which he was himself a prominent member. Rather than continue his attempt to reach the distant Allied lines, Pagani was persuaded to make instead for the Karen hills to join an English major who was operating a resistance there. This he finally managed to do after journeying through some of the roughest jungle he had ever seen. The major was Hugh Seagrim, the saintly and legendary leader of the Karen resistance.*

---

* When a strong Japanese punitive expedition later began taking savage reprisals against the Karen villagers, Seagrim gave himself up to save his followers from further punishment. He was taken to Insein and executed.

Pagani was employed as an envoy by Seagrim in his efforts to keep the Karens loyal and organised. In this role the Karens reported 'Corporal Ras', as he was known by them, to have been 'brave to the point of recklessness'.[3] After a brush with the Japanese he decided to revert to his earlier plan of getting through to the Allied lines, reporting the POW camp conditions, delivering a report from Seagrim and rejoining the conventional fight. Accompanied by four Gurkhas and an Indian lance *naik*, Pagani managed to get across the Sittang river and right down to the central plains of Burma and the banks of the Irrawaddy, being passed from village to village by friendly Karens. However he was betrayed by native Burmans while attempting to cross the great river and fired on by them. He was wounded, captured and finally after two months of hospitalisation and confinement at Prome, sent down to Rangoon. Pagani pretended to be an American Air Force lieutenant who had been shot down over Burma and he managed to keep to his story despite extended interrogation and torture by the *kempeitai*. He later survived strafing by Allied Hurricanes during a move south and was finally rescued by advancing Allied troops. 'What did I gain from my escapes?' he later asked himself, 'Earlier release from the hands of the Japanese, and the knowledge that I was a better man than they . . .' His was a spirit which remained unbroken.[4]

The second successful escape began in horrific and ended in tragic circumstances. It concerned a group of ten POWs in 'F' Force who were based at Songkurai, in many ways the worst of 'F' Force's five main camps in which, as has been noted, cholera took a dramatic toll and where Lieutenant Abe, the local Japanese engineer in charge, was conspicuous for failing to stop the brutal treatment handed out by his subordinates. One of the group which later made the escape bid was found to be a cholera carrier after a glass-rodding test and was moved, on Japanese orders, with the genuine cholera cases to an isolation camp on the far side of the railway trace. The move took place at night and when daylight came it disclosed the horror of the camp having been a cremation area for the cholera-stricken native labour force and it was now seen to be littered with partly cremated bodies. The move to this site, one of the escape group later reported, 'was altogether the most inhuman thing I have ever witnessed'.[5]

The escape plan was suggested as a way of bringing the appalling conditions in the Songkurai camp to the notice of the outside world. The group which planned the escape included five men from 18th Division, three who had belonged to the Singapore Fortress units and had a little local knowledge, together with an Indian fisherman from Chittagong who had been taken prisoner by the Japanese and spoke some Urdu. The party left camp on 5 July at the height of the cholera outbreak intending to strike due west for the coast, little realising that a 1,200 ft mountain range, dense with jungle and with no tracks across it, lay in their path. By 28 July their food had run out and one of their number whose tropical ulcers had turned gangrenous could not be found; it was assumed that he had walked out into the jungle to die. Four days later a second man died in the night, followed three days later by another, who succumbed, it was presumed, to heart failure.

After six weeks of struggling westward through the jungle the party, now reduced from ten to five, had been virtually without food for two weeks though they had plenty of water available. They finally reached the river Ye and started to build a raft to cross it, but in their weakened state this construction task took three days. They finally launched their raft successfully into the apparently slow-running river but soon reached a gorge which smashed the craft to pieces. The five finally struggled ashore, minus all their equipment and totally exhausted. It was at this stage that they saw their first humans, Burmese hunters who took them to their settlement at Karni, fed them and then moved them on to the village of Arkan, three on foot and the two sicker members by boat. They were welcomed, showered with gifts of fruit and given a chicken curry. The following day, 21 August, they were arrested by two Japanese soldiers and some Burmese policemen; the headman of Karni had betrayed them. In almost seven weeks of freedom half their number had been lost and the survivors were half starved and very sick. They were interrogated first at Ye by the *kempeitai*, then at Thanbyuzayat by Colonel Banno and a *kempeitai* sergeant major. Later they were returned to Moulmein, ending up in the jail hospital. They were subsequently transported to their original camp at Songkurai from which at the end of October they were moved down to Singapore. Ultimately, after further periods of hospitalisation and lengthy interrogations, the escapers were finally brought to trial. All were reduced to the ranks and received long sentences of penal servitude; but they escaped the death penalty.

The contrast between these two cases and the others which generally ended in summary execution is remarkable, but perhaps explicable. Corporal Ras Pagani had been picked up hundreds of miles away from the 18 kilometre camp at which he had been based. In the circumstances his claim to have been the pilot of a US plane was apparently credible and his ready acceptance by the American group of POWs at Rangoon added further verisimilitude to his story. The sparing of the 'F' Force group of escapers seems more difficult to explain, though one of the party took the view that Colonel Banno and his officers rather admired them for having defied the jungle for as long as they did. He also claimed that the spirited defence argued on the escapers' behalf by the interpreter, Captain Wild, actually reduced Banno to tears. In addition the escapers were only indirectly under local command, being really the responsibility of General Arimura's headquarters in Changi rather than the subordinate railway administration up-country. In Singapore the Japanese authorities tended to behave a little more correctly in relation to their prisoners and by June 1944 when the survivors' trial finally took place, the Pacific War was rapidly turning against the Japanese. Perhaps their more lenient treatment was the result of a certain uncharacteristic circumspection on the part of the Japanese concerned; or was it indeed admiration for their exploits which accounted for the lenient treatment and led the sentencing judge to give each of the convicted escapees a small bag of sweets and tell them to take care of their health? One of the survivors attributed the almost moderate Japanese behaviour to the civilised circumstances of Singapore as compared to the ruthlessness, unpredictability and barbarity to which their captors reverted in the jungle.[6]

However, for most POWs the idea of physical escape did not hold any great attraction. On the other hand a kind of psychological liberation from the appalling circumstances of their captivity was available. Some escaped mentally into the beauty of their surroundings when they had time to take in the wild grandeur of the tropical rain forest which surrounded them. Others lived through the torment of the 'speedo' period by feeding on the 'fat in their minds' as one captive put it; the memory of the full and varied life they had led before the war took over their existence, and into this other life they could again pass mentally to escape momentarily from the drudgery and horror of their environment. For such people there would be bizarre moments, even during gruelling physical work, when the mind would detach itself from the miseries of the body and travel along some incredible flight of fancy, not unlike that of those religious sects for whom the mortification of the flesh is the necessary prelude to spiritual exaltation. But the escape of others was more pathological; there were the men who reacted to the ordeal by a total withdrawal from what little social life remained in the primitive hutments of the camps, who would lie on the bamboo slats of their sleeping platforms staring at the roof in a state of almost cataleptic withdrawal and inactivity. 'Atap staring' was a strange phenomenon of the railway episode and one British commanding officer wrote that in all the cases he knew of it, the men concerned died.[7]

However, even at this point in the railway travail when the monsoon was at its height, the 'speedo' pressure at its most intense and disease and debilitation were the common lot of the labourers, the administrative and disciplinary framework of the camps managed to hold together at a primitive level, despite the immense strains put upon it. Meals, however inadequate, continued to be prepared; the sick were afforded rudimentary care; the dead were generally given a burial and the basic norms of social behaviour were observed, though selfish and at times despairing attitudes inevitably developed in the camps worst affected by the shortages of food, the appalling conditions and the working practices demanded by the Japanese engineers and guards. At one stage the morale and discipline at Songkurai, where the Japanese had been particularly savage and there had been over 600 deaths, seemed to have reached the point of almost total collapse.[8] The sense of utter hopelessness and despair was moderated for some prisoners only by the slenderest of contacts with the outside world, the gossamer thread of hope which was provided by the news broadcasts on the radios still operated in a few camps along the line. However there was a second factor which gave fresh reason for hope for those who were aware of its existence, and a renewed chance of life to many sick prisoners who were not. This was the aid that was now getting to some of the camps via the underground organisation in Thailand.

It will be recalled that the efforts of the International Red Cross to have the Japanese agree to regular shipments of relief supplies to the South East Asian prisoners had met with almost total failure. The directly-despatched Red Cross parcels which did get through to them, however welcome, were a tiny fraction of what was required. Lacking sanction for these external efforts, the Red Cross concentrated its energies on working through the representative of the Protecting Power. In Burma, as the official record reported, 'no means of helping either prisoners of war or civilians could ever be devised' though, as we have seen, one Red Cross consignment did get through in December 1943, consigned from the Swiss consulate in Bangkok; but in Thailand the consul was able to organise considerable assistance, supplying drugs, food and local currency to the prisoners through the good offices of the local Catholic mission. The Japanese seemed content enough with this arrangement but the Apostolic Delegate in Indo-China became increasingly nervous about it, fearing that if the Japanese discovered all that was going on they might curtail the privileges which his mission enjoyed. The Swiss consul bought much of what was later distributed on the black market and for a time received permission to distribute these supplies to the camp leaders.[9]

However the main agency for the collection and distribution of aid to the prisoners in the Thailand section of the railway was a Kanchanaburi merchant who later became a legend along the line. This was Mr Boonpong Sirivejjabhandu who operated under the aegis of the underground 'V' organisation. The embryonic 'V' organisation first established contact with the railway camps in September 1942 when a lance corporal belonging to 54 Brigade Group Company RASC, one of the first units to have been sent up to the railway, was surreptitiously handed a note signed 'V' while on a ration collection detail from Ban Pong to the camp at Nong Pladuk. The note said that civilian internees in Bangkok had heard that POW conditions were not good and asked for details. After much debate about the authenticity of the note, the OC of the RASC company at Nong Pladuk camp decided to reply to it and included information about other camps along the line so far as he knew them and also details of all Japanese movements on the railway which had been noted.

Thus began a monthly exchange which persisted for most of the war in which the POWs supplied details of camp conditions, medical requirements and (until June 1943) Japanese dispositions and movements, to which the 'V' organisation replied with world news, drugs and money. The 'V' organisation was run by a Bangkok-based Englishman, K G Gairdner, who was one of about 200 British subjects who had been interned in January 1942 in a camp run by the Thai authorities in the grounds of the University of Moral and Political Sciences in Bangkok. Gairdner was reasonably well treated and his agents for the exchange of messages and smuggled goods and money were his Chinese employee K S Hong and Gairdner's Thai wife Millie; being locals they were able to move about freely. The messages were generally exchanged via the RASC driver who took Japanese NCOs from Nong Pladuk to Ban Pong each week. Since this particular RASC company's drivers were frequently used for trips up-country, they were well placed to provide accurate information to the 'V' organisation and to take messages to more northerly camps on its behalf. Thus 'V' sent 'small packet' drugs, news and money (250–400 Ticals monthly) to enable the POWs at Nong Pladuk to buy the more bulky medical requirements in Ban Pong. Later in 1943 when it became clear that the 'Speedo' was having such disastrous effects, Gairdner arranged a loan of 12,000 Ticals subscribed by private individuals in Bangkok which was smuggled to the prisoners in piles of 20 Tical notes (the highest denomination which the Japanese ever allowed the POWs), concealed in a bag of tapioca flour which Mrs Gairdner passed to the prisoners in front of a Japanese guard.[10] In return regular reports of the camps and the distressing conditions of their inmates were passed back to Gairdner's organisation and from him via various diplomatic contacts to the outside world and the Allied authorities. So although the British Red Cross journal *The Prisoner of War* was unable to include in the list of Japanese POW camps which featured in its July 1943 issue, a single one in the area of the railway and was in general attempting to present a reassuring picture for its readers,[11] in fact the intelligence authorities in Calcutta and London were building up a comprehensive and most disquieting picture of the situation. By April 1943 the British government had received a list of the camp sites compiled by the Swiss consul and it had become clear just how remote and isolated most of these were. In June they received alarming reports of the conditions of prisoners in the Kanchanaburi POW hospital and at Chungkai to which hundreds of sick men were then being sent from the up-country jungle camps. The news was kept from the public at large in the Allied homelands since it would only have caused distress to relatives and no government action could be promised which would have alleviated the situation. However a strong diplomatic protest was made via the Protecting Power; but it only met with a denial that the conditions were as stated.[12]

It was at this stage that Boonpong Sirivejjabhandu began to make his invaluable contribution. As the news filtered through to 'V' of the conditions in the up-country camps, Gairdner kept up his Nong Pladuk contact while two of his British internee colleagues, E P Heath of the Borneo Company and R D Hempson of the Anglo Thai Corporation undertook to expand the medical aid as far up-country as possible. Via another friend of one of them, Boonpong was contacted and became involved in the 'V' organisation's work.[13] He was reputedly a captain in the *Seri Thai* organisation[14] and was initially the contractor for supplying the camps with such canteen goods as the Japanese permitted, but rapidly became identified with the prisoners' cause and throughout the latter part of the construction period he would take supplies of food, drugs, cash and even wireless batteries ('canary seed' as they were known), to camps a considerable distance up-river. There were other camp traders, of course, but as one purchaser later put it, Boonpong's 'prices were always the lowest and his profits the slightest'.[15] However it was his illegitimate operations as part of the 'V' organisation which were so significant. He cashed cheques, advanced money against any remaining personal valuables which the prisoners still had and, of course, supplied invaluable drugs and cash to the camp commandants. The additional food which Boonpong was able legitimately to sell was literally a life-saver; but it was his activity as a 'V' agent in providing medicines and money which was so invaluable, involving, as it did, enormous risk-taking on his part. His barges did occasionally get a substantial distance up-country, but it was principally in the lower reaches of the Kwai that they were most active. However, since it was to the base hospitals in these areas that the seriously sick patients from the north were evacuated, they ultimately benefited as well. In Tamarkan camp, for example, which became a base hospital in May 1943, the death rate rose at one stage to five per day; but by November it had dropped to one per week, in part as a result of supplies from Boonpong who at this time was sending the camp 5,000 Ticals in cash and about 7,000 Ticals-worth of medicines and drugs each month.[16] The camp commanders took great care to keep their 'V' contacts secret and despite the suspicions of the *kempeitai* being aroused on several occasions, some unpleasant interrogations and numerous breaks in contact as the labour force was moved around, the network managed to continue operating throughout the war and became integrated with the efforts of the Swiss consul to get supplies to the camps. Gairdner's employee Hong who was the important early contact was said to have been a most unlikely undercover agent: he was Chinese, wore a white solar topee, had a large and noticeable wart on his face and wore semi-European clothes.[17] After the war the Red Cross reimbursed those who had contributed to the local fund-raising which had been very substantial: over 100,000 Ticals in cash and medicines was reported to have been supplied to four of the southern camps alone.[18] At war's end several members of the 'V' organisation received awards for their efforts* which were not only a remarkable example of local initiative, courage and daring, but were amply justified by the impact they had

---

* Boonpong is widely believed to have been awarded the George Medal and his obituary in *The Times* records this; but there is no official record of this award ever having been made.

on sickness rates in the camp hospitals, as numerous medical officers would readily testify.

For the Japanese railway authorities, neither the cholera epidemic, nor the escape attempts, nor the appalling physical conditions under which their workers were operating had any impact on their unwavering determination to have the line completed by the stated date. Their insistence that the work continue round the clock despite the ever-lengthening sick list remained unshakeable. However, the physical difficulties seemed always to be conspiring against them. Although every additional kilometre of track laid down was a triumph for the railway organisation, it nevertheless took them a further kilometre away from the base areas whence came the supplies for the camps and the materials for further construction; and while the onset of the monsoon rapidly made transport by land an enormously difficult affair, it was some time before the river levels rose sufficiently to make boat traffic possible to the up-country camps where the critically important work on the line was now concentrated. Nor had the large number of reinforcements made any great difference to the speed with which the construction could be progressed. The 'F' and 'H' Force reinforcements of April and May 1943 arrived, together with thousands of native workers, already debilitated by their long approach march, just in time to be hit by the worst of the monsoon and the cholera which accompanied it. The situation had rapidly been reached in most of the up-country camps where the number of men in hospital was greater than the number available for work. The Japanese themselves later acknowledged that at this period it was not uncommon to have 50 per cent of men on the sick list. The example of Songkurai camp, admittedly worse than most, is worth noting; in late July out of a strength of 1,300 men, 1,050 were on the sick list, with the Japanese nevertheless calling for a workforce of 280.[19] Such a demand had now become as unrealistic as the railway's August completion date.

To add to the concerns of the Japanese, they once again had trouble with the overall command of the railway organisation. General Takasaki, who had taken control of the project when General Shimoda was killed, caught malaria at the end of April and by the end of June he too, like so many of the workers under his control, became a sickbed casualty. Imperial GHQ decided to send out a specialist to survey the project in detail; the officer selected was Colonel Kato, a chief planner from the Railway Bureau. Kato completed his inspection and in July the Tokyo authorities issued revised instructions based on his recommendations.[20] No. 4 Special Railway Construction Corps from Malaya was reorganised and put in charge of transportation as far as Kinsaiyok. 9 Railway Regiment was then able to concentrate its entire resources on the area up to Konkoita which became the designated junction point for the two stretches of track. 5 Railway Regiment moved its headquarters up to Kyandou near the Burma–Thailand frontier and put all its energy into the Nikhe operations. More importantly the completion date for the entire operation was put back to the end of October 1943. Major General Ishida Eiguma was put in overall charge; he took control of the project in August and confirmed that it would be completed in two months' time.[21] It was an invaluable reprieve for all concerned but the decision, however inevitable it may have been, was wildly discordant with the ever-deteriorating strategic situation.

12

Relief Deferred

To use prisoners-of-war and with their cooperation to complete the task constituted a unique phenomenon in world railway construction
Yoshihiko Futamatsu

IN MARCH 1943 Allied bomber aircraft began attacking Moulmein, causing a panic exodus of Burmese ox-cart convoys across the border into Thailand. Moulmein was a nodal point near the southern extremity of the Burmese railway system which the new line from Thailand was intended to join. In the same month and again in April and May the bombers paid premonitory visits to the Thanbyuzayat area where the northern headquarters of the railway project was located, before droning on to coastal targets further south. Then at 2.30 p.m. on 12 June, during a sunny break in the monsoon rains, six Liberators appeared from the north over Thanbyuzayat, broke into two formations of three, wheeled about and began a bombing run on the town. One scored a direct hit on the well which served the prisoners' camp and hospital; 12 POWs were killed, among them were representatives of all the Allied nationalities held there. However, the planes missed the 14 long huts, indistinguishable from the surrounding Japanese barracks and storehouses, in which lay about 3,000 sick prisoners. On one side of this base hospital was the railway with its sidings and stores, on two others were the Japanese lines and on the corner of the fourth the Japanese had built an ammunition hut.

On 15 June six Liberators again visited Thanbyuzayat. In the meantime slit trenches had been prepared around the hospital huts and air raid evacuations had been planned. On this occasion the main camp area was the target for the bombing and strafing runs which the Japanese opposed from prepared positions with fire from automatic weapons. In this raid 17 prisoners were killed and over 40 were

155

injured. Soon afterwards the Japanese moved their headquarters and the POW administration of No. 3 Group away to less vulnerable and conspicuous sites at camps further from the town, while the prisoners' hospital was moved to Retpu camp, 30 kilometres up the line. The threat of air attack was now to be added to the tribulations of the prisoners and the casualties at Thanbyuzayat were unfortunately not to be the last. 'There are few things so testing of morale as being bombed in a POW camp', one Australian in No 3 Group noted. For the Japanese, however, this fresh threat operated at quite a different level; it meant that their new railway, still incomplete and so important to their plans, was already identified and proving to be well within the range of the Allied Liberators, now present in eastern India in considerable, and still growing, strength. The great reach and payload of these heavy bombers meant that no section of the new line was likely to be free from their attention. The logistic strategy of the Japanese which involved developing communications by land to replace the sea lanes, which they had neither the merchant ships to maintain nor the fighting ships to protect, was already being negated by the changing force balance in the region. What made the situation even more grave was the fact that the Burma strategy of the Imperial Army was also in the process of change from one of passive defence to an alternative which involved a pre-emptive attack on the British base at Imphal. Such a reordering of strategic priorities would make great demands on the supply system to the Japanese forces in Burma of which the railway along the Kwai was to be such an important part.

It will be recalled that the commander of the Japanese 18th Division, General Renya Mutaguchi, had been opposed to the idea of a follow-through of the initial Burma campaign with a drive into Assam when this idea, code-named Operation 21, had been first examined in July 1942. However the first Chindit expedition had exposed the error of believing that the hills separating India and Burma were an adequate protection for Japan's western Imperial boundary. Mutaguchi was promoted GOC 15 Army in March 1943, the month after Wingate's men had first marched into Japanese-held Burma to cut the enemy's communications to the northern front. The new Army Commander's determination to invade India to establish a new defensive line based on the Imphal plain seems to have been a direct consequence of Wingate's costly and relatively unsuccessful incursion. There were few more ardent converts to the offensive strategy than the man now responsible for the defence of upper Burma. Mutaguchi pleaded the cause of his Imphal offensive to

General Kawabe of Burma Area Army who gave his agreement to the general concept. A series of operational planning conferences was held of which the Burma Area Army conference which opened in Rangoon on 24 June 1943 at the height of the cholera-ridden 'speedo' further south, was the most important. When HQ Southern Army examined the proposal, the VCGS, General Inada, was not particularly impressed by it. At a subsequent detailed planning meeting Inada repeated his criticisms, saying that more attention should be given to supply matters and that to rely on the capture of the Imphal stores as supplies for the second phase of the operation, as Mutaguchi was proposing, was 'to skin the racoon before you caught him'. The view of IGHQ was that Imphal should possibly be taken, but only 'if we investigate the rear set-up thoroughly'. There was a general coolness about the move from Imphal into Assam but Mutaguchi was no wit deterred from this larger objective by the lack of enthusiasm shown by the senior officers above and around him and as time went on the opposition to his aims steadily diminished.[1]

However there was considerable strategic wisdom in the general caution and the concern for the supply situation which senior officers at all levels had expressed when hearing of Mutaguchi's extravagant plans. The merchant shipping situation was now little short of disastrous; between March and July 1943 a further 147 Japanese merchant vessels were sunk, in the main by the far-ranging American submarines, depriving the scattered garrisons of the use of a further 600,000 tons of freightage, one-tenth of the pre-war total. There was at least the consolation that it would be some months before the weather would improve sufficiently to allow Allied aircraft to range freely over the new railway. August was to bring the worst of the monsoon rain to the border area in which the construction effort was now concentrated; but in the following month it would lessen dramatically at the Burma end of the project though the river levels would remain high for some time thereafter; so it was likely that the work might proceed more rapidly with supplies able to get up-river with greater ease. Nevertheless the new commander of the project, General Ishida, still had major problems ahead of him before he could report the line as ready for operation, the principal one being the continuing difficulty of assembling an adequate work force owing to the high sickness and mortality rates which persisted even after the dramatic rage of cholera deaths had begun to subside at the end of June. In the final analysis dysentery and diarrhoea were to account for more prisoner deaths than cholera, certainly in the 'F' Force camps near the border. Indeed the plight of the prisoners in this group continued long after cholera was defeated.

By mid-May, it will be recalled, the monsoon had rendered impracticable the line of communication southward for 'F' Force, and the failure to weatherproof the track north into Burma probably accounted for the appalling conditions during the worst of the monsoon when the force was almost isolated. When the evacuation of the sick southwards by road became an impossibility the British force commander, Lieutenant Colonel Harris, pressed for a southward evacuation by river as soon as the water level was high enough. There were then about 3,000 seriously sick prisoners in the force who could not receive adequate treatment in the jungle camps. The Japanese considered this proposal at length but finally opted for a move to a hospital camp in Burma which was to be established at Tambaya, about 80 kilometres away. Their orders were for the move of 1,700 patients and staff by road and rail via three staging camps. Movement tables were issued by the IJA authorities and the advance party moved off at the end of July. However, what followed turned out to be, in Harris's words 'the normal Japanese administrative mess'.

In the first place the selection of patients to go was exceedingly difficult for there was little point in sending those who would not survive the journey. On the other hand, those who were not sent would surely die if left in the working camps. Once again the medical officers were faced with agonising choices and without the foreknowledge of the unnecessary hardship which was an inevitable consequence of the mismanagement of the move. To make matters worse, hardly had the advance party set off than the Japanese announced that three of the five 'F' Force camps were to close, the men being concentrated in Upper Songkurai and Songkurai in such a regrouping as would provide 800 fit workers at each of the camps. Thus the sick men who had been adjudged too ill to make the journey had now to move in any case. An added complication was that in order to provide the required numbers of fit men at each camp, it was necessary to create mixed camps of fitter Australians with less fit British. The confused moves, made with little notice and in conditions of considerable hardship, merely accelerated the deaths of the many sick who had to take part in them. Upper Songkurai was originally the Australian camp of 396 men and up until the end of July it had lost only 23 men, 14 of them to cholera. However it filled up to a strength of 1,685 in the first week of August, many of the incomers being either men who were too ill to move to Tambaya, or else those who should have been moved there but for the arbitrary Japanese ceiling of 1,700. From the start of August until Upper Songkurai was finally vacated at the end of November the camp had a further 490 deaths. In Songkurai itself the situation was even worse, deaths there averaged almost ten a day during August with dysentery and allied complaints claiming over half of them. Nor did the group selected for the move to Tambaya fare any better; 43 of the 1,700 patients died during the journey into Burma and a further 748 during the six months of the camp's occupation.[2]

The pressure exerted by the engineers to complete the construction remained unremitting despite the rate at which the camp cemeteries were spreading. Towards the end of August the 'F' Force commander was told that unless the work parties produced by both camps were doubled in size, all prisoners, sick as well as fit, would be turned out of the camps into the jungle to fend for themselves, thus making way for native workers who would take over from them. Colonels Harris and Dillon, the British and Australian commanders and Captain Wild, their interpreter, were given the opportunity a few days later to put their case to the commander of the 5th Railway Regiment. Ultimately they were allowed to retain two-thirds of the accommodation surrendering the rest to the labour reinforcements; but the threat had been real enough. 'It is a grim recollection', Colonel Harris's report notes, 'that we were able to make available a third of our accommodation only by taking into consideration the number of deaths which would inevitably occur in the next few weeks.'[3]

'H' Force was meanwhile enduring similar privations; moves to new camps and fresh work seemed to be the order of the day and as always it was the seriously ill prisoners who suffered most from the moves, if indeed they managed to survive them. Towards the end of July, for example, the Japanese decided that Hintock Valley camp should be evacuated to Hintock River camp about four miles away. Parties of sick were sent down daily, but as there were no fit men to help or carry them, they had to walk the four miles unaided over difficult country. Of a party of 110 walking sick who left on one day, 17 were dead within 48 hours. Some while later a party of fit men was spared to bring down the remaining 22 of the seriously ill. The commander recalled that, 'throughout this period it never stopped raining and the result was disastrous. All the men later died'.[4] Although the new camp was near the river which meant that food was more plentiful and even milk was available for the sick, the damage was already done to the men's health and the death rate remained high. Towards the end of August a party known as 'No. 1 Subsection' of 'H' Force and including all the remaining fit men from all the 'H' Force camps was put together and despatched to work up in the border area near the 'F' Force concentration. Its move to Konkoita was the all-too-common experience of mismanagement and misinformation which had characterised the original journey of the force up from Ban Pong. It began with a journey in railway trucks up the new line to Takanum and then a series of marches through the rain with bivouacs at Tamuron Port, Krian Krai and finally at Konkoita where the ex-hausted marchers had to clear a patch of secondary jungle before they could make their camp. The camp site at Konkoita proved to be an excellent one but the railway work was as arduous as before and the pressure on the workforce as unrelenting as ever. 'The brutality shown by some of the engineers was, if anything, worse at Konkoita than hitherto and protests only resulted in further excesses', wrote the Force commander.[5]

The coolie forces which were now being crammed into the camps in the border area where the last stretch of the line was being completed were faring even worse than the Allied prisoners. 'K' and 'L' Forces, improvised from the remaining medical personnel in Changi, were attempting to do something for these desperately neglected workers. It has already been noted that many in these medical teams found themselves occupied less with treating the sick than with general labouring duties around the camps, a role for which some of them were entirely unsuited having been spared inclusion on earlier Thailand details on account of their age or sickness. Some 'K' Force personnel were not allocated to coolie camps at all. One party of two medical officers and a dental officer were despatched to an anti-cholera unit at Wanyai where they had to dig swill pits and drains to carry water from the river to the camp as well as work in the labora-tory. This proved too arduous for the medical officers, one of whom was in his mid-fifties, and both fell sick. The dental officer was then moved to the Japanese camp nearby where he spent his time treating Japanese personnel and, it has to be added, stealing drugs from a well-stocked dispensary which supplied medicines to Japanese hospitals up and down the line, and passing them on to an 'H' Force camp nearby. The dental officer was well treated in this camp as the sole prisoner among the Japanese but when the suspicion of stealing drugs centred on him he was removed to Kanchanaburi for investiga-tion and was lucky to avoid being executed.[6]

'L' Force consisting of 15 medical officers and 100 orderlies was not despatched from Singapore until 23 August 1943. Like so many of its predecessor parties its members were inexplicably told that there was no need to take medical equipment since they were going as a medical reinforcement to an established hospital from which they would return to Singapore in about three months. However, taking account of the rumours passed on by Korean guards returning from up-country because of a cholera outbreak, the Force commander requested additional medical equipment from the POW stores at Changi, but this was refused by the RAMC authorities who were still styled 'DDMS Malaya Command'. The mixed British–Australian force accordingly left with sufficient medical stores only for the requirements of its own personnel for two or three months. As had happened so frequently before, it was at the railway transit camp at Ban Pong that the true circumstances of this mercy mission began to dawn. The members of 'K' and 'L' Forces were, in fact, part of a Japanese medical organisation run by a Major Kudo, known as the *Kudo Butai* which had already established a series of primitive coolie hospitals at Ban Pong, Kanchanaburi, Wanyai, Tamajo and Nikhe in Thailand and at Tarden, Apalon, Mezali and Anakwin in Burma. The two hospitals at Kanchanaburi in Thailand and those at Apalon and Anakwin in Burma were larger base hospitals. 'K' Force personnel were already working in these hospitals and about 60 per cent of the 'L' Force staff were now allocated to them, the remainder supplementing the doctors and orderlies in the POWs' own hospitals. They were detailed into parties irrespective of which force they had originally belonged to and were frequently moved about by rail, river and on foot.

By this stage in the railway operation a very rough and ready medical evacuation system for the sick native labourers was in operation. Initially the coolies had died in their thousands in the working camps, particularly during the cholera outbreak, but now when they became sick they were moved, usually after a delay of some days, to one of the smaller hospitals. Those who recovered went back to the camps and those who remained seriously sick were later collected and evacuated to one of the base hospitals, though this happened infrequently before the railway was completed, particularly in the up-country areas. However conditions even in the base hospitals were very poor, though with the arrival of 'K' and 'L' Forces, improvements were progressively introduced; nevertheless it was some time before these had an appreciable impact on the alarmingly high death rates.[7] Some appreciation of the scale and character of the problems in the coolie base hospitals along the railway may be gleaned from the situation at No 2 Coolie Hospital based at Kanchanaburi.

This hospital was situated between the newly constructed railway line and the service road which ran parallel with it about 100 yards away. The hospital huts were built on some paddy fields and these were opened as a base hospital in June 1943. Each of the hospital's atap huts was in the charge of a native *mandor* who was responsible for discipline, cleanliness, feeding and general administration. He had two fit native assistants who carried the food from the cookhouse, issued it to the patients and were supposed to keep the huts clean. The *mandor* and his assistants were paid by the Japanese but made a good deal more from bribes and the disposal of dead men's kit. A Japanese captain was in charge of the hospital and he was assisted by a medical lieutenant, but they only visited the huts once a week. In actual daily charge was a non-medical corporal who 'knew no medicine but would prescribe treatment for all and sundry'. The Japanese dispenser apparently had no knowledge or training in dispensing. He generally met any request for drugs with abuse and often with physical violence. Every morning there was a lengthy battle in order to obtain drugs for the sick. A British doctor explained the reason, 'It must be understood that a good price could be obtained for quinine and other drugs from the Siamese and the less he issued the more he could sell outside. Siamese prostitutes who visited the IJA weekly were usually paid in quinine.'[8]

When the first 'L' Force personnel arrived at the hospital at the end of August 1943 the conditions were chaotic, hygiene and sanitation were practically non-existent, the latrines were open and swarming with flies and the camp flooded with their contents during the rain. There was no uncontaminated source of water and when cholera broke out all visits to the river were forbidden and the camp had to rely on a Japanese pump and filter for its supplies. When the pump broke down the coolies sometimes went as long as four days without water being provided. Dysentery was rife in the camp and there was no isolation in the wards for the dysentery cases. The hospital featured one hut 12 metres by 6 metres, known locally as 'the death house' to which all patients in the hospital too sick to look after themselves and to crawl to the latrines were transferred. They would lie on the mud floor of this hut in indescribable filth. They received no medical treatment of any kind, and since the Japanese forbade the issue to them of any food, no coolie survived for more than a few days. The strength of the hospital varied from about 1,500 to 3,000 and in the period June to August 1943, according to native accounts, some 3,000 coolies died, sometimes as many as 50 in one day.

This was the situation when, in late August 1943, an Australian medical officer and about 20 British and Australian nursing orderlies arrived and set about trying to remedy the situation.[9] It was to be a long haul and this, it has to be remembered, was a base hospital near Kanchanaburi, an administrative centre in a productive agricultural region with good communications. What made the position even more tragic for the Malayan coolies was that some of them, believing the recruitment stories of the good conditions in Thailand in which they would be operating, had brought their wives and children with them. Mortality among the children was very high and some of the women whose husbands died contracted fresh marriages in the hope of a little security, only to have their new spouses die as well. Coolies who attempted to run away were generally caught and given a severe beating.

In the northern section things were a little easier for both prisoners and native labourers. Many of the latter escaped back to their villages, as has been noted. In addition the Burmese authorities were now taking an anxious interest in the welfare of their nationals who were working on the project. They organised inspection teams to visit working camps and found, as Ba Maw later reported, that the accessible ones were well organised and healthy. However there appears to have been considerable difficulty in their labour officer and inspection teams getting to 'the numerous small out-of-way camps where conditions continued to be most primitive and even brutal'.[10] However the Burmese Premier's Director of Press and Publicity was rather more forthright; he stated bluntly that the government's labour inspectors 'were not allowed to visit camps in the interior'. He quoted the case of two young labour officers who managed to get as far down the line as 173 kilometres from Thanbyuzayat. This took them into the heart of 'F' Force country where the conditions were appalling and the death rates were frighteningly high. They were detained there for four months and only obtained their release with the greatest difficulty to return to Rangoon with harrowing tales of their experiences. There they were apparently very politely warned that any report of the true state of affairs might involve them with the Japanese military police. Nevertheless, they did give a first-hand account of what they had witnessed to the Government, explaining that for months the labour conscripts had had no-one to whom they could relay their grievances.[11] Sadly, the reports were nothing new and only confirmed the stories that had been circulating for some time. Premier Ba Maw claimed that his administration very seldom knew the full truth in time and even when they did, 'the fast-crumbling war situation prevented us from acting really effectively'.

However the concentration of the workers along the final stretch of the line around Konkoita did finally indicate that the railway ordeal was nearing its end. On 17 October 1943 the two stretches of rail, one snaking down from Thanbyuzayat, the other up from Nong Pladuk, finally linked up at Konkoita, 262 kilometres north of the Thailand terminus and about 40 kilometres from the Burma border, amid deep forest. The Japanese celebrated the final junction with as much formality and ritual as they could muster in the primitive conditions and on 25 October they held a special 'opening-to-traffic' ceremony at which Lieutenant Colonels Sasaki and Imai, the commanding officers of 5th and 9th Railway Regiments respectively, completed the construction by driving specially-made gun-metal dog spikes into an ebony sleeper before stepping forward to the GOC Major General Ishida and reporting their task at last completed. The Chief of Staff of Southern Army witnessed the ceremony along with men from both railway regiments. Locomotive No. C5631, bedecked with two crossed flags, one Japanese and one Thai, in front of the smokestack and pulling three open trucks encased in specially constructed wooden frames and roofed with atap (immediately dubbed by the irreverent POWs 'the flying Kampong') and occupied by Japanese officers in their best khaki uniforms, moved quietly up from the south east to the junction point. One prisoner at Takanum noted that a high screen of freshly cut bamboo branches had been erected along the side of the track where it passed an 'unbelievably squalid coolie camp' about a mile down the line, presumably to hide the unsightly spectacle from the view of the high ranking visitors. At the junction point the Southern Army military band, brought north for the occasion, struck up the Japanese national anthem. 'Even now', wrote Futamatsu 37 years later, 'the inspiration of that moment is something I cannot forget.'[12] A pylon had been set up in the enclosure at the ceremonial site to mark the occasion; but more ominously the Japanese had also positioned an anti-aircraft gun post in the jungle nearby. Furthermore it appears that their original plan for the ceremony had been that Premier Ba Maw from Burma and Prime Minister Phibun Songgram from Thailand should ride the first train from each end of the line and greet each other dramatically at the border. But on the due day Ba Maw was advised not to travel because it was believed that a major Allied air attack on the railway was planned.[13]

13

The Impermanent Way

Although the importance of the completed railroad was very great from the standpoint of supply for Burma, and, although the Burma Area Army entertained great hopes of it, the anticipated capacity failed to materialise due to its short period of existence after its completion
Colonel Takeo Kurahashi

THE MAGNITUDE of the task which the Japanese had now forced to completion and the scale of the effort required in the tropical and undeveloped corner of the world in which the activity was concentrated, is perhaps best comprehended by an examination of some of the railway statistics collected after the war.

Japanese engineers stated that the completion of the line involved the building of 4 million cubic metres of earthwork, shifting 3 million cubic metres of rock and the construction of 14 kilometres of bridgework.[1] The bridging expert Futamatsu adds that 60,000 cubic feet of bridging timber had been used, together with 650,000 cubic feet of timber poles; while the blasting of cuttings and the like had consumed about 300 tons of explosives. Over 300 lorries had been used on the treacherous supply road and for communication with the nearby villages, though of more general use throughout the year were the 700 motor boats and sampans which had been requisitioned locally for waterborne supplies. Engines for the now-completed line were drawn from the Thai, Burmese and Malayan stock and were supplemented by about 35 locomotives shipped over from Japan and converted for local use. Finally, supplementing the human muscle which was wasted with such prodigality, were the 400 elephants and their *mahouts* who had been enlisted and set to work beside the human toilers.[2]

The manpower balance sheet is hard to complete with total

reliability for the Japanese destroyed many of their own records and forbad the POWs to keep any. Official records of 'F' and 'H' Forces do exist however and it is very plain from these at what cost in lives the strategic railway had been constructed. By the time of the official opening ceremony on 25 October 'F' Force had lost about 2,200 men, one third of its original strength; for 'H' Force the figure was somewhat lower at about 20 per cent and for the other main groups along the line there were smaller but still substantial proportions who had perished during the course of construction.

Before the relatively small No 5 Group in Burma was merged with the much larger No 3 Group and began its journey down to Thailand, it had lost about 23 per cent of its strength, the highest mortality rate, at about 28 per cent, being suffered by the locally-enlisted Asian 'Dutch' troops, and the lowest at about 14 per cent by the Australians. The American contingent under Lieutenant Colonel Thorp had 98 of its men die, 21 per cent of its original 456. Many of the survivors were sorely ravaged by their experience and in appalling physical shape. One 'F' Force prisoner recorded that before captivity he had weighed about 14 stones. In November 1943, while still recovering from his latest attack of fever, he tipped the makeshift camp scales at eight stones ten pounds and during his time on the railway he had suffered from beriberi, pellagra, dengue fever, malaria, dysentery, blackwater fever, jaundice, scabies, ringworm, tropical ulcers and tropical pamphlicus.[3] Not surprisingly, life was to ebb away from the emaciated frames of hundreds more as a result of the railway ordeal before the final Allied victory and the release of the prisoners from their camps.

However the greatest losses but the hardest to measure were undoubtedly those suffered by the native labour forces, the Burmese and Malayan coolies who were still dying in great numbers even after the line had been completed. Many of their deaths went unrecorded and only the most general indication can be given of the scale of the tragedy which their loss represented for the communities concerned. Literally thousands had perished in the up-country camps; in Nikhe for example, 6,000 coolies were admitted to the hospital there of whom 1,750 died. Cholera had been a major killer but dysentery also took a frightening toll.[4] Major movement of the sick to the base hospitals was not possible until the railway was completed and even then the journeys took place in conditions that were so primitive (60 patients to a railway truck was not an uncommon loading) that many arrived too traumatised to survive for very long. In No 2 Coolie

Hospital Kanchanaburi, about 5,000 coolies died during the seven month period from September 1943 to May 1944, an average of 20 to 25 per day, though in the following 11 months when British doctors and orderlies were in charge of the main part of the hospital the situation improved considerably, deaths totalling about 600 for the whole period and averaging one to three per day.[5]

The official opening of the railway was marked by a day's holiday for the workers and a special issue of extra food, Japanese tinned milk, fish and margarine. Some also got an issue of cigarettes. At Kinsaiyok the Japanese dynamited the river and allowed the prisoners to have a celebration meal with the haul of over one hundred kilograms of fish. The military band made other stops along the line, giving concerts to motley groups of Japanese, Siamese, Tamils and Allied POWs and even introduced some Western music in its programme – one diarist noting that selections from *Carmen* and *The Merry Widow* were included with more traditional Japanese compositions in the concert at Takanum. A brothel train also visited the Japanese and Korean personnel in their camps dotted along the line and on several occasions the girls gave cash and cigarettes to the destitute POWs. The Japanese ordered that religious ceremonies should be held in honour of those who had died that the railway might be built. In Nos. 3 and 5 Groups in Burma, large inscribed crosses were erected at the cemeteries and Colonel Nagatomo read a letter of condolence to the assembled prisoners in 55 kilometre camp which his representatives repeated at others. The Burma-side workers also had two days' rest.

At Takanum the Japanese colonel addressed his oration directly to the grave of a British captain before bowing and returning to his assembled troops. The sight of the Japanese dressed in their best uniforms and accoutred with their ceremonial swords laying wreaths at the graves of prisoners in whose death they had been the major factor was a spectacle which most of the assembled captives found difficult to take. In the opinion of the Australian war correspondent at Aungganaung 105 kilometre camp in Burma it was 'one of the most nauseating displays of Japanese hypocrisy that we were ever called upon to witness'.[6] This perhaps betrayed a slight misunderstanding of the Japanese approach to war and to the duty of the individual. But now, at last, the intense pressure on the workforce eased off and with the great improvement in the weather, supplies were able to get through again via the now dry service road and the river whose level remained relatively high for some weeks to come. In most places the diet improved and some labourers were fortunate enough to get an issue of clothing from the Japanese. The working parties were reduced in size and were generally concerned with railway maintenance, stacking timber fuel, strengthening embankments and so on. Some maintenance groups, as for example, that composed of No 5 Group men in Burma, worked on a day-on, day-off basis.

Once the railway was completed the Japanese Malayan POW Administration began to withdraw the shattered remnants of 'F' and 'H' Forces back to their base at Singapore. Many of course had already been evacuated from the working camp to the base hospitals long before this. Sick members of 'H' Force had been arriving at the belatedly-constructed Kanchanaburi hospital in parties of 100–150 from about the end of August to the end of October. In early November the balance of 'H' Force, now numbering some 800 men also travelled down to Kanchanaburi and by the middle of the month the first contingents, gaunt and sickly but nevertheless classed as fit, were back in the Sime Road camp in Singapore. They were followed by the fitter of the men from the base hospital at Kanchanaburi which had also been receiving the 'F' Force patients transferred to it from Tarsao and Chungkai since the end of September. In November the evacuation of 'F' Force from further up the line began. The resources of the hospital were sorely pressed in taking the sick from both groups and additional huts had to be taken over from the coolie camp hospital nearby. At one point the hospital housed over 2,900 patients; but just as it looked as though admissions would outstrip the available space, the evacuation of 'H' Force patients began. Many of the 'F' Force sick had a great distance to travel; some had been evacuated, it will be recalled, to a base hospital at Tambaya in Burma when communications with Thailand had been entirely disrupted by the monsoon. It was decided to leave behind at Tambaya 300 of the sickest and weakest men; but for some of those whom it was decided to evacuate, the journey south on crowded, open, flatcars, was the last journey they would make. The arrangements for their transfer to Kanchanaburi were, their commander reported, 'disgraceful, no attempt being made to provide reasonable amenities, food or water for the fit or sick, and fourteen men perished on this journey'.

As 'H' Force vacated the Kanchanaburi hospital, so it was taken over by the 'F' Force medical staff and as the patients were returned to relative fitness in the improved conditions which applied there post-monsoon, so they also were moved down to Singapore. By 22 December 1943 all of 'F' and 'H' Forces, except 700 very sick patients at Kanchanaburi, had returned to Singapore and these 700 were transferred to another hospital in the area. The conditions at this second hospital were good, the Japanese adjutant of 'F' Force, who commanded the camp, cooperated with the 'F' Force doctors, the rations were adequate and, since the medical authorities had been able to retrieve the medical stores which the Force had been forced to leave at Ban Pong on its march up to the line, satisfactory treatment of many of the sick was now possible. The hospital was finally closed in April 1944 with the remaining 'F' and 'H' Force personnel being returned to Singapore. Here at least conditions were reasonable with Lieutenant Colonel Newey, who came down with the first of the 'H' Force parties, reporting 'kindly treatment and every consideration that circumstances would permit in the way of feeding, hospital facilities etc'.[7]

By the turn of the year the remaining labourers on the railway were also being regrouped at the southern end of the line and by March 1944 they were concentrated into main camps at Chungkai, Tamarkan, Kanchanaburi, Tamuang and Nong Pladuk where conditions were immeasurably better than they had been on the line itself. The Japanese also began to make arrangements to transfer 10,000 of the Thailand-based prisoners to Japan for work in heavy industries there. The labour shortage in the homeland was now so acute that despite their own manpower predicaments, the military were granting deferments of conscription to certain categories of workers and the domestic labour force was being supplemented by 381,000 Koreans and a growing number of university students and technical and middle school pupils.[8] The fittest of the prisoners therefore represented a very valuable supplement to what was available, if only the means could be found of transporting them to Japan, an increasing difficulty as the year wore on.

From May 1944 onwards parties of varying strengths were also sent back up the line for maintenance work, besides repairing damage caused by Allied bombing. Since the healthiest of the prisoners had already been earmarked for Japan, this work fell to the less fit but while conditions were reasonable this did not matter overmuch. However, the numbers now involved with maintenance were not sufficient to attract traders up river with canteen stores and with over-use of the railway, the maintenance demands grew. In some camps the worst of the brutalities of 1943 reappeared; the sole redeeming feature of the situation being the relative ease with which the sick could now be evacuated to hospital by train.

The Japanese had now reorganised their own railway maintenance assets. 5 Railway Regiment had been moved to northern Burma and taken over the operation of the Myitkyina line which was now being regularly attacked by Allied bombers; 9 Railway Regiment moved up to replace it and took over responsibility for the new line as far south as Nikhe, with the lower half of the line in the charge of 4 Special Railway Corps from Malaya. The importance of the new line to Japanese plans was evidenced by the fact that as soon as the inaugural train had passed through on its way to the northern terminus, it was followed by a second carrying supplies to the Burma front. Although the railway had been completed in accordance with the revised timetable, its availability had been eagerly awaited by the planners of the Imphal offensive. The pressure which had been placed on General Ishida and his workforce and the haste with which they had got the line into operation was very evident from the standard of the completed structure. The early work at both ends, in the relatively flat country around Thanbyuzayat and between Nong Pladuk and Kanchanaburi, had been carried out reasonably well with a sound road bed and wide cuttings where they were required. But as the construction progressed so the standards deteriorated: sleepers sank flush into the foundations, cuttings were barely wide enough to allow a train to pass, collapses occurred, there were landslides into the cuttings and some of the bridges, built quickly with green timber for speed rather than durability, were in a very bad state.

Long journey times were an inevitable consequence. One train coming south from Tambaya with an 'F' Force party including many sick, took five days to reach Kanchanaburi, averaging three miles an hour, being delayed by the inability of its two engines to manage the gradient without some of the human cargo disembarking and walking to the next station. This was presumably in the border area where the gradient was 29/1000 rather than the 25/1000 originally specified. At other times the train ran out of fuel and the prisoners had to dismount again from the flatcars and roam about the jungle gathering wood to enable the boilers to get up a fresh head of steam.[9] No doubt the prisoners' low priority for use of the line and of its accumulated stocks of wood fuel were also factors in the snail's pace of their progress south. One POW noted wryly that at times the rails were up in the air above the sleepers, at others the sleeper would be up in the air with the rail attached. He noted that they were not even regularly laid, but were 'just like so many matches tossed down by a giant hand'.[10] Numerous eye-witness accounts record derailments; one mentions 13 trucks which had rolled off the line and lay abandoned at the foot of an embankment; another noted how the driver was obliged to take curves in the track very slowly and that the more dangerous of the bends were marked with the wrecks of previous derailments. Caution was also necessary with the bridges, particularly the flimsier wooden structures which, since the maximum axle load was about ten tons, had to be negotiated at dead slow speeds. On the other hand, once the flatter regions of the line were reached, and providing no higher priority traffic demanded use of it, the trains could travel at 30–40 miles an hour on a track that was solidly constructed. There were no stations as such but merely points on the line at which there were passing loops and sidings with unloading areas and fuel dumps, given names quite arbitrarily from the nearby village if there was one or a physical feature named on the map.

Prime Minister Tojo had apparently given formal permission for the 1944 Burma offensive while he was taking a bath. The head of the Military Affairs Bureau had approached him for authorisation of this urgent matter and Tojo had fired questions at him from his bathtub through the glass partition which led to the dressing room where Colonel Nishiura Susumu waited. Among his queries was one demanding whether the supply situation for the offensive was all right. The staff officer went away to check and when he returned with an affirmative answer Tojo set his seal onto the document.[11] However the reality was that the supply situation was already giving cause for serious concern. The logistical planners had long since given up the hope of getting anything other than reinforcing units and war material to the Burma theatre; the attrition of the merchant marine had seen to that. Now, just as the monsoon had eased sufficiently to allow the railway to be completed a few days ahead of the revised deadline, the Allied bombing offensive against the supply system supporting the formations in Burma was resumed with fresh intensity. Even before this the slow progress in the building of the line had forced compromises and risks with the logistical build-up. Southern Army planned to give Burma Area Army 140,000 tons of supplies for the Imphal Operation: 36,000 tons of field ordnance supplies, 21,000 tons of field motor transport supplies (the oilfields at Yenangyaung in Burma were supposed to provide the rest), and 63,000 tons of field freight supplies to supplement the rice which was all that the Burmese economy could be relied upon to provide locally. In view of the railway's unfinished state, it was planned to transport two thirds of these requirements by sea during the period May–October 1943 when the monsoon conditions would inhibit enemy air action, using small, coast-hugging wooden craft. The remainder was to be brought north via the new railway when it was completed.[12]

As to the reinforcing formations which were to move into Burma for the planned Arakan and Imphal offensives (Ha-Go and U-Go as the Japanese called them), several accounts record that seven or eight divisions and also Corps and Army troops moved into Burma via the new railway during the first half of 1944. No doubt both the commander of Burma Area Army and the railway regiments themselves would have liked this to have been the case. In fact the Area Army had already received some of its reinforcements by the start of 1944 and it was, in any case, not to receive any more than six extra divisions before the whole campaign closed. Furthermore, since the Burma–Siam railway had fallen behind schedule, other land routes had to be used for the despatch of some of them, in addition to the limited use of the sea reinforcement route by which 24 Independent Mixed Brigade made its way to Tavoy before taking over as the Tenasserim garrison force and then moving north to play a vital role in resisting the Chindits at Indaw. 54th Division was also transported by sea from Java to Rangoon, where it moved quietly behind 55th Division ready for the Ha-Go Arakan offensive. But other reinforcing units had to make their way with greater difficulty overland. 31st Division from Malaya having moved up into Thailand by train had to complete its journey into Burma by marching along the service road beside the as yet uncompleted railway. This route was practicable for foot soldiers and pack animals, but useless for motor transport during the rains. However it did give the troops access to ready-made billets along the line and a rudimentary food supply organisation.

The reason for the urgency with which the Japanese drove their labour force to get the line completed can be deduced from the state of the troops who had perforce to march through the monsoon down the muddy track alongside it. 'They were exhausted' one prisoner noted, 'and were driven even harder than we were. In addition to carrying full kit, arms and ammunition, they dragged little field guns, four or more to a battalion.'[13] One company marching at twice the prisoners' speed, overtook a party of 'F' Force who were trudging up the track in the Takanum area to their working camp. They 'were as bedraggled and filthy as we were. Fifty were harnessed to a cart loaded with heavy equipment',[14] one of the 'F' Force group observed, while an Australian fellow-prisoner at the Burma end of the line remarked that 'our own men toiling on the railway watched with grim satisfaction that was tinged with pity the ordeal of this Nippon cannon fodder struggling to the front in such primitive conditions'.[15] It took the division a month to labour up the supply road with its equipment.[16] Led by Major General Sato, 31st Division was going to have the longest approach march of all the Japanese formations, for it was destined to conduct the attack on Kohima, 1,000 miles to the north of the Three Pagodas Pass, though one of its units, the *Retsu Butai*, was spared the first part of the exhausting approach march, travelling up via the newly completed railway in December 1943.[17]

A sister formation, 15th Division, also had to make its way overland to its appointed battleground in Burma. The division had been due to arrive in northern Burma on 17 June but it was held back on labouring chores in Thailand for months on end building an all-weather road between Chiengmai in northern Thailand and Toungoo in Burma, by order of Southern Army which clearly gave a higher priority to rear area communications than did General Mutaguchi. The division, under Major General Yamauchi, had previously served in central China where it had been equipped with motor transport, but on the way to Burma it had to switch to pack animals since part of the division's route lay across the difficult border hills. The division's artillery was also changed to mountain guns which could be manhandled across the broken and roadless terrain. Anti-tank guns were mostly left behind in the belief that they would not be needed at Imphal, and one commander even left one of his two mountain guns and its ammunition hidden on the banks of the Chindwin because movement across the grain of the land was such an exhausting business.[18] Aside from this misjudgment, one of the division's three infantry regiments, its artillery regiment and most of the divisional transport was still in Thailand when D-Day for the Imphal offensive arrived.

Many of the smaller supporting units for the Burma offensive made use of the short railroad which crossed the Isthmus of Kra at its narrowest point between Chumphon in the Gulf of Thailand and Kra Buri facing the Andaman Sea. By coincidence this prisoner-built line had been completed on the day of the 'opening-to-traffic' celebration at Konkoita. Its use obviated the long sea journey around Singapore but involved the combined use of rail, water and land and still exposed its users to the sea journey north to Rangoon. Because of the complications of loading and unloading, this route was used exclusively for troop transport. Nevertheless, as many as 300 reinforcements were moved to Burma along it each day, a total of 22,000 men by February 1944.[19] Eventually 2nd Division, destined initially as the

Bay of Bengal coastal garrison, and 53rd Division, which was to reinforce Major General Honda's 33rd Army on the northern front, were transported into Burma via the new railway. However, the range of alternative supply routes which the Japanese were forced to use testifies to the problems which the late completion and poor supply potential of the new line produced for the logistical planners in Singapore.

The Imphal offensive finally began on 15 March 1944 and the battle for control of the Imphal plain raged for almost three months; not until 7 June did Japanese resistance finally crumble and the pursuit by General Slim's 14th Army begin. When the diseased, disorganised and starving remnants of General Mutaguchi's divisions scrambled back across the Chindwin, his 15th Army had suffered the greatest defeat to date in the Allied fight-back in the Pacific war. The casualties to the Army were 65,000 of its initial strength of 115,000 men and the two divisions, 15th and 31st, which had plodded by foot into Burma and to their general's chosen battlefield, had lost respectively 80 per cent and 65 per cent of their men in dead or wounded. These two divisions and three others had been temporarily destroyed as effective fighting formations. More important still, for the first time in modern Japanese military history, a divisional commander had retreated from the battle line, directly contravening an Army order. Sato's 31st Division had been starving, its artillery and heavy infantry ammunition was exhausted and its commander had resolved to withdraw it to a point where it could receive supplies. 'I'm not going to have my men act as fodder for Mutaguchi's imperial dreams', Sato had raged at the visiting Army Chief of Staff. 'He sent me no rations, no ammunition, nothing except orders to advance. What am I supposed to advance with?'[20]

Although engineer Futamatsu records that the opening of the Burma–Siam railway coincided with enemy air raids which immediately damaged the line's carrying capacity, it was not until 1944 that the new railroad became a regular target for the Allied bombers. In fact, it mattered little to the Allied cause if it received only intermittent attention, providing other targets on the supply route to the forward Japanese divisions were attacked and interrupted; the new line was only as important as the other links in the supply chain. The Burma–Thailand railway system as a whole had three inherent weaknesses. There was a dearth of side lines over which traffic might be run if the main marshalling yards of such centres as Bangkok, Pegu and Mandalay were put out of action. Vulnerable bridges were also a significant feature of the system with 126 in Burma alone which were over 100 feet long and a further 176 of more than 40 feet. Finally there was a long stretch (which included the new line) of 420 miles of isolated track which if broken at any point would sever the Burmese and Thai systems once again.

In the early post-monsoon period it was the communications system within Burma itself and the major communication centres such as Rangoon, Mandalay, Pegu and Bangkok, together with the major bridges within range, on which the bombing offensive was concentrated. The bombing of any two successive bridges inevitably isolated the intervening track and trapped the rolling stock which could then be destroyed. The Japanese consequently had to effect a transfer of materials by detours around the breaks, a slow process with inevitable delay in supplying the front line with its requirements. However, the bigger targets which the important railway centres represented were the ones visited most regularly. The Japanese were particularly sensitive to attacks on Rangoon which became one of the most heavily fortified areas in South East Asia. Heavy anti-aircraft defences and batteries of searchlights were concentrated at the vital points and the larger part of the Japanese fighter strength in Burma was based at Mingaladon and other airfields close by.

So far as the 414 kilometres of the new line were concerned, their vulnerabilities were those of the two national lines writ even larger: the line had 63 bridges that were more than 50 metres in length and a series of vulnerable points, in particular the engine sheds, shunting yards, workshops and junctions at Nong Pladuk and Thanbyuzayat, on which the attacks in early 1943 have already been recounted. Bombing and strafing attacks by the Liberators began again in 1944 and were especially heavy in the early months, but declined as the monsoon descended. During this period the Japanese had their labourers building locomotive shelters at the stations and watering points and constructing spur lines into the jungle where they could be hidden. A Japanese engineer's trace of the railway[21] shows 14 stretches of concealed track below Hin Dat and numerous sections of loops line bypassing the main bridges at the Burma end. Once the line began to be raided regularly by the air forces, traffic came to a complete halt during the day and operated only at night. However in the early stages the main effect of the attacks was less the actual physical damage caused but rather the extent of the disorganisation produced. The bombing, unless directed at extensive terminal facilities, was not particularly accurate and if a bomb missed the single narrow track it would often discharge itself harmlessly in the jungle or the river. However, if a strafing attack took place, it could be particularly dangerous since the trains were often carrying between two and five trucks of ammunition, which were generally in the middle of the train, and also petrol which, for safety's sake, was usually loaded in the rear. But even when attacks were unsuccessful, or not pressed home because of poor visibility, their effects could still be considerable: shipments were held up, schedules were dislocated and bottlenecks were caused which immobilised and delayed as many as ten trains at a time. Given the single track nature of the operation, dislocation was as severe for the 'up' as for the 'down' traffic.

When the original specifications for the line were drawn up it had been intended that it should carry 3,000 tons of cargo daily in each direction. However, this standard had to be reduced to 1,000 tons as construction difficulties were encountered. Nevertheless, there was no single month throughout the entire period of the railway's operation when it managed to deliver even this reduced amount and during the majority of its operation it was carrying less than half this tonnage. During its first full month of operation it managed only 7,600 tons of supplies.[22] The cause is not difficult to ascribe. As one Japanese commentator has admitted, 'The record immediately after opening was a terrifying one . . . in the 55 kilometres between Plankashi (Brankassi) and Konkoita there were some 60 derailments, and 31 in one round trip on the 37 kilometre section of track between Apalon and Anankwin.'[23] As the prisoners had already noted, even two wood-burning engines could not deliver sufficient power to take some of the gradients; since stores, unlike passengers, could not be invited to dismount, the only solution was to reduce the tonnage carried still further. The consequence was that the railway was unable to deliver the one-third of the combat supplies for the Burma Area Army's 1944 offensive that had been assigned to it. Forty-eight thousand tons of ordnance and other combat supplies should have been transported along it before the combined offensive began; but by the end of January only a little more than half that amount had got as far as Thanbyuzayat; from there this vital war *matériel* had to be laboriously ferried across the Salween estuary and then had to cross the Sittang river which was under regular air attack, before it even reached the main railway terminal at Pegu. According to Colonel Kurahashi, a logistics officer of the Area Army, as late as March 1944 the reserve munitions of Burma Area Army (sufficient for one engagement by about two divisions and amounting to about 50 per cent of the total allocation) still had not arrived because of the bad condition of the Thailand–Burma Railway. 'Shipment over the Thailand–Burma Railroad did not meet with any degree of success', he later noted, 'Consequently, the Army initiated the Imphal operation with only two-thirds of the scheduled supplies.'

To make matters worse a considerable proportion of the ammunition which did get through to the forward supply depots of the three divisions assaulting Imphal was destroyed by Allied bombing.[24] In the opinion of Lieutenant General Numata Takaze, Chief of Staff of Southern Army, strategic bombing up to the time of the Imphal offensive did relatively little damage to the new railway 'the efficiency of which was marred by the defect in the hurried original construction.' This was a view with which the former Chief of Staff of Burma Area Army Lieutenant General Naki Eitari concurred, though in remarking that the railway 'worked fairly smoothly'[25] he clearly was unaware of the frantic efforts that were needed to transport even the 400 tons a day which was all it managed to deliver during the first six months of 1944. This, it must be realised, was only two trains per day and fell ridiculously short of what had been planned. However the fact remains that although the railway consistently failed to deliver what was demanded of it throughout its period of operation, the number of trains which the authorities managed to run from the south up to Thanbyuzayat increased steadily throughout 1944; in November 1943, the first full month of operation only 45 trains had made the journey, but by December the following year the monthly total was 115 with almost a tripling of the tonnage carried by the five trains a day which were then getting through. Plainly, Allied air power might well have been playing a role in keeping the railway below its planned effectiveness; but it was certainly not stopping it from delivering increasing quantities of supplies as the year went on.

Nevertheless, by late 1944 the supply situation of Burma Area Army was grave in the extreme. Following the disastrous reverse at Imphal, General Kimura had effectively lost northern Burma. He had also now received the last reinforcing formation he was going to get, 49th Division, which had travelled up via the new railway. The supply specialists in Singapore knew that about 60,000 additional troops were available as reinforcements for Kimura's understrength divisions and that they could supply weapons and ammunition for about three divisions, together with 45,000 tons of supplies, 500 lorries and 2,000 pack animals. The problem was getting them to him. The supplies risking the sea route to Rangoon had now been reduced to a trickle. Since the port approaches were now being regularly mined and the risk of attack from the air was always increasing, large vessels had long since terminated their run at Penang in Malaya, if indeed they ventured beyond Singapore at all. Substantial merchant craft were too precious a commodity to risk unnecessarily.

The combined air and submarine assault on Japan's cargo vessels was now reaching a crescendo: the loss of 162 ships in the last three months of 1943 had been serious enough but in the first three of 1944 the sinkings increased to 274, over a million tons' worth of merchant shipping; by the end of the year the total lost was to rise to 2.3 million tons. Every expedient resorted to by the hard-pressed naval line of communication had its downside. Inadequate ship maintenance caused by the lack of bottoms and over-use led to breakdowns, while running without lights and using less safe routes to avoid detection increased the risk of accidents. Tokyo's domestic plight was now so desperate that even younger primary school children were being mobilised to support the war effort. In October 1944 the number of 12 to 14 year olds involved in war work was already over 700,000; it rose to over a million and a quarter by February 1945.[26] But despite the desperate manpower shortage which these extreme measures signified, large numbers of ex-railway prisoners organised initially as 'Japan parties' were left waiting at Saigon or were transferred to Singapore because no vessels were available to take them to the Japanese homeland. Some were still stationed at the two ports when the war ended.

If the sea route for resupplying Burma Area Army was not viable, the railway from Thailand was hardly a satisfactory alternative; now under regular air attack it could only manage to deliver 15,000 tons of supplies in a good month. The true measure of the extent to which it was failing to meet Burma Area Army's logistical needs at this critical juncture was the decision of the supply specialists to get the bulk of Kimura's reinforcements to him once again by sea. 60 coastal vessels under No 38 Harbour Unit at Rangoon used the cover of the monsoon to run the gauntlet of aircraft and submarine patrols and the risk of mines to deliver 30,000 fresh troops by October 1944 to stiffen the defending divisions. The irony was that some troops were rapidly withdrawn again the following month to shore up other sections of Japan's crumbling imperial dam.[27]

The steadily increasing effectiveness of the air action against the railway was the result of a number of factors. One important contribution was made by the Commanding Officer of 159 Squadron RAF,

Wing Commander Blackburn whose unit had been formed in 1942 as a Liberator squadron and transferred to Burma at the end of the year where it had operated ever since. By experimenting with cruise control and extra fuel tanks Blackburn had managed to increase the bomb load from 3,000 lbs to 8,000 lbs at the aircraft's maximum range of 1,100 miles, a great enhancement of its hitting power; which meant that all of the railway and indeed the connecting line as far as Bangkok were now within fully-loaded heavy bomber range. These techniques were employed by the British squadrons and those of the American 7th Bombardment Group. When 99 and 215 squadrons converted to Liberators in the latter part of 1944 they were able to add their weight to attacks on the railway. From March 1944 Beaufighters of 27 and 177 squadrons were also able to get to targets along the line and to the main termini at Bangkok and Chiengmai. Armed with 20-millimetre cannon and machine-guns, these aircraft proved ideal for attacking rolling stock and locomotives which were costly for the Japanese to replace and time-consuming to repair. The railway engineers responded by building a system of bullet-proof pens and shelters for their locomotives. However in January 1944 a third squadron arrived which was equipped with rockets which proved quite successful in dealing with even the protected engines. The Beaufighters were a very effective element in the war against the railway, and were nicknamed 'Whispering Death' by the Japanese.

Another factor increasing the effectiveness of the bombing of the narrow railway track was the introduction of the spiked bomb which had been used by the Allies and the Germans in North Africa but which reached its full development in the Burma theatre. The problem of bombs delivered in low altitude attacks tending to ricochet off the track and explode harmlessly elsewhere has already been noted. After several attempts at a solution the spiked bomb was developed. The modification was a 17 inch steel spike screwed into the nose fuse cavity of a standard 100 lb demolition bomb which then screwed into the track bed on impact and detonated. Tactical planning called for them to be dropped in pairs at half-mile intervals along the track. The B-25s used them with great effectiveness. However the American Bombardment Group halted its bombing missions after 11 January 1944 and was switched to transporting fuel to the forward bases in China. It was perhaps this easing of the attacks upon it which saw the railway almost double its effectiveness between July and the end of 1944, raising the tonnage delivered from 70,000 in the first six months of the year to 113,000 in the last.

Attacks on the railway yards and workshops caused great disorgan-isation with an average three-day delay before any running traffic could be restored and a week before the normal flow could be re-sumed. Damage to the track itself could generally be repaired within a couple of days though it caused great disruption to traffic movement while the damage was dealt with. Attacks on bridges brought even greater disruption, though the time taken to repair them could vary greatly depending upon the type of structure involved, the local topo-graphical conditions and so on. The Japanese nevertheless demon-strated considerable flexibility and originality in improvising alterna-tive structures and repairing damage. In many cases bridges were not repaired at all, but bypass structures were substituted. Repairs were often hurried and resulted in further degradation of the overall sys-tem. Other expedients were the use of a ferry system of small boats or squads of coolies to carry cargo across temporary footbridges. The engineers nevertheless claimed that even large bridges could be re-paired in 10–20 days; this by the determined exploitation of the two resources which they still had aplenty – timber and manpower. They generally maintained an adequate supply of timbers cut to the required lengths in the vicinity of each bridge and, of course, they exploited their captive labour force without respite. For example, in 1944 they maintained the 100 kilometre section of line between Bran-kassi and the Nikhe area and its 100 associated bridges with a force of 10,000 labourers dispersed in 60 camps. Once a bridge was hit repair work would begin the instant the raid was over and would continue night and day until it was complete. The average bridge took a week to rebuild with coolies transporting the stores in the meantime. One bridge in this section was 200 metres long and when damaged in a raid the Japanese rebuilt it in two weeks, working three shifts of 500 men throughout the period. The scale of the activity involved can be imagined when it is realised that on occasions there would be as many as 20 bridges hit in one day. Japanese records indicate that bombing destroyed ten bridges between Thanbyuzayat and Nikhe during 1944 and 1945; two of them were put out of action ten times and three others seven times each. In the same section 16 locomotives were damaged and 192 waggons, 114 of them beyond repair.

The main workshop and railway sidings at Nong Pladuk were also now attracting the attention of the bombers and with similar tragic results to those which had attended the first major raid on Thanbyu-zayat. Indeed the position of the unmarked prisoners' compound at Nong Pladuk was not unlike the situation at Thanbyuzayat described earlier; it was bounded on one flank by sidings, on another by workshops and on a third by supply sheds and anti-aircraft batteries – all major targets and quite close to the unprotected POW huts. On the night of 6/7 September Liberators carried out an attack on the workshop and marshalling yards at this important terminus. In the first wave the Japanese assets were attacked accurately and successfully, including three ammunition trains which lay in the sidings alongside the camp. Then the second wave attacked, hitting the targets once again and all apparently going according to plan. The operational record of one of the later attackers reported: 'Arrived over target to find it well on fire and dropped own bombs straight across the station and into the hutted camp at 0200 hrs from 9,500 feet. Opposition futile and return uneventful.'[28] It was a most successful raid, but also a disastrous and tragic one from the prisoners' viewpoint for two sticks of bombs fell across the camp; the ultimate casualty toll was 100 dead and 400 wounded. After vigorous protests the Japanese commander eventually allowed the prisoners to build slit trenches. From this time on the POWs, crowded into the camps at the southern end of the line, were continually at risk from air raids. There were further deaths and more men wounded as they sat out the final months of the war in better supplied camps which enabled their general physical condition to improve but whose regular targeting by the heavy bombers imposed an alternative psychological strain on the inmates. When 7th Bombardment Group returned from its 'Hump' duties towards the end of October, the Strategic Air Force once more concentrated its attacks on the strategic railway; the Allies were now advancing on the Burma front and the Japanese were desperately trying to improve this supply line to the theatre. In November the heavy bombers made 697 sorties against bridges and rail facilities, dropping 1,000 tons of bombs.

However as 1945 began, two improvements in bombing technique reduced the risks to the prisoners a little and improved the effectiveness of the raids immeasurably. The first was the development of a dive-bombing technique which for all its increased effectiveness, indicated just how technologically crude were the bombing practices then in use. As the originator of the technique in 7th Bombardment Group explained it, the pilot pulled out of his gradual dive 50–100 feet above his target and then released his bomb: 'It was all guesswork, for there was no bombsight ... I noticed a row of rivets in front of my seat extending out across the nose of the plane. This was my bomb sight.' When that row of rivets was aligned with the target, the bomb was released. It apparently was a most successful aiming method.[29] The second improvement was rather more sophisticated, this was the AZON bomb – the progenitor of the 'smart bombs' of modern airforces. The AZON was a standard 1,000 pound munition but with a special tail assembly containing a gyro and solenoids to hold it steady and a radio and servo motor to steer it. The bomb could be steered right or left by radio signals from the plane dropping it. There was no provision for controlling range, however, hence the name AZON – 'azimuth only'. However it was ideal for long narrow targets like bridges and railroads and from 15,000 feet it could be steered two or three thousand feet to left or right with errors as small as five or ten feet being capable of detection. AZONs arrived in Burma in autumn 1944 and wherever a target defied conventional destruction, the AZONs of 493 squadron were used to take it on.

Throughout February 1945, the Group's history reports, the squadron was engaging important targets on the Burma–Siam railroad and its precision tactics were soon being used to help destroy the most notable of the railroad's bridges, the steel and concrete bridge at Tamarkan, together with the all-wooden supplementary bridge alongside it. These were subjected to major attack on seven occasions from the end of 1944 to June 1945. During the first three raids the bridges suffered only superficial damage, the weather being bad for two of the raids. On the fourth attack the wooden bypass bridge was seriously damaged but only minor damage was caused to the main steel structure. However, nine days later on 13 February 1945 a low level attack by the B-24s of 493 Squadron USAAF knocked down three of the eleven spans as well as putting the wooden structure out of action. When the next major attack came in on 22 April the wooden bridge was in mid-repair. The night attack was pressed home for seven hours and damaged both structures once again. Two days later, in a raid of unparalleled ferocity and concentration, 40 B-24s took on all the main bridges in a 200-mile sector of the railway, using low level techniques, dive bombing and employing the AZON bombers from great heights. The raid claimed 30 bridges destroyed, 6 damaged and the approaches to seven others torn up. One Japanese account suggests that after the damage caused on 22 April the Maekhlaung steel bridge was not brought into operation again, though the much repaired wooden structure continued to be patched up.[30] British photo reconnaissance indicated efforts to get both bridges working once more and so the RAF Liberators returned to the attack on 24 June 1945 causing further damage and putting both structures out of action.

The June raid was the last which the Tamarkan bridge was to suffer; when the Liberators returned to the Kanchanaburi district the following month their main task was dropping propaganda leaflets; the bombing on this section of the railway was over. The air effort against the railway system had been a very costly operation. The planes were flying enormous distances to get at this single railroad; the round trip was about 2,000 miles, the equivalent of a flight from London to Naples, and the long haul was not always successful or without cost. In the period from January 1944 until the end of the war 34 British and 29 US strategic bombers were lost, many of them in the vicinity of the railway. The Japanese defences were ingenious but seldom effective enough to deter or negate attack. They had orthodox anti-aircraft defences and also, resorting to rather desperate improvisation, deployed remote control land mines against low-level air attacks on bridges and stretches of line. Additionally, they turned flatcars into flak wagons with machine guns and light anti-aircraft guns deployed on them, sometimes firing from fixed positions and sometimes as part of a moving train.

For the attacking aircraft, even when ack-ack defences were not a problem, targets could not always be located, and when pinpointed they were not, without the AZON device, always easy to hit. Mechanical failures in the heavy bombers also degraded their effectiveness from time to time. An example might be the railway mission of 355 Heavy Bomber Squadron on 24 August 1944 for which three Liberators were unable to take off owing to mechanical failures, one returned to base still bombed-up when its rear turret became unserviceable, one missed its target because of an unserviceable compass, two could not see their primary targets owing to cloud and one aimed its bombs at the line but saw them fall on the opposite bank of the river. Only three of the twelve bombers could report damage to the line. Reports very frequently referred to the difficulty in sighting primary targets because of mist and haze.[31] In the end, however, the immense investment in bombing the railway system paid off; at no stage did the strategic line, on which so many hopes were pinned, live up to the expectations of its planners.

14

Defeat and Deliverance

One's emotions were almost numb, after such long suppression of hopes and fears. One could hardly realise that the moment for which one had waited with such desperate but such doubtful hopes had come at last. It was over: we were free again ...
Dr Robert Hardie, Medical Officer Tamaung Camp, 17 August 1945.

IT IS CLEAR that after the great expectations which they had entertained of it in 1942, the dismal performance of the Burma–Siam railway in the period prior to the Imphal offensive came as a great disappointment to the Japanese. No doubt their hopes of it were more modest when it came to support for the two other major engagements of the Burma campaign, the battles of the Mandalay Plain and of the Sittang breakout. However, neither of these was an ambitious, offensive operation occasioning high expenditure of fuel and ammunition and requiring the provision of substantial reserves, as Imphal had been; the former was a stubbornly-fought defensive battle and the latter an attempt by the Japanese to free 28th Army from encirclement in southern Burma. Furthermore, the railway actually significantly improved its supply performance in the second half of 1944.

In the event neither of the two major battles ended in Japan's favour. In the Mandalay Plain engagement Slim's Army crossed the Irrawaddy river on three fronts and at Mandalay and Meiktila inflicted major defeats on the Japanese 15th and 33rd Armies. It is difficult to compute their total losses, but it seems that between January and March 1945 these two armies lost 12,900 men, 6,000 of them killed.[1] Meiktila had been the advanced supply base for all Japanese forces in central Burma as well as the focal point for communications with the south. General Kasuya defended it resolutely, but by March 1945 the town was in Allied hands; the Japanese lost 10,000 men in its defence, 5,000 dead and 5,000 wounded. Only 47, mostly wounded, were taken prisoner.

When General Kimura had begun his planning for the defence of the Irrawaddy shoreline, a plan which was to go disastrously wrong, it had already been clear that not a great deal could be expected from the new railway. The historian of the Burma campaign records that by this time, although General Kimura had been charged with the considerable responsibility of ensuring the security of all southern Burma, which was, of course, the gateway to Indo-China and Malaya so far as the Allies were concerned, he was told that he had to plan *jikatsu jisen* for his command.[2] This meant subsisting on his own and fighting on his own. It was an instruction with which other Japanese overseas commanders were becoming familiar and was eloquent of the inability of metropolitan Japan any longer to sustain its far-flung garrisons. Seaborne supplies now reaching Rangoon were minimal and the effectiveness of the new railway, which had reached its maximum in November and December 1944 when in each month over 20,000 tons of munitions and supplies were carried along it, fell away rapidly thereafter with January's total dipping down to 11,400 tons and the decline being dramatic and irreversible thereafter. Nor were these supplies getting as far west as the Burmese capital, for the Allied airforces were managing to keep an average of nine bridges unfit for use between Rangoon and Pegu from January to May 1945.[3]

Fortunately General Kimura had received his major reinforcements of both men and supplies in the latter half of 1944 before the use of the railway for significant traffic had become out of the question; but even then it had been falling far short of meeting his needs. The consequence was that the logistics planners in Singapore had once again to seek alternative ways of getting the support up to Burma. They had about 60,000 men available as reinforcements, together with weapons and ammunition for three divisions, 45,000 tons of supplies, 500 lorries and 2,000 pack animals. Ultimately a great deal of this went up by sea. No 38 Harbour Unit at Rangoon risked encounters with British submarines and aircraft to run a fleet of 60 small vessels which transported 30,000 fresh troops to fill out the depleted and demoralised divisions of Burma Area Army.[4] However, some of them were soon pulled back to meet threats elsewhere in the Philippines and Indo-China. Kimura did receive one complete and valuable reinforcement via the railway in the period before the struggle for the plains of central Burma began. This was 49th Division which became a very necessary strategic reserve for the Area

Army, though it never had the opportunity to operate as a single formation throughout the entire campaign, being used as a stock of reserves to be thrown into action piecemeal as different threats developed. For example, the division's 168 Regiment fought first with 56th Division against four Chinese armies in Yunnan, losing over 600 men, before it was moved south and pushed into the Meiktila battle where it was almost destroyed. Similarly 153 Regiment was used initially against the East Africans at Seikpyu and then later in the fighting at Letse. When the struggle on the central plains was finally concluded, it could not be said that this railway-delivered reinforcement had not made an effective contribution to the Japanese defence; by mid-April 49th Division was reduced to 1,600 men and a single mountain gun.[5]

After their success at the battle in the Mandalay Plain, General Slim's forces began the race for Rangoon down the railway axis from Meiktila hoping to capture the Burmese capital before the monsoon began. 4 Corps spearheaded this task since it was already concentrated at Meiktila and was a fully mechanised formation capable of rapid exploitation. The Corps was supplied entirely by air in the first stage of its advance, as were its leading elements for the entire dash to the capital. However, the Japanese wisely did not fight to keep Rangoon; it would have been an encounter of desperation, for no eastward withdrawal from the port would have been possible if they then lost it. The capture of Rangoon was completed by 5 May 1945 and the engineers soon had the port facilities in operation again. By the middle of June it was receiving 3,000 tons of supplies daily, the tonnage that the railway had been originally scheduled to deliver for the Japanese but had never managed to achieve. It had always made better sense to supply Rangoon by sea; but first one had to command the ocean which approached it and this the Japanese had managed only briefly.

As the Burma campaign now drew to a close, the railway in whose construction the Japanese had taken such pride and whose traffic was to have propelled them into India, became progressively the route by which their casualties received their release from this tormenting theatre of war. It was also the escape route for some of the Japanese administrative departments in Rangoon to make their way to the safety of Bangkok and by which Subhas Chandia Bose's 'Provisional Government of Free India' and the Japanese Burma puppet Ba Maw also ultimately got away from Burma. Bose showed some concern for the security of Rangoon with its large Indian population by leaving a garrison of 5,000 Indian National Army troops to maintain order until the British arrived. Ba Maw seemed to have no similar solicitude and as for the Commander-in-Chief of Burma Area Army himself, he left by plane on 23 April without even telling his local garrison commander, Major General Matsui.[6] Matsui decided to leave the doomed city and join the defence at Pegu, so he gathered his garrison troops and the fittest 300 of the POWs from Rangoon jail, some Liberator crewmen and the redoubtable Ras Pagani among them, and made off east as well. It was some weeks before the military situation forced Ba Maw to take the train down the much battered railway to Bangkok but when he did so he found it a memorable experience. 'Some of the longer bridges', he noted, 'skirting and even in places overhanging the gorges or steep river banks were simply breathtaking ... This journey will remain as one of the deepest experiences of my life.'[7]

The Rangoon exodus was followed, after a gap of some weeks while both sides regrouped, by the final engagement of the Burma campaign, Japan's last of the war in Asia; a final desperate struggle by the Japanese as they sought to extricate 28th Army from its entrapment in the hills and swamps between the mighty Irrawaddy and Sittang rivers and keep it in touch with the remainder of the Area Army and the railway escape route. 33rd Army had already got away to the east and it launched diversionary attacks to try to assist the breakout of 28th. These failed, as did the breakout effort itself. In the whole of the breakout battle the Japanese suffered 16,900 casualties, nearly 10,000 of them killed and, a remarkable statistic for the Japanese, 1,400 taken prisoner. Total Allied casualties were a little over 400, 95 of them killed. It was the most exceptional exchange rate of the entire campaign and an explicit demonstration of the total superiority in the theatre which the Allied forces had now achieved.

In the meantime the Burma–Siam railway itself had been put in a state of defence. 24th Independent Mixed Brigade was established as the garrison force and defensive positions had been prepared along it. Further forces were deployed along the Tenasserim coast to resist a possible seaborne assault. By this stage there had been several major reorganisations of the railway workforce. All except railway maintenance parties and those deployed to dig Japanese defences had long since left the line. Those from the Burma section had travelled down to Kanchanaburi, marvelling at the engineering difficulties which their fellows in the south had had to contend with and realising, as Major Apthorpe did, how fortunate they had been to work in Burma.

Even 'K' and 'L' Forces, sent up to Thailand to treat the coolie forces, had long since been replaced in their medical role by dressers recruited from the Malayan Medical Service and trained on a two-week course by Japanese doctors at Kanchanaburi. Later some locally qualified doctors were also brought up to the coolie hospitals; altogether over 700 medical staff of one sort or another were brought up from Malaya for this work. However, although 'K' and 'L' Forces had been relieved of their medical responsibilities in August 1944 and warned of an imminent move back to Singapore, they were held in the base camp area and retained on general labouring duties until March 1945 when they were handed over to the Thai POW administration and immediately enjoyed improved conditions.

Those of the Japan parties for whom shipping space could be found had long since departed for further labouring duties on the Japanese home islands. They could hardly have known when their voyages began that their lives were to be at risk once again from Allied aircraft and even more menaced by Allied submarines. On 6 September 1944 a force of about 2,300 prisoners had been put aboard two ships, *Kachidoki Maru* and *Rakuyo Maru* at Singapore for a journey to Japan in a convoy which ultimately totalled seven transports, two oil tankers and six supporting vessels. On 12 September submarines attacked the convoy; an escort and the two tankers were sunk, and then the *Kachidoki Maru* and the *Rakuyo Maru*. Because of the slowness with which the *Rakuyo Maru* sank the prisoners were able to get on deck safely and, since the Japanese crew were rescued by the escorting destroyers, the prisoners were able to take over the abandoned life-boats. Some were later picked up by Japanese destroyers, Others, including the boat containing Brigadier Varley, were not seen again. Some 150 survivors of the sinking who had clung to rafts and wreckage were later rescued by American submarines and finally reached Australia. They provided the first authentic 'open source' information on conditions in the railway camps. Early in 1944 a large number of postcards and letters had been received from prisoners in the Far East almost all uniformly stating that they were in good health and being treated well. This encouraging news had been so completely at variance with what the Government's secret sources knew to be the case that Foreign Secretary Eden had made a statement in the House of Commons at the end of January indicating 'that the true state of affairs is a very different one so far as the great majority of prisoners in Japanese hands is concerned'. He spoke of the railway and road building work they had been forced to carry out and reported that there had been some thousands of deaths.[8]

The statement naturally caused widespread shock and anxiety but it had been carefully concerted with the other Allied governments as a means of bringing pressure on the Japanese government. In April 1944 a special Inquiry Centre had been set up in London, rather belatedly in the view of many, to deal with relatives' queries, but little additional information was available, certainly none that could allay individual concerns. However with the rescue of the survivors from the *Rakuyo Maru* there was news aplenty, both about general conditions in the railway camps and about the fate of individuals. A statement on 31 October announced the rescue of survivors and then on 17 November, after the rescued POWs had been fully debriefed and their stories corroborated and authenticated, Sir James Grigg, Secretary of State for War in the House of Commons and Acting Prime Minister Forde in Australia gave carefully coordinated statements which presented the full horror of the Burma–Siam railway story, the appalling working conditions, the disease problem, the poor diet and the mortality rate, 'the lowest estimate of deaths' said Sir James, 'being one in five'. The short question and answer session which followed ended with a request from a member of the House that a copy of the Secretary of State's statement should be sent 'to Dublin for the benefit of the Japanese consul-general who is residing in that city'.[9] The point had not been reached at which the Allied governments had any other than diplomatic weapons with which to protect the interests of their captive citizens. The previous year Sir James had explained to the House that 'the only indubitably successful step is to beat the Japanese'. That remained the situation.

Nevertheless, for many of the POWs who had worked on the railway, in their final year of captivity, physical conditions were immeasurably improved; the food was better in the Thailand plains camps, conditions were easier and there was less work to be done. Other groups had suffered badly; the 1,000 who had been detached to build a road through the Tenassarim jungle to Mergui, or the 500 detailed to build defensive positions on the railway near the Burma border. Discipline had tightened noticeably as 1944 ended; camp fences were strengthened, embankments were built around them to block the prisoners' view, petty regulations were imposed. In January 1945 all officer prisoners were concentrated at Kanchanaburi, leaving the warrant officers and NCOs to run the soldiers' camps, assisted by medical officers in the hospitals. Finally in June 1945 the Japanese decided to move the officers away from the railway area altogether and began to transport them in parties of 400 to Nakhon Nayok, north east of Bangkok where a camp had to be built from scratch together with a motorable track leading to it. An advance party of 450 began the move. An added complication was that the new camp was apparently sited right in the middle of a Japanese defensive position from which 30,000 troops were actively preparing to resist any further Allied advance. Some of the prisoners made their final move to Nakhon Nayok via Bangkok station where a blackout was in force. There, and on other parts of their railway journeying in this final phase of captivity, they came across increasing numbers of Japanese casualties being moved down the new line and then on to the main Thai railway system for hospitalisation in the Bangkok capital. Despite their own harsh treatment at the hands of the Japanese, many POWs were deeply moved by the plight of the wounded. 'They were in a shocking state', wrote one, 'I have never seen men filthier. Their uniforms were encrusted with mud, blood and excrement. Their wounds, sorely in-flamed and full of pus, crawled with maggots.'[10] Another learned from a badly-wounded Japanese officer who was still clutching his sword, that he had been 98 days on the journey from Burma and that the sustenance he received from some sympathetic Allied prisoners was the first time he had received food and water except by his own exertions. Japanese sick and dead littered the main Bangkok railway station and one fatigued POW eye-witness remarked that watching some of them detrain there by the light of oil lamps and a guttering candle was like looking at a mad picture by Goya.[11] Approximately 10,000 Japanese wounded were evacuated to Thailand while the new railway was in operation.

The improvement in the physical conditions in the prisoners' camps was accompanied by increasing psychological tension as 1945 wore on. Barbed wire appeared around many camps, machine-guns were mounted at the perimeter, facing inwards. Tension mounted still fur-ther as news and rumours of an ever-worsening war situation for the Japanese were passed around the camps. The attitude of the Japanese guards seemed little changed except that they appeared more moody. Some prisoners were of the view that in the event of an Allied landing the POWs were likely to be slaughtered by their captors as part of their last stand in South East Asia. Another theory was of a death march of fit prisoners away from the war theatre, with the sick being killed off first. In some camps there were well-concerted plans for a break-out by the prisoners if the threatened massacre seemed imminent. In Nakhon Nayok officers prepared to defend themselves with sharpened bamboo staves and one of the Korean auxiliaries, realising that he too was under threat, offered to transfer to the prisoners the few weapons which the Koreans controlled.[12]

In early August, at about the time when the last surviving diseased and starving remnants of the Japanese 28th Army had reached the relative safety of the east bank of the Sittang river, the United States dropped the first atomic bomb on Hiroshima. It destroyed about 26 square kilometres of the city by blast and fire and killed about 80,000 people. Three days later a second bomb was dropped in the northern outskirts of Nagasaki causing rather less structural damage but about 70,000 deaths. To complete the catalogue of Japan's woes, the USSR now declared war and began a whirlwind campaign through Manchuria. The majority of the prisoners were largely unaware of these events and certainly knew nothing of the debate that raged within Japan's Supreme War Direction Council over whether the Allied demand for unconditional surrender should be agreed to. They were equally ignorant of the fact that it had required the intervention of Emperor Hirohito himself to still the disagreement in the Council and decide in favour of surrender. As it was, the Commander-in-Chief Southern Army, Field Marshal Count Terauchi, in his typically independent manner, was determined to ignore Tokyo and fight on. It required the despatch of three Imperial princes to the main overseas command centres to ensure the compliance of the local commanders. It was Prince Chichibu who flew to Saigon and persuaded Terauchi to bow to the imperial will.

No-one realised at the time what a very close call it had been for those who had survived the railway ordeal, for Terauchi's orders appear to have been that all prisoners were to be killed in the event of an Allied assault on South East Asia proper, and such an assault was planned for 6 September. The relative isolation of the officers' camp at Nakhon Nayok and the lack of a working wireless set there meant that news of progress in the war was more the result of rumour than of fact. However, the possibility of a massacre of the prisoners appears to have been strengthened by a report passed to a POW interpreter by one of the more friendly Koreans, believed to be named Haraya, to the effect that he had seen an order notifying the local Japanese commander that he was to shoot the prisoners and the Koreans if the Allies should attack. Such an attack was expected in Thailand on about 21 August. The desperate breakout plans were based on this information.[13] The timing of the atomic bombing of the Japanese

cities was thus critical for the prisoners' survival; but of equal importance was the fact that they fell to atomic rather than conventional
bombing. The cataclysmic character of the new weapon which had
been unleashed on the Japanese people at least gave its armies an
opportunity to withdraw without dishonour from a war which they
could not win and could otherwise have ended honourably only by
continuing the struggle until all their fighting men had been erased.
As a prisoner on Java later put it, 'Only changes initiated and
endorsed by the nearest human equivalent to a God of his people
could succeed, in the circumstances, to relieve the fanatical military
forces of their compulsion to fight to the last'.[14] This not ignoble
justification process probably saved the prisoners' lives, though the
manner in which they learnt of their survival and freedom was in an
altogether lower key.

In Kanchanaburi rumour had been rife for days that the war was
over and on 15 August Boon Pong cycled past the camp and whispered the message that confirmed it; but it was not until the evening of
the 16th that the Japanese commander called the hut leaders together
and gave them the news. Additional food supplies and medicines were
quickly acquired and within a few days the Swiss Red Cross representative from Bangkok had visited the camp. However, as long as a
week after their captivity had been brought formally to an end, the
Kanchanaburi POWs were reminded of its worst horrors when 1,500
prisoners arrived in the camp from the Burma border area where they
had been digging Japanese defences at a frantic pace in the last days of
the war. Half British and half Dutch Eurasians, they were diseased
and emaciated and at their last gasp. Some had died on the rail
journey down when they were technically already free men. 'It was
just like the old days all over again', wrote one observer, 'sick and
dying men, many quite incapable of walking from the trains to the
camp ... We have the food and drugs for them now, thank Heaven,
but I am afraid that many have gone too far for us to be able to do
much for them.'[15]

At Nakhon Nayok the POWs heard of their freedom a day earlier
when, in the absence of the much hated local Japanese commander,
Captain Noguchi, his deputy passed the news of the surrender to
Lieutenant Colonel Toosey. On the evening of 16 August the British
interpreter at the camp translated a speech by the Japanese colonel
commanding the prisoner of war groups in Thailand. 'His Imperial
Highness has decided to stop fighting,' it ran, 'you will soon go home.
We are responsible for your safety until you go. You can sing your

national anthem and hoist your flags.'[16] At Ubon near the Thai–Indo-Chinese border, to which some railway prisoners had been moved for work on an airfield at which they had been digging trenches, their first signal of a changed situation was not being called for work on 15 August; the following day they learnt the reason why. At Saigon, where some men from the railway were still awaiting their transport to Japan, no official announcement was made to the now-officerless parties; their usual guards were merely replaced by much older men and they were contacted by the local French community. At Tamuang, another camp now being run by the warrant officers and NCOs, the Regimental Sergeant Major was called in by the Japanese and briefly informed that the war was indeed over and that the prisoners were now responsible for their own discipline.

In the main Changi gaol camp in Singapore the information came via a secret wireless set which gave the news on 15 August; the Japanese officially confirmed it on the 17th. The first hint for those in the less settled camps around Singapore island came when work parties were not sent out. Official confirmation of the war's end soon followed. It was, of course, a huge relief for all the surviving prisoners, but like so many events so deeply longed for it was also something of an anti-climax. Long-withheld personal mail and stocks of Red Cross goods were soon handed over to the prisoners but there were no victorious Allied troops in sight and it was circumspect for them all to remain in their camps and keep their jubilation within bounds; their guards, after all, had not been defeated in battle. Indeed, the SEAC Commander Mountbatten was so concerned at the risk of local disobedience to the surrender message that he issued an 'unshakeable order' that no camp was to be approached until he was certain that the surrender was holding and had sent a special signal to go ahead.

The planning for the recovery of prisoners of war and internees (RAPWI as the responsible organisation was called) had started in April 1945. It had been planned that small control staffs would operate with each formation headquarters as the armies advanced. However, the ultimate suddenness of the surrender threw these plans awry, just as they did the clandestine operations of Force 136 which was planning insurrection in the occupied territories and of 'E' Group which was dedicated to helping prisoners to escape. The early clandestine operations had been hampered by the hostile attitude of the British government to the Thai administration and by the competitive and uncooperative attitudes of the British and American undercover organisations. However, once agents had been inserted into Thailand they were able, despite their capture and imprisonment, to make contact with the *Seri Thai* organisation and pass details of the POW camps back to the Allied authorities. Thus, once the surrender was officially announced and Mountbatten was negotiating its details in Burma and Malaya, 'E' Group was able to provide him with a map of the locations and strengths of the POW camps in his command 'that astounded the Japanese by its completeness, its accuracy and its superiority to their own scrappy information'.[17] Leaflets were dropped to the Japanese camp authorities, the local population and the prisoners, in that order and with a necessary interval between the first and the third. The leaflet operation – 20 tons of leaflets were dropped over camps in Burma and Thailand – was known as Operation Birdcage and it was followed by Operation Mastiff which dropped men and supplies into the camps.

The full cooperation of 'E' Group, OSS and Force 136 swung behind the RAPWI operations, the Siam Country Section of Force 136 acting as its 'father and mother' for its entry into the country, its supplies and its communications. There were about a dozen different RAPWI areas and teams on the basis of which about 50 four-man units were briefed to go into the camps and arrange for the evacuation of the prisoners and the notification of their relatives. Back in Britain the families' Red Cross journal *The Prisoner of War* had long since been replaced for families of men who were in Japanese hands by a publication devoted to their interests alone, *The Far East*. These long-suffering relatives, starved of information since the fall of Singapore, were now able to read in the September 1945 issue's editorial, 'The long night is ended. The grim silence is broken. Cables are streaming in to their parents and wives from prisoners and internees announcing their release after years of captivity. Soon they themselves will follow.' Meantime 1,000 tons of medical supplies, food and other stores were dropped to the camps, doctors and medical orderlies visited them; briefings were given on the world situation, the atomic bombing of Japan and the ending of the war; contact was made with the local Thai towns and villages and trading flourished again. Three and a half years of isolation from the civilised world had finally come to an end.

On 27 August Japanese delegates in Rangoon signed a preliminary agreement which enabled instructions to be sent out through Field Marshal Terauchi ordering local Japanese commanders to assist and obey the British commanders of the reoccupation forces. By 28 August five RAF C-47 aircraft had landed at Bangkok's Don Muang airport and the first batches of POWs were flown to India and their onward journeys home.[18] This was the beginning of a daily succession of planes which took prisoners from the Bangkok area with the active assistance of the Thai administration. On 30 August the Singapore prisoners had been contacted by relief teams parachuted into Changi airfield. On 5 September 5th Indian Division landed with a number of RAPWI personnel and the evacuation began soon afterwards. Indeed the speed with which the evacuation operation was undertaken was the cause of some surprise and consternation. In the first instance the scale of the problem was underestimated; 10,000 RAPWI were expected in Singapore but in the event 37,000 were processed and evacuated by the small British RAPWI Control Team on the island, assisted by teams, from the Field Army Nursing Yeomanry and YWCA. The result was that when the large Australian PW Reception Group, consisting of a Brigadier and 1,272 all ranks arrived, the 6,000 Australians with whom they were supposed to deal, had already departed.[19] Indeed, many reached Australia before fresh uniforms and clothing could be got to them, causing Mr Forde, the Minister for the Army, to call for a report on whoever was responsible for the 'neglect to supply clothing to these men and who has consequently brought disrepute upon the army for its treatment of returning prisoners of war'.[20] The Indian PW Recovery Mission, again commanded by a Brigadier, also arrived after most of its prisoner nationals had departed from Singapore. However, both missions were needed to deal with the considerable numbers still being transferred to Singapore from Thailand and Malaya. The small No 2 RAPWI Control Staff in Singapore had done extremely well; in exactly three weeks after the reoccupation of the Island it had evacuated 34,225 fit POWs and internees by sea and hundreds of sick by air.

By the end of September 53,700 had been evacuated from the whole region, a total which rose to 71,000 by the end of October and reached 96,500 by May the following year, leaving only 30,000 Dutch internees in Java, victims of the confused and turbulent political situation there. However for the great majority of ex-railway prisoners the ordeal was now over and their return to health was rapid. By November 21,000 had arrived back in the UK, all showing huge weight gains; two stones seemed about the average, though one lieutenant from Changi managed to put on three stones in eight weeks. A soldier who came back to Southampton aboard the *Corfu* with 1,500 of his fellows from Thailand brought a Siamese duck back with him which was said to have contributed 163 eggs to the POW diet in the previous 18 months.

Unfortunately the RAPWI Control organisation which dealt so rapidly with the evacuation of the railway prisoners had no brief for the thousands of native labourers who had been their fellow workers on the line, about whom there was in any event scant documentation. When Burma and Malaya were reoccupied RAPWI gave emergency aid to them and left the rest to the incoming military administrations concerned. In the case of the Burma end of the line this meant that although the Japanese surrendered in mid-August, it was not possible for the military administration to take responsibility for the railway section of its territory until two and a half months later, when two medical officers were sent up the line. A reception and medical centre was set up at Thanbyuzayat and a transit camp at Rangoon; but only 3,000 to 3,500 workers were found. The rest of the 40,000 who had still been on the line at the surrender had now melted away. It was assumed that they had escaped as Japanese authority collapsed and tried to make their own way back to the plains of Burma, some no doubt dying in the jungle on the way.

Once the remnants of the force had been brought down to the northern terminus, their further repatriation posed additional problems; rail communications from Moulmein northwards were entirely disrupted and the roads, still affected by the monsoon, were little better. Evacuation by sea to Rangoon was tried but since few ships were available, powered lighters and barges were pressed into service. Travel by these proved so difficult and hazardous in the monsoon conditions that the dispersal rate was very slow and many of the workers declined the transport offer, preferring to take their chances overland, walking through the rice-shortage district of Thaton. The administration shipped rice across from Rangoon to prevent these wretched, penniless people from looting supplies as they went along.[21] It was more difficult for the workers taken originally from Malaya to make their own way home and quite impossible for the numbers of Javanese among them. A group of ex-POWs who volunteered to stay and care for and ultimately repatriate these workers found 35,000 of them still on the railway. They were mostly Tamils but there were other local racial groups among them. 25,000 were collected into camps in Kanchanaburi and a further 10,000 in the Chumphon area of the Isthmus of Kra where the Japanese had set up a workers' hospital; 'nothing but a ghastly charnel house' was how it appeared to a Force 136 agent who visited the area soon after the surrender. In November this Kra group was evacuated to Alor Star in northern Malaya where its members were fed and given medical attention prior to the journey home. The Kanchanaburi group was not repatriated until January 1946 when it left by rail for a Bangkok reception centre whence two ships made regular journeys to the Malayan ports taking 800 of them on each trip. These wretched people returned to a Malaya whose economy had been devastated by the Japanese occupation, whose social fabric had been rent asunder and where the communist insurrection, set to last until 1960, was already developing.

15

Brought to Account

Human history advances with bleeding feet
Chinese merchant on the river Kwai

THE BURMA–SIAM railway was built at enormous cost in human life and attendant social damage. So far as the POWs are concerned the balance sheet is relatively easy to draw up. A total of 61,806 of them were taken up to work on the railway project; at least 12,399* of these had died by the end of the war, 20 per cent of the total. By comparison Japan achieved the conquest of Malaya, Singapore and Burma at the cost of 5,500 lives – but lost a further 183,000 trying, with the help of the railway, to retain Burma alone. British railway deaths amounted to 6,904; 2,815 Australians perished in Burma and Thailand; the total of Dutch dead was well in excess of 2,000 and the bodies of 337 US prisoners were repatriated at the end of the war.

The highest mortality had inevitably been during the 'speedo' period when the combination of monsoon conditions, hard work, poor food, cholera and dysentery had seen roughly 7,000 prisoners die in six months. 'F' and 'H' Forces had taken the severest toll, losing respectively 45 per cent and 27 per cent of their overall strength. For the British element of 'F' Force the mortality rate was highest of all at 61 per cent; the worst rate for any force of Australians on the railway was 39.3.[1] Individual camps also acquired gruesome records of which that of Songkuri, with 678 deaths between May and November 1943, is about the worst. For individual regiments their losses during captivity contrasted strangely with their casualties in battle; 5th Suffolks, for example, had 34 men killed in action against the

---

* The total was certainly greater; men were dying long after the railway was completed and even after the surrender had been announced.

Japanese, but lost a further 271 while prisoners in Japanese hands and their sister battalion, the 4th, lost 90 in the fighting but a further 321 as prisoners on the railway, en route to Japan or while working there.[2] 9th Battalion Royal Northumberland Fusiliers had 15 men killed in action but lost ten times as many in captivity where they formed the rail-laying party at the Thailand end of the line. The Argylls on the other hand suffered a double sacrifice, losing 244 men in the Malayan campaign itself and then a further 187 in the incarceration which followed it; this was 45 per cent of their strength and, with a further 162 wounded, was a grievous loss for a single battalion to bear.[3]

For all the units involved, the deaths in captivity were only part of the account. The returning prisoners found that there were great problems of readjustment to be overcome, a three and a half year trauma in their lives to be bridged and a bizarre period of unimaginable hardship and suffering to be connected with their ordinary post-war lives. Some would find it difficult to stop talking about their experiences as prisoners, others would find it impossible to recount them at all; some would become chronically claustrophobic, others agoraphobic. Anxiety and depression would be constant conditions for a proportion; while nightmares would disturb the sleeping hours of others. One US marine troubled initially by nightmares after his release from Thailand had to enlist the help of his doctor 29 years later when they returned to plague him. Then there were the physical disabilities with which the men had to learn to cope, the amputees who struggled to resume their civilian occupations; the sick and debilitated who required extended hospitalisation before they were returned to health, like the Argylls officer who, despite a recuperative sea journey back to UK, was then hospitalised, still suffering from malaria, avitaminosis, hepatitis, enlarged heart and ulcerated intestines.[4] As a group the ex-POWs suffered from chronic depression and anxiety states more often than those not incarcerated and generally suffered higher rates of morbidity after the war than prisoners interned in Europe, where conditions were less harsh.[5] 'It is obvious', concluded the most celebrated doctor among them, 'that many prisoners of war will suffer for the remainder of their lives from disabilities related to their grim ordeal.'[6]

However, the native labourers on the railway suffered both greater losses, in raw numbers and as a proportion of those employed, and the communities from which they came endured greater social dislocation, than was the case with their fellow workers from the Allied forces. There are rough totals for the local workers whom the

Japanese brought up to the railway, but of the numbers who perished there only the most general estimates can be made. The Japanese kept few accurate records and certainly preserved none, there were few individual graves, most bodies being incinerated or buried *en masse* and since many of these coolies were illiterate, no account of their experiences was produced. At the northern end of the line the labour agencies of the Burmese administration produced, according to U Aung Min, Deputy Director of Labour at the time, a total of approximately 178,000 native labourers. It is clear that many of these deserted at the earliest opportunity when the conditions of work became obvious to them, but equally plain that many thousands died of disease and malnutrition, particularly when cholera swept through the camps in 1943. One estimate is of 40,000 deaths in the Burmese labour force.[7] The official historian of the British military administration which took over after the Japanese surrender suggests a death ratio 'probably reaching three out of seven among those drafted from Burma',[8] which would put the total at about 75,000. This figure seems high and could well not account for many who escaped from the camps and managed to get back to central Burma whence most of them came, though some would certainly have died in the attempt. Along the railway trace itself there was evidence of some 3,700 who were buried in a cemetery at Thanbyuzayat and a further 8,400 at other graveyards along the line. About 40,000 were still present along the railway at the time of surrender.

The numbers brought up from the south were much smaller and totalled 91,000, drawn mainly from the rubber estates of western Malaya, but also a few thousand from Java. The records of the Japanese Labour Department headquarters of 4th Railway Corps show almost 33,000 of them as having died and 21,600 as being on the railway awaiting repatriation in 1945.[9] It seems likely that both figures are underestimates, as are those given by *gunzoku* engineer Futamatsu, both for totals employed and numbers deceased. The official historian suggests that as high a proportion as one in two of those recruited in Malaya may have died on the line and notes that 35,000 were awaiting repatriation at war's end.[10] Other commentators record the deaths among the Tamil labour force alone as between 25,000 and 50,000. The truth is probably nearer to the higher figure. A fresh mass grave containing the remains of about 700 bodies, probably Tamil coolies, was unearthed as recently as November 1990 in a plot of land about 100 yards from Kanchanaburi Town Hall.[11]

The most significant measure of the loss is the impact it had on the rural Indian population of Malaya from which the labourers had been largely drawn. The demographic trends need to be treated with a little caution because of the 'Klondike' nature of Malaya's economic development as palm oil, tin and rubber were successively developed by immigrant labour; moreover there was a freeze on Indian immigration from 1938 onwards. However, the facts are that the Indian population of Malaya stood at 621,847 in 1931 and in normal circumstances might have been expected to reach 800,000 by 1947; but the census of that year recorded it as having declined to 577,616, a drop of 3.6 per cent. By comparison the other racial groups had increased by at least 25 per cent; even the Indian community in Singapore (from which there was little railway recruitment) went up by 35 per cent. There was admittedly some panic flight to India by the well-to-do in the days prior to the war and some recruitment to the Indian National Army in the occupation's early stages, with casualties at the opening stages of the Imphal campaign; but these factors cannot account for the very specific nature of the decline which was limited almost solely to the rural Indian community in the estates, where the overall population declined by 20 per cent. In the three western rubber growing states of Perak, Selangor and Negri Sembilan, through which ran the railway line to Thailand, the decline was 25 per cent.[12] One survey of 11 estates in Perak recorded that of 1,146 men taken to Thailand by the Japanese, only 545 returned. This was a terrible blow for the rural Tamil community to bear; it now had 5,730 widows and 9,341 children who had lost one or both of their parents.[13] Women (always a minority in a labour force imported on period contracts) and children over 10 now represented over half the workforce. The statistics represented not simply the tragedy of many of the men not returning from the railway work; their absence during the latter part of the war denied many families their sole breadwinner and had its impact on birth rates and on the mortality rates among young and old when the estate administration collapsed in 1943.

When the war ended and the scale of the distress could be appreciated, public and private bodies moved in to help. Voluntary welfare agencies reconstituted the Indian orphanages in Penang to which many of the destitute children were consigned. By 1947 the Government had arranged to distribute a grant of $1.5 million to the widows and dependants produced by the railway tragedy; this was a sum greater than the whole of its routine annual social welfare budget.[14] The Congress Party of India also sent a medical mission to Malaya to help relieve the distress. This was a political organisation, anti-colonial in its attitude to both Britain and Japan. Its official report on the mission carries the dedication: 'In memory of One Hundred Thousand Malayan Indian victims of the Siam Death Railway.'[15] Many fewer than this estimate actually died on the line, but in terms of total impact on the Tamil community the figure may not be too preposterous an exaggeration.

The railway project, for all its subsequent notoriety, was by no means the worst example of Japanese treatment of prisoners of war or subject peoples in the areas occupied by its armies; but it was certainly not the best. On Blakang Mati island off the southern tip of Singapore (now redeveloped as the leisure island of Sentosa) 1,000 prisoners were held throughout the war, operating a supply base for the Japanese airforce. Accommodation was good, the food was generally adequate and there was no reduction in rations for those who were sick. Only four men of the 1,000 died in three and a half years of captivity, two of these by drowning and the other two after they had already been evacuated to Changi. By contrast, only six men survived of the 2,500 who were imprisoned in the Sandakan area of North Borneo in late 1944. Equally the men of 'Gull' Force, captured on Ambon in late 1942, were starved and maltreated to a degree experienced by few other of the 21,000 Australians who were imprisoned by the Japanese. Their death rate at 77 per cent was twice that of the least fortunate group of their fellow countrymen on the Burma–Siam railway.

The railway was notable neither for any extreme of brutality in the treatment of its labour force, nor indeed for any leniency towards them. What made it singular was, first of all, its scale. As an operation employing well over 300,000 men drawn from a remarkably heterogeneous background of race, nationality and culture it was unique in the short-lived Japanese empire. More than that, it was a noteworthy example of single-minded determination to achieve a military purpose at whatever cost in the lives of prisoners of war, or civilian labourers; for the same generalisation applies to the coolie forces as well. It would not be too sensational to record that the death toll of this latter group reached horrific proportions at times; however this was generally an incidental consequence of the main Japanese purpose and never an end in itself. Although the civilian railway workers perished in their thousands they were never the victims of an orgy of savagery such as had taken place in China in the Rape of Nanking; nor indeed did they suffer the planned atrocities of the kind for which the bacteriological research establishment, 731 Unit at Harbin, achieved its reputation for scientific barbarity. There were, however, some particular atrocities perpetrated by junior Japanese medical staff at one of the coolie hospitals at Kanchanaburi.[16] By and large the extremes of brutal Japanese behaviour ended when the last railway line was laid, the workers even receiving some minor presents and a brief holiday to celebrate the occasion. In general, what most characterised the Japanese approach to the interests of their workforce was insensitivity and neglect. Their relentless determination to build the railway and their general unresponsiveness to all human factors which might have given them pause and perhaps reduced the feverish intensity of the 'speedo' period, is a factor to which we must return. All that is necessary to record at this stage is that once Imperial General Headquarters had confirmed two critical decisions – to build the railway using a captive labour force and to mount the offensive into India – the fate of many of the labourers was already sealed; the terrain, the climate and the lack of food did the rest.

There was, nevertheless, a series of other factors which exacerbated the inevitable human disaster. Significant among these was sheer maladministration. Administration in war is never easy; it is concerned, like its peacetime equivalent, with the inevitably complex business of managing people and things in an intractable physical environment, but it stands alone in having to do this when an opponent is doing his damnedest to make the process difficult. This was true of many aspects of the railway operation, where enemy action cut the sea supply lines, damaged the line itself, helped disaffect the local population and, by developing fresh threats to the Japanese position in Burma, made extra demands on its overstretched operational units. The overall quality of the POW guard force was not high, no doubt because of the manpower required for the fighting formations. Among the guards were men who were too old to manage affairs competently and some who lacked the strength of personality to cope with the rigours of the local situation; in addition alcoholics, sadists, womanisers and plain criminals were all represented among the Japanese guards, and the relatively isolated circumstances of their lives which gave them considerable responsibility with relatively little supervision meant that providing the railway work progressed satisfactorily, other aspects of their responsibility were generally ignored. The obsessive secrecy of the Japanese military also complicated administrative matters, while the general unwillingness of their administrative headquarters to cooperate with each other was bound to work to the disadvantage of the prisoners and no doubt contributed to and accelerated the death of many. The worst examples of these influences at work are seen in the experiences of 'F' Force about which we have the most complete authoritative account and which, of course, suffered most grievously during its short period in Thailand.

Misinformation about the original move from Changi, whether designed to enlist the active support of the prisoners, to conceal the true purpose of the move from the world at large, or simply to impose a blanket of security on the activity, certainly caused the inclusion and subsequently the death of many of the sick members of the party and was the reason for the exclusion of valuable equipment which was later desperately needed. The journey up to the Nikhe area was punctuated by administrative failures ranging from totally unsatisfactory feeding arrangements to insufficient transport, badly planned marches and ultimately poorly located camp sites at which there was insufficient accommodation. As the report of Colonel Harris summarised it, 'The IJA Administration within "F" Force attained a standard of inefficiency which is almost beyond description.' In the event the move back to Singapore proved to be as much an administrative disaster as the journey up, 'The arrangements for the first part of this journey were disgraceful,' Harris noted and concluded that, 'the arrangements for the second part of the journey had not improved since April.' At least part of the problem stemmed from the unwillingness of the Thai POW administration to cooperate with those of 'F' and 'H' Forces which were still responsible to Singapore. Prisoners on the railway, as soldiers everywhere do, often spent a great deal of time merely waiting; but for starving and sick men to be kept waiting for hours in the heat of the day as they frequently were on the journeyings of these two forces in particular, was often itself the cause of fatalities.[17] There are numerous parallels between the administrative shortcomings, associated insensitivity and random brutalities in 'F' Force's journeying and the Bataan 'death march' of US and Filipino prisoners in the Philippines.

The Japanese camp staff were not universally poor but varied greatly in ability and conscientiousness and were, of course, the supreme arbiters of the fate of their prisoners. Some were hard but fair, as was Sergeant Major Saito, in direct charge of the prisoners at Tamarkan; others were venal and corrupt like Major Kudo who commanded the *Kudo Butai* which included the medical reinforcements 'K' and 'L' Forces sent north to succour the native labourers. Often they were weak men, as Colonel Banno proved to be, easily dominated by their subordinates. Among the guards were rank incompetents of whom Officer

Cadet (later Second Lieutenant) Onishi was a prime example. He 'appeared to us', wrote Colonel Harris, 'to be mentally deficient. It is probable that much can be put down to the uselessness of this individual.' There were also sheer sadists among them, of whom most ex-prisoners could cite examples. The Korean auxiliary Toyama was a particularly unpleasant specimen, belabouring prisoners with a steel-shafted golf club for no good reason when he first encountered them at Ban Pong and a bane to all who came under his supervision thereafter. Lieutenant Naito of Retpu camp was another; although he spoke good English and could be reasonable towards the prisoners when sober, he was notoriously vicious when drunk, as he often was. Language difficulties compounded the administrative problems and led to beatings when guards thought they were being slighted or deliberately misunderstood. In the command circumstances which prevailed, the view of a senior Allied medical officer on the siting of latrines or the arrangements for water supply would be ignored in favour of the diktat of a Japanese lance corporal. Issues of 'face' often determined such decisions which frequently had literally fatal consequences.

There were occasions where local circumstances, particular personalities and, especially, the labour strategies adopted, enabled some of the POW commanders to achieve reasonable working relationships with their Japanese overlords and therefore to save their men from unnecessary suffering. The best examples of this occurring are probably Brigadier Varley and Lieutenant Colonel Nagatomo at Thanbyuzayat and Lieutenant Colonel Toosey and Sergeant Major Saito (Saito's boss Lieutenant Kosakata was less tractable) at Tamarkan; but this was always subject to the engineers being satisfied with the working arrangements and the progress being made. However, it often seems to have been the case that the senior Japanese officials and commanders did not know what was going on at the level of the individual POW or civilian labourer and perhaps did not care. No other explanation could account for Futamatsu's assertion that in respect of rations and health the POWs were treated as well as the Japanese, for his complaint of the unreasonable 'constant fault-finding' of the POWs, or for the apparent surprise of Lieutenant Colonel Imai at the inadequacy of their diet when he encountered some British POWs eating their midday meal on a hill road near Wanyai. As Futamatsu records the incident Imai 'stepped up to them directly without ceremony and peeped into a tasty lunch box'. Surprised to find it contained only rice he asked the prisoners if there was not anything else for them to eat and when it was confirmed that there was not, he apparently wasted no time in getting something done about it. But the care of the labour force was not Imai's responsibility and Futamatsu does not record whether any improvement resulted.[18] When formal inspections of POW compounds took place they were generally carefully stage-managed by the local guards to give the best impression.

The food and medical situations were both aspects of the distressing conditions in the railway camps over which the camp authorities had only partial control. One of the effects of the Japanese occupation of South East Asia was totally to dislocate the regional systems of food production and distribution. While in peacetime the region as a whole was generally self-sufficient in food grains, during the war production fell dramatically, and distribution became entirely disordered with the disappearance of traditional markets and the Allied campaign to interdict communications. The situation was exacerbated by the rampant inflation induced by the Japanese monetary policy. So serious did the situation become in Singapore that a mass evacuation of 300,000 people was ordered out of the island into Malaya. Several new towns were set up, one at Endau in north east Johore, the idea being that these should become agricultural communities self-sufficient in food. Incredibly, even Burma, a rice surplus economy, was short of food; the 1943 rice crop was reported to have been about a million tons short of consumption needs.[19] Though it was believed that the peasantry had hoarded grain from previous years, that facility was not available to the railway camps. Inevitably, when supplies were short, the prisoners and the labourers, rather than the Japanese, were the ones who received less. Occasionally both went short. There is even an account of prisoners and Japanese guards conspiring on several occasions to steal from waylaid ration trains. The shortages also meant high prices for what was available, so the camp canteens could buy less with their modest funds. When the total failure in communications produced by the 1943 monsoon is added to these difficulties, it is not surprising that the labour force went hungry and that the prisoners in particular were chronically malnourished.

There were also some extenuating circumstances concerning medical supplies and facilities. The domestic drug supply situation in Japan itself had rapidly fallen prey to Allied blockade and bombing, though little in the way of medical supplies was in any case destined for the garrisons in Burma and Thailand. Medical facilities were not a factor to which the Japanese military accorded a high priority and the medical cover for their operational units was quite inadequate. When the engineer regiments took on the responsibility of providing medical facilities for the native labour forces as well, it was obvious from the outset that they would be unable to cope and that a major tragedy was in the making. The price of medicines also increased dramatically as the war continued. This meant that it became more costly for the Japanese to supply them and also more expensive for canteen funds to purchase them if the opportunity arose. The supply of medicines also was affected by transport difficulties during the monsoon. In addition cholera struck before the Japanese were really prepared to deal with it and anti-cholera serum was produced in sufficient quantities just as the epidemic was abating. However, the Japanese did have the world's stock of quinine in their hands; but while some camps received enough to treat malaria attacks, they were never supplied with sufficient to provide a general prophylactic dose. The fact remains, too, that 'V' organisation agents like Boon Pong did manage to keep a minimal supply of medicines going when the Japanese failed to and both Japanese dispensaries and Red Cross stocks held medicines which the camps badly needed but which were withheld from them. This was certainly the case with the base area camps. Medicines were, of course, an important item of barter as inflation continued and the money economy began to lose its usefulness. There was also straightforward criminal abuse: one prisoner recorded a Japanese guard as having a set of pyjamas and curtains made from Red Cross supplied surgical lint. Yet it should not be imagined that all the cases of sickness were the result of Japanese neglect and their failure to provide the necessary drugs. Even an army as well supplied with doctors and medicines as the British Eastern Army in Burma still suffered exceptional sickness rates in this infamously unhealthy region. In early 1943 one of the brigades in the Arakan lost 69.6 per cent of its strength to malaria alone, while in 1944 in 14th Army the admissions to medical units largely on account of malaria alone equalled the strength of a standard division each month.[20] But while these men went sick, unlike the railway labourers, they did not often die.

Japan had signed and ratified the 1907 Hague Convention which included provisions on the treatment of prisoners of war. It was noted earlier that although it had never ratified the much more detailed 1929 Prisoners of War Convention, it had nevertheless agreed to observe its provisions. Perhaps the Allies, recalling Japan's chivalrous treatment of European captives in the Russo–Japanese war and humanitarian acts in providing medical facilities, for example, at

Gallipoli in the First World War, hoped that Japan would honour this agreement. The Convention itself contains 97 articles, 73 of them dealing directly with the treatment of prisoners held captive. The great majority of these were breached by the Japanese at some time or other, and many constantly, so far as their railway prisoners were concerned. At the War Crimes Trials which took place after the Allied victory many of the POW guard staff and railway engineers were arraigned. According to a Japanese account there were 120 individual indictments, 111 guilty verdicts and 32 capital sentences delivered against those concerned with the railway. 64 prison camp guards and 6 men from the engineer regiments were among those found guilty and 27 of them received death sentences.[21] Among those hanged was the Korean *heiho* Toyama, Lieutenant Abe, the chief engineer at the infamous Songkurai camp, Lieutenant Colonel Nagatomo in charge of No 3 Group in Burma and Captain Noguchi who had commanded the officers' camp at Kanchanaburi. A life sentence went to Captain Tarumoto, in charge of 8 Company's engineers at Chungkai.

Yet criminals and sadists aside, and discounting the local difficulties and administrative shortcomings which beset their activities, there was a dreadful inevitability about the way the Imperial Japanese Army of the early 1940s treated its prisoners of war, given its cultural and social background, the military philosophy and training system under which it operated and the moral corruption to which the possessors of absolute power are proverbially susceptible. Its concern to adopt and reflect Western military norms which had been so evident in 1905 and at the time of the First World War had largely disappeared by the onset of the Second. What is more, the chivalrous conduct towards European prisoners of war which the military observers had noted in 1905 had not always extended to Asian ones. In this first essay against a European power they had desperately needed to prevent others going to Russia's help. There may well have been more than a little calculation in their distinctive treatment of Russian captives.[22] Paradoxically, the increased technological sophistication of Japan's armed forces which gave them the appearance of conformity with Western military practices, concealed a belief system and military doctrine which were proceeding in a quite different direction. Cooperation with the Western powers had been replaced by hostility to them as the commericial and imperial interests of the two sides clashed and the West's policies seemed increasingly racial. Issues such as new US immigration laws, the rejection of the racial equality clause in the Convenant of the League of Nations, together with the closing of Western-controlled markets to Japanese goods encouraged those who were already of the view that the white man would never treat the Japanese as equals. Britain's ditching of Japan in favour of the United States over the 1922 Naval Treaty appeared to confirm this. In their turn, the Japanese belief in their distinct and special qualities was itself essentially a racist concept almost carrying the implication that they were 'a different species of animal from the rest of humanity'.[23] Once battle was joined in 1941 racial and national self consciousness were heightened and the war was increasingly seen in racial terms. 'The present war is a struggle between races', a Japanese military orientation pamphlet issued in 1941 declared, 'and we must achieve the satisfaction of our just demands with no thought of leniency to Europeans.'[24]

However the racial factor was but one element in the fundamental discordance of the two opposing military systems. Complementing and expanding its was the clash of oriental and western cultures. 'Oriental culture', ex-Ambassador to Tokyo, Joseph Grew, later explained to the American public, 'stands as the antithesis to luxury. To many Japanese, culture means a Spartan ability to endure hard work, hard living and hard fighting ... They look upon us as boastful, vain-glorious, rich and flabby. They think that we are physically soft.'[25] The rapid and spectacular victories of Japan echoed these sentiments and appeared to underscore its spiritual superiority over the effete materialism of the West. This in itself did not bode well for the Japanese treatment of their prisoners, the representatives of this racist and decadent Western society.

Moreover, all of the educational and social conditioning of the Japanese soldier gave him a value system which clashed fundamentally with that of his captives. From middle school onwards his beliefs had been moulded to value social obligations at the expense of individual liberty; a willingness to die for one's country was not simply an attitude developed during military training, it was inculcated in the civilian school classrooms. From 1925 onwards active service officers were assigned to all middle and most senior schools and military training became a regular part of the curriculum. At a time when Western armies, and indeed Japan's own, were becoming more technology-dependent, the emphasis of Japan's military training was upon non-material factors, 'spirit', 'loyalty', 'sacrifice' and 'obedience'. The military had also become despotically authoritarian as it sought to transmit the *bushido* code of the *samurai*

to a traditionless mass army of farm workers and clerks. Some Western perceptions were that *bushido* was analogous to 'chivalry', but it
had many differences, most notably it was certainly not a code of
honour which required the strong to protect the weak and it had no
tradition of mercy and compassion. *Bushido* stressed loyalty and self-
sacrifice and the virtue of suicide rather than surrender. It also gave a
respectable position to the notion of 'revenge' as a function of loyalty
and duty.[26] This complex of selfless virtues was beaten into the
Japanese soldier by a system in which corporal punishment was institutionalised and almost ritualised.

When the products of such a system took charge of an amazingly
large force of unwounded Allied prisoners it is perhaps understandable that they should have been surprised that the prisoners were not
only unashamed of their situation, but actually wanted their Governments and families to know of their dishonoured position. By contrast, the wives of some Japanese soldiers had actually committed
suicide as their husbands went off to war so that they would be entirely
free to do their military duty. Equally, some officers and men had
their funeral rites performed before they left for active service so that
their selfless intentions would be clear. It is difficult to see how a field
army which took such a negative attitude to living in defeat and to the
very concept of 'prisoner of war' could have had any interest in a
convention which gave it obligations to what it regarded as such a
shameful class of soldiers. The senior officers in IGHQ in Tokyo were
well aware of their obligations, as their belated attempts to conceal
their failure to live up to them by staged propaganda films and inter-
views made very clear.

These artificial and unnatural traits fell away to some extent as
time progressed, but never sufficiently to make the railway labourers'
lives any more than merely bearable during the construction phase,
when Japanese determination was at its most pronounced and vari-
ants of 'You do not understand. The railway is to be built at all costs.
You will work for the Japanese until you die', were given as explanation to many prisoners. This was the period when physical punishment was at its most extreme and when many guards were under a
specific remit from their officers to make their prisoners' lives as mis-
erable as possible and to break their spirit.[27] Nevertheless, it was the
military objective itself – the railway's completion – which dominated attitudes and conditions and accounted for the worst excesses
along the line, just as the overriding military purpose occasioned the
suffering of the Japanese troops before Imphal and Kohima. The

Imperial Army had a maxim, often repeated by its captured generals when asked to account for the persistence of their attacks on 14th Army's positions long after their value had been exhausted: 'a battle is won in the last five minutes', they uniformly declared.[28] It was this conviction in the supreme importance of endurance and stamina which underlay the formidable fighting qualitites of the Japanese and combined with their readiness to accept death without demur to produce such high casualty rates in battle for themselves and in labour along the railway for their prisoners.

And yet there was at least one Allied captive in Thailand who, having served in both World Wars, found his experience of Japanese captivity in the Second preferable to the conditions of combat in the First.[29] Basil Peacock concluded that a prisoner on the Kwai had at least some chance of survival by his own efforts if he did not despair, had some luck and followed his basic training as a soldier. Terrible as the Kwai casualty figures were over three years, they did not approach those of infantry units on the Western Front in the First War. There, 18th Division, that late reinforcement for the fated Singapore garrison whose men were the largest British component of the railway labour force, had also taken part in the Battle of the Somme where its thirteen battalions took 3,115 casualties in a single day. This was accounted such a low figure given the success it had attained that its units were used over and over again as 'stormers' for the rest of the war. By comparison with this Flanders lottery some might have preferred to take their chances on the Kwai. This might have been particularly true of officers whose ranks had borne a high proportion of the casualties on the Somme (60 per cent of those engaged on the first day as compared with 40 per cent of the men). On the Kwai it was the other ranks who did the dying. In 'H' Force the death rate for British and Australian officers was 6 per cent; for the men it was over 30 per cent. In 'F' Force three Australian officers died as compared with 1,065 other ranks.[30] But only those who had served in both environments would have thought to make the comparison, for most it was irrelevant. What the POWs found particularly offensive and insufferable about the Kwai experience was not that the sickness, suffering and death were in themselves excessive: it was that they were not part of the accepted order of things according to Western mores and the conventions which they thought Japan should accept, and that the ordeal also took place in the context of sustained humiliation and degradation which drove some to the point of despair.

As to the Japanese treatment of their civilian labour force, no rationalisation based on military mores and anti-Western attitudes is possible. The peoples of South East Asia deserved much better of their liberators than the misuse they received at the hands of the armies of Japan. For many Japanese, particularly the military and the civilian officials overseas, the concept of a Co-prosperity Sphere was little more than a convenient cover for the pursuit of Japan's own imperial interests. The coolie forces on the railway were only one group of South East Asians among many who were ruthlessly exploited by the Japanese. That Japan's war actually hastened their political emancipation has not lessened the local nations' bitter memories of this wartime episode and has proved an enduring obstacle to the development of modern Japan's political role in the region. It has taken Japan's leaders a long time to come to terms with Asian perceptions of Japan's wartime excesses; but there are signs that they are at last doing so. In May 1991, in the course of a ten-day tour of South East Asia, Prime Minister Toshiki Kaifu expressed his sincere contrition at 'Japan's past actions, which inflicted unbearable suffering and sorrow upon a great many people of the Asian-Pacific region'.[31] It was the most direct apology yet delivered and perhaps the prelude to Japan at last advancing to the adoption of a more complete and conventional foreign policy in the region.

In any overall evaluation of the conduct of the Japanese in regard to the suffering and death of her railway labourers, perhaps we should recall that war has a way of forcing decisions about priorities on governments, however unwilling they may be to take them; it focusses attention on central, war-fighting issues to which civilian priorities and interests, including those of POWs, are inevitably subordinated. We might instance what was happening in the British-governed state of Bengal in north eastern India in 1943 at the time of the worst horrors on the railway. Bengal too was in the grip of famine and cholera from which its rural peasants were dying like flies. The total deaths have never been computed, but they were certainly in excess of a million people. The desperate situation was not alleviated until General Wavell, who has already made a fleeting appearance in this account, took over as Governor General, in the month the Japanese completed their railway, and began to give the crisis some priority. In a telegram to the Prime Minister he declared that the 'Bengal famine was one of the greatest disasters that has befallen any people under British rule and damage to our reputation here both among Indians and foreigners in India is incalculable'.[32] A similar outcry to that which followed Japan's ill-treatment of her civilian labour force had occurred 40 years earlier when Britain had concentrated thousands of Boer civilians into camps at the time of the South African War. It had been intended to house the Boers in comfort and safety so that the war could be more effectively prosecuted; but the administration soon ran into difficulties. In the ensuing tragedy more than 20,000 died, mainly in measles and typhoid epidemics which the victims were too mal-nourished to survive. This figure represented something approaching a quarter of the women and children of the old republics of Orange Free State and Transvaal. The concentration camp policy seemed at the time a perfectly reasonable war measure, though as the *Times History* put it, 'whether on the broad grounds of expediency it was an absolutely necessary measure is one of those questions which perhaps can never be answered finally'.[33] However, the social impact was immense and still leaves a scar on the mind of the Afrikaner.

Little is now left to bear witness to the desperate activity which took place on the banks of the Kwai in 1943. At the end of the war much of the line was dismantled; the British Army took up a short connecting section at the border itself, while the rails which ran from the Three Pagodas Pass down to Thanbyuzayat were reputed to have been sold off by Karen and Mon tribespeople.[34] The Thailand section ulti-mately became the property of the Thai government and the State Railways finally dismantled the up-country stretch from the border as far down as Namtok (Tarsao as the POWs knew it) and upgraded the remaining 124 kilometre stretch that linked with the Bangkok line to operational permanent way standard. As part of this restoration the much-bombed Tamarkan bridge was also repaired; the middle piers were rebuilt and the original three spans of curving girders were replaced by two of parallel chord type, supplied under a reparations agreement by Japan Bridge Company Limited of Osaka. A major all-weather road now serves the area where once the railway was briefly the only year-round means of land communication; but the restored line still carries some local traffic as well as a considerable freight of tourists brought in by the expanding long-haul package holiday trade. They visit the beautifully maintained war graves and the Buddhist-run railway museum at Kanchanaburi and ride the train past the Chungkai War Cemetery and over the still spectacular Wampo viaduct (see Frontispiece). Further north they can visit the Australian memorial at Hell Fire Pass which recalls the epic struggle that took place there, or take a long-tailed boat trip up the river to Kinsaiyok waterfall where the site of the railway labour camp is now a national park with paths which meander through a teak forest planted in 1950 which now bears little trace of the railway which once ran through it.

Further still up-country the old camp at Konkoita and much of the embankment immediately to its south is now submerged under the dam waters of the Khao Laem hydro-electric scheme which features Japanese turbines embedded in the hillside generating the power. Near Tarsao, at the River Kwai Village Hotel, British tourists share the swimming pool with Japanese, dine next to them in the open-sided dining room which looks down on the ochre waters of the Kwai, or jostle with them and the Australians for drinks at the bamboo decorated bar. As they sip their refrigerated beers the Japanese perhaps recall the skill and valour of their wartime railway regiments and their extraordinary engineering achievement, while the ex-prisoners among the other tourists, now a dwindling band, perhaps remember a little grimly where it was, as a celebrated prisoner-artist later expressed it, that they first grasped the 'thorny but true measuring stick against which to place things that did or did not matter in life'.[35]

References

NOTE. IWM indicates Imperial War Museum, London, PRO Public Record Office, London.

Preface

1. J. Stewart, *To The River Kwai*, (London, Bloomsbury, 1988), pp. 145–49.
2. Particular examples are L. Rawlings, *And The Dawn Came Up Like Thunder*, (Rawlings Chapman Publications, 1972), H. R. Charles, *Last Man Out*, (Marlborough, Crowood, 1989) and E. R. Hall, *The Burma–Thailand Railway of Death*, (Armadale, Graphic Books, 1981).

Chapter One: The Explosion of Japanese Power

1. This analysis is based on F. C. Jones, 'Japan: the military domination of Japanese policy', in M. Howard (ed.), *Soldiers and Governments*, (London, Eyre and Spottiswode, 1957), pp. 117–18.
2. H. Kublin, 'The 'Modern' Army of early Meiji Japan', *Far Eastern Quarterly*, Vol IX, (1949), 38–40.
3. P. Fleming, *The Siege of Peking*, (London, Hart Davis, 1962) p. 165.
4. P. Towle, 'Japanese Treatment of Prisoners in 1904–5 – Foreign Officers' Reports', *Military Affairs*, (Oct 1975), 115–17.
5. E. J. Drea, 'In the Army Barracks of Imperial Japan', *Armed Forces and Society*, Vol 15, No 3, (Spring 1989), p. 337.
6. J. Morris, *Traveller in Tokyo* (London, Book Club Edition, 1945), p. 135.
7. S. Ienaga, *Japan's Last War* (Oxford, Blackwell, 1979), pp. 157–59.
8. A. D. Coox, 'High Command and Field Army: The Kwantung Army and the Nomonhan Incident 1939', *Military Affairs*, (Oct. 1969), 302–12.
9. Drea, *op.cit* pp. 339–400.

Chapter Two: The Western Bastion

1. Cited in N. J. Bailey, *Thailand and the Fall of Singapore*, (London, Westview, 1986), p. 100.
2. This view is widely supported, e.g. C. Cruickshank, *SOE in the Far East* (Oxford, 1983), p. 121; A. Gilchrist, *Bangkok Top Secret* (London, Hutchinson, 1970), p. 192 and J. B. Haseman, *The Thai Resistance Movement During the Second World War* (Bangkok, Chalermnit Press, 1988), pp. 35–6.
3. C. A. Fisher, 'The Thailand–Burma Railway', *Economic Geography* (1941), Vol 23, 85–7.

Chapter Three: The Labour Forces

1. The Japanese version of this exchange was printed in the *Manchester Guardian* on 17 April 1942. Cited in J. Leasor, *Singapore: The Battle that Changed the World*, (London, Hodder and Stoughton, 1968), p. 253.
2. P. Calvocoressi, G. Wint and J. Pritchard, *Total War* (Harmondsworth, Viking, 1972), p. 997 and S. W. Kirby *et al., The War Against Japan*, Vol. 5, p. 542.
3. Cited in C. Thorne, *Racial Aspects of the Far Eastern War of 1941–1945*, (London, 1982), p. 346.
4. M. Shinozaki, *Syonan – My Story* (Singapore, Times Books, 1982), p. 43.
5. Quoted in Ienaga, *op. cit.* p. 49.
6. Combat regulations quoted in W. W. Mason, *Official History of New Zealand in the Second World War: Prisoners of War*, (Wellington, 1954), p. 188.
7. Y. Futamatsu *Account of the Construction of the Thai–Burma Railway*, trans. C. E. Escritt (Escritt collection IWM), p. 2.
8. M. Tsuji, *Singapore – the Japanese Version*, (London, Mayflower Dell, 1966), p. 246.
9. U. Hla Pe, *Narrative of the Japanese Occupation of Burma*, Data Paper 41, (Cornell, South East Asia Programme, 1961), p. 15.
10. Burma Intelligence Bureau, *Burma During the Japanese Occupation*, 2 vols, (Simla 1943 and 1944), esp, Vol 2, pp. 136–7.
11. Ba Maw, *Breakthrough in Burma: Memoirs of a Revolution 1939–46*, (London, Yale University Press, 1944), pp. 290–2.
12. U. Hla Pe, *op. cit.* p. 18.
13. Haseman, *op. cit.* p. 16.
14. C. C. Brett, *The Burma–Siam Railway* SEATIC Bulletin No 246, 1946, IWM and Y, Futamatsu, *Across The Three Pagodas Pass* (Tokyo, Yamamoto Press, 1985), trans. C. E. Escritt, ms. IWM p. 154.

Chapter Four: Planning The Impossible

1. Fisher, *op. cit.* pp. 86–8.
2. Ewart Escritt, 'The Thai–Burma Railway' *Royal Corps of Transport Review*, (June 1988), 33, based on correspondence with Y. Futamatsu.
3. The evidence is that of Mr Hiroike, formerly Chief of Staff of Southern Army's Field Operations Control cited in Y. Futamatsu, 'Recollections of the Thai–Burma Railway', privately printed 1980, trans. and ed. C. E. Escritt, Escritt collection, IWM.
4. R. D. H. Jones, 'Notes on the Organisation of Japanese Railway Regiments, unpublished ms. dated 24 Nov 1945. IWM.
5. A. Kuar, *Bridge and Barrier: Transport and Communications in Colonial Malaya 1870–1957*, (Singapore, OUP, 1985), pp. 171–2.
6. Y. Futamatsu, *Recollections*.
7. E. Protheroe, *The Railways of the World* (London, Routledge, 1911), p. 622.
8. L. Allen, *The Independent Magazine*, 10 March 1990, p. 7.
9. Futamatsu, *Three Pagodas*, p. 109.
10. P. A. Tyler, 'Water Chemistry of the River Kwai, Thailand' *Hydrobiologica* III, (1984), 65–73.
11. HMSO, *Colonial Report for the Malayan Union 1946–7* pp. 108–9.
12. Burma Intelligence Bureau, *Burma During the Japanese Occupation*, (Simla, Government of Burma, 1943), Vol. 1, p. 75.
13. B. Peacock, *Prisoner on the Kwai* (London, Blackwood, 1966), p. 9.
14. R. Hardie, *The Burma–Siam Railway: The Secret Diary of Dr Robert Hardie 1942–45*, (London, IWM, 1983), p. 24.

15. J. Crosby, *Siam: The Crossroads* (London, Hollis and Carter, 1945), p. 143.
16. Based on figures in D. Nelson, *The Story of Changi Singapore*, (West Perth, Changi Publication Co., 1974), and Brett, *op. cit.* pp. 22–3.
17. Ba Maw, *op. cit.*, p. 291.
18. Wigmore, *op. cit.*, p. 547.
19. D. P. Apthorpe, 'Diary of the British Sumatra POW Battalion', unpublished ms. 1945, IWM (DPA 4/2), p. 4.

Chapter Five: The Battle Begins

1. The U.S. Strategic Bombing Survey, *The War Against Japanese Transportation 1941–45*, (London, Garland, 1976), p. 2.
2. *Ibid.* p. 47.
3. Haseman, *op. cit.*, p. 23.
4. Futamatsu, *Three Pagodas*, p. 154.
5. Ba Maw, *op. cit.*, p. 292.
6. Futamatsu, *Three Pagodas*, ch. 30.
7. This was the judgment of Major J. F. Clegg, OC 318 Independent Railway Bridging Company, in a post-war survey cited in Brett, *op. cit.*
8. V. Toose in *Barbed Wire and Bamboo* (Journal of NSW, Queensland, Victoria, Western Australia ex-POW Associations), Aug 1977.
9. Futamatsu, *Three Pagodas*, p. 207.
10. *Ibid.*, ch. 19.
11. P. N. Davies, *The Man Behind the Bridge: Colonel Toosey and the River Kwai*, (London, Athlone, 1991), p. 102.

Chapter Six: Lives on the Line

1. F. A. E. Crew, *History of the Second World War. The Army Medical Services Campaigns*, Vol. 5. *Burma* (London, HMSO, 1966), p. 22.
2. F. A. E. Crew, *History of the Second World War. The Army Medical Services Campaigns*, Vol 2. *Malaya* (London, HMSO, 1957), p. 104.
3. *Ibid.* p. 115.
4. E. E. Dunlop, *The War Diaries of Weary Dunlop* (London, Lennard, 1987), p. 176.
5. H. R. Charles, *Last Man Out*, (Marlborough, Crowood, 1989), p. 87.
6. Hla Pe, *op. cit.*, pp. 18–19.
7. Futamatsu, *Three Pagodas*, pp. 162–5.
8. Apthorpe, *op. cit.*, p. 8.
9. Brett, *op. cit.*, p. 24.

Chapter Seven: Isolation

1. Dunlop, *War Diaries*, p. 126.
2. H. Satow and M. J. Lee, *The Work of the Prisoners of War Department During the Second World War*, (The Foreign Office, 1950).
3. R. Garnett, *P.O.W. The Uncivil Face of War*, (Newton Abbot, David and Charles, 1988), p. 94.
4. Quoted in Towle, *op. cit.*, p. 115.
5. *Ibid.*, p. 116.
6. Satow and Lee, *op. cit.*, p. 7.
7. R. Rivett, *Behind Bamboo*, (London, Angus and Robertson, 1952), p. 245.
8. Satow and Lee, *op. cit.*, p. 147.

9. *Ibid.* p. 133.
10. R. Braddon, *The Naked Island* (London, Werner Laurie, 1953), p. 178.
11. Hardie, *op. cit.*, p. 50.
12. Dunlop, *op. cit.*, p. xv.
13. Medical Officer Kevin Fagin, quoted in H. Nelson, *Prisoners of War: Australians under Nippon*, (Sydney, ABC Enterprises, 1985), p. 61.
14. Wigmore, *op. cit.*, p. 547.
15. Hall, *op. cit.*, p. 87 and 91.
16. Charles, *op. cit.*, pp. 184–93.

Chapter Eight: Speedo – the Plan

1. Futamatsu, *Three Pagodas*, p. 226.
2. *Ibid.* p. 223.
3. *Ibid.* p. 228.
4. C. E. Escritt, 'The Death of General Shimoda', ms. note, 1985, Escritt Collection, IWM.
5. RAF Narrative, *The Campaigns in the Far East: Vol III, India Command Sep 1939 – Nov 1943*, Ministry of Defence, p. 61.
6. Nelson, *op. cit.*, pp. 202–215, and Brett *op. cit.*, Appendix B, p. 22.
7. Futamatsu, *Three Pagodas*, pp. 231–6.
8. *Ibid.*, pp. 248–9.

Chapter Nine: Reinforcements

1. Dunlop, *op. cit.*, p. 213.
2. Futamatsu, *Three Pagodas*, p. 249.
3. Hla Pe, *op. cit.*, p. 18.
4. Brett, *op. cit.*, p. 26.
5. Ba Maw, *op. cit.*, pp. 292–4.
6. Burma Intelligence Bureau, *op. cit.*, p. 207.
7. Hla Pe, *op. cit.*, p. 18.
8. Burma Intelligence Bureau, *op. cit.*, p. 207.
9. Brett, *op. cit.*, p. 24
10. Chin Kee Onn, *Malaya Upside Down*, (Singapore, Jitts and Co., 1946), p. 59.
11. Ibid., p. 60.
12. Dunlop, *op. cit.*, p. 213.
13. J. Coast, *Railroad of Death*, (London, Commodore Press, 1946), pp. 129–30.
14. S. W. Harris, 'History of F Force' in Brett, *op. cit.*, p. 45.
15. Wigmore, *op. cit.*, p. 573.
16. Stewart, *op. cit.*, p. 65.
17. Braddon, *op. cit.*, p. 172.
18. T. H. Newey, 'Report on H Force', unpublished ms., IWM p. 1.

Chapter Ten: 'Speedo–Worko'

1. Crew, *Medical Campaigns* Vol. 2., *Malaya* p. 161.
2. Apthorpe, *op. cit.*, p. 6.
3. Wigmore, *op. cit.*, p. 553.
4. C. H. Lee, unpublished ms. IWM p. 28.
5. Tyler, *op. cit.*, pp. 65–73.
6. Harris, *op. cit.*, p. 47.
7. Hardie *op. cit.*, p. 94.

8. J. Huston, 'F Force Medical Report', unpublished ms., Australian War Memorial Ref SU554/9/1.
9. Dunlop, *op. cit.*, p. 250.
10. Crew, *Medical Campaigns*, Vol. 2., *Malaya*, p. 170.
11. T. H. Newey, *op. cit.*, p. 5.
12. E. S. Benford, 'The Rising Sun On My Back', privately printed, IWM.
13. Hardie, *op. cit.*, p. 109.
14. Lee, *op. cit.*, p. 28.
15. Dunlop, *op. cit.*, p. 336.
16. Wigmore, *op. cit.*, pp. 587–8.
17. Harris, *op. cit.*, pp. 52–3.
18. *Ibid.* p. 49.
19. Dunlop, *op. cit.*, p. 289.
20. Benford, *op. cit.*,
21. Wigmore, *op. cit.*, p. 569.
22. P. J. D. Toosey, 'Report on Prisoner of War Camps in Malaya and Thailand', unpublished ms., IWM, p. 8.

Chapter Eleven: Ending the Torment

1. D. P. Apthorpe, 'Report on Treatment of British POWs in Burma, Siam and Indo-China', unpublished ms., IWM, para. 10.
2. I. Morrison, *Grandfather Longlegs*, (London, Faber and Faber, 1947), p. 205.
3. *Ibid.*, p. 89.
4. *Ibid.*, p. 211.
5. J. Bradley, *Towards the Setting Sun*, (Chichester, Phillimore, 1982), p. 57.
6. *Ibid.*, pp. 108–110.
7. A. A. Apthorpe, *The British Sumatra Battalion*, (Lewes, Book Guild, 1988), p. 113.
8. P. Shaw, *Brother Digger*, (Richmond, Greenhouse Publications, 1984), p. 103.
9. Satow and Lee, *op. cit.*, pp. 140–7.
10. C. E. Escritt, 'Note on the 'V' Organisation', unpublished ms., Escritt collection, IWM.
11. British Red Cross POW Dept., *The Prisoner of War*, July 1943.
12. Satow and Lee, *op. cit.*, pp. 140–7.
13. Escritt, ''V' Organisation', p. 6.
14. R. A. N. Davidson, 'POW on the Siam Burma Railway' *News Bulletin of 4th Gurkha Rifles Officers' Association* (1987), 55–6.
15. Coast, *Railroad of Death*, p. 123.
16. Toosey, *op. cit.*, p. 8.
17. Davidson, *op. cit.*, p. 56.
18. A. E. Knight, 'Personal Experience of 'V' Organisation', unpublished ms., 1958, IWM, p. 7.
19. Brett, *op. cit.*, p. 16.
20. Escritt, *Shimoda*.
21. Futamatsu, *Three Pagodas* ch. 31 and *Recollections*, p. 9.

Chapter Twelve: Relief Deferred

1. L. Allen, *Burma: The Longest War*, (London, Dent, 1984), p. 157–66.
2. T. Wilson, 'Sickness and Death Rates' in 'Report of SMO 'F' Force', unpublished ms., IWM.
3. Harris, *op. cit.*, p. 56.

4. Newey, *op. cit.*, p. 8.
5. *Ibid.*, p. 9.
6. J. F. N. Clarkson, 'Atrocities', unpublished ms., IWM, p. 2.
7. W. B. Young, 'Report to Colonial Office', unpublished ms., IWM and H. C. Benson, 'Report on History of 'L' Force POW Thailand', unpublished ms., 1945.
8. Young, *op. cit.*, p. 7.
9. *Ibid.* pp. 5–13.
10. Ba Maw, *op. cit.*, p. 293.
11. Hla Pe, *op. cit.*, p. 19.
12. Futamatsu, *Recollections*, p. 1.
13. Ba Maw, *op. cit.*, p. 295.

Chapter Thirteen: The Impermanent Way

1. Wigmore, *op. cit.*, p. 588.
2. Futamatsu, *Three Pagodas*, p. 96.
3. R. Burton, *The Road to Three Pagodas*, (London, Macdonald, 1963), p. 135.
4. Wigmore, *op. cit.*, p. 588.
5. Young, *op. cit.*, p. 13.
6. Rivett, *op. cit.*, p. 249.
7. Newey, *op. cit.*, p. 10.
8. D. MacIsaac (ed.), *The United States Strategic Bombing Survey*, (London, Garland, 1976), Vol VIII, p. 104.
9. Stewart, *op. cit.*, p. 149.
10. Dunlop, *op. cit.*, p. 270.
11. Allen, *op. cit.*, p. 166.
12. T. Kurahashi, *Burma Operations Record: Outline of Burma Area Line of Communication* (Japanese Monograph No. 133), (Military History Section, HQ Armed Forces Far East, Feb 1952), p. 13.
13. Peacock, *op. cit.*, pp. 133–34.
14. Stewart, *op. cit.*, p. 79.
15. Rivett, *op. cit.*, p. 197.
16. Kurahashi, *op. cit.*, p. 13.
17. Brett, *op. cit.*, p. 37.
18. Allen, *op. cit.*, p. 248.
19. Turahashi, *op. cit.*, p. 13.
20. L. Allen, *Sittang: The Last Battle* (London, Macdonald (Arrow ed.), 1976), p. 127.
21. C. E. Escritt, 'A Japanese Engineer's Trace of the Thailand Burma Rail Link', Escritt redrew and translated the map and produced an accompanying commentary. IWM.
22. Brett, *op. cit.*, p. 36.
23. K. Tsukamoto, 'Maeklaung Steel Bridge' in *Railway Fan* No 246, (Dec 1981), translated by C. E. Escritt, unpublished ms., IWM, p. 9.
24. Kurahashi, *op. cit.*, appended Table No. 2, p. 2.
25. *SEATIC Historical Bulletin No. 242*, (Singapore, 1946), p. 33.
26. MacIsaac (ed.), *op. cit.*, p. 104.
27. Allen, *Burma*, p. 391.
28. PRO Air 27, 1758.
29. C. H. Fritsche, 'B 24 Liberator' in R. Higham and C. Williams (eds.), *Flying Combat Aircraft of the USAAF and USAF*, (Ames, Iowa State University Press, 1978), Vol II, p. 55.

30. K. Tsukamoto, 'Maeklaung Steel Bridge' in *Railway Fan* No 247 (Dec 1981) translated by C. E. Escritt, unpublished ms., IWM, p. 22.
31. PRO Air 27, 1752.

Chapter Fourteen: Defeat and Deliverance

1. Allen, *Burma*, Appx. 1, p. 645.
2. *Ibid.*, p. 390.
3. S. W. Kirby, *et.al., The War Against Japan,*. Vol IV, p. 401.
4. Allen, *Burma*, p. 391.
5. *Ibid.*, p. 466.
6. Allen, *Sittang*, pp. 33–7.
7. Ba Maw, *op. cit.*, p. 296.
8. *Hansard*, Commons, Vol. 396, Col. 1030.
9. *Ibid.*, Vol 404, Cols. 2244–2247.
10. E. Gordon, *Miracle on the Kwai* (London, Collins (Fontana), 1965), p. 162.
11. Peacock, *op. cit.*, p. 253.
12. G. S. Gimson, private communication to the author based on diary entry made soon after the surrender from information supplied by the interpreter concerned.
13. *Ibid.*
14. L. van der Post, *The Night of the New Moon* (London, Hogarth, 1971), p. 128.
15. J. T. Barnard, *The Endless Years* (London, Chantry, 1950), p. 159.
16. I. McA. Stewart, *History of the Argyll and Sutherland Highlanders 2nd Battalion 1939–45*, (London, Nelson, 1947), p. 140.
17. M. R. D. Foot and J. M. Langley, *MI9 Escape and Evasion 1939–45*, (London, Futura, 1980), pp. 303–4.
18. D. Ripley, 'Incident in Siam', *Yale Review* (Winter 1947), Vol 36(2), 273.
19. *A Report on RAPWI in Malaya and Singapore.* Held in MOD Library, London, pp. ii–iii.
20. Quoted in Wigmore, *op. cit.*, p. 638.
21. F. S. V. Donnison, *Military Administration in the Far East 1943–46*, (London, HMSO, 1956), p. 283.

Chapter Fifteen, Brought to Account

1. J. Beaumont, 'Gull Force comes home', *Journal of the Australian War Memorial*, No. 14, (April 1989), 51.
2. W. N. Nicholson, *History of the Suffolk Regiment 1928–46*, (Ipswich East Anglian Magazine Ltd., 1948), p. 231.
3. I. McA. Stewart, *op. cit.*, pp. 146–165.
4. Gordon, *op. cit.*, p. 181.
5. Beaumont, *op. cit.*, p. 51.
6. E. E. Dunlop, 'Medical Experiences in Japanese Captivity', *British Medical Journal*, (1946), Vol 2, pp. 481–86.
7. Brett, *op. cit.*
8. Donnison, *op. cit.*, p. 281.
9. Brett, *op. cit.*, p. 25.
10. Donnison, *op. cit.*, p. 281.
11. *The Independent*, 18 November 1990.
12. M. V. Del Tufo, *Malaya: A Report on the 1947 Census of Population*, (London, Crown Agents, 1949).

13. Gamba, *The History of the Plantation Workers of Malaya 1946–58*, (Singapore, Donald Moore, 1962), p. 13.
14. Malayan Union, *Annual Report of the Malayan Union 1947* (Kuala Lumpur, Government Press, 1948), p. 86.
15. C. S. R. Sastri, *Congress Mission to Malaya*, (Tenali), 1947.
16. J. N. F. Clarkson, 'Atrocities', unpublished ms., IWM.
17. Harris, *op. cit.*, p. 54.
18. Y. Futamatsu, *Account of the Construction of the Thai–Burma Railway, Mainichi Shimbunsha*, (1955), ms. translation C. E. Escritt, IWM. pp. 132–37.
19. Burma Intelligence Bureau, *op. cit.*, p. 186.
20. Crew, *Medical Campaigns*, Vol V, *Burma*, p. 618.
21. Tsukamoto, *op. cit.*, p. 4.
22. Towle, *op. cit.*
23. E. D. Reischauer, *The Japanese* (Cambridge, Mass., 1978), p. 411.
24. M. Tsuji, *op. cit.*, p. 246.
25. J. C. Grew, *Report from Tokyo* (London, Hammond and Hammond, 1972), p. 30.
26. This explanation draws on S. L. Falk, *The March of Death* (London, Robert Hale, 1964).
27. Toosey, *op. cit.*, Appendix 'D', p. 2.
28. *SEATIC Historical Bulletin* No. 242, p. 33. Lieutenant Generals Numata, Naka and Konomura answered the question in almost identical terms.
29. B. Peacock, 'The Somme and the Kwai' in *Peacock's Tales*, (Wallington, Fleetwing, 1970).
30. H. Nelson, *Prisoners of War: Australians under Nippon*, (Sydney, ABC, 1985), p. 61.
31. *The Independent*, 4 May 1991.
32. P. Moon (ed.), *The Viceroy's Journal* (London, OUP, 1973), p. 54.
33. *The Times History of the War in South Africa 1899–1902*, Vol V, p. 66.
34. Stewart, *op. cit.*, p. 144.
35. The judgment is Ronald Searle's.

Bibliography

Unpublished Sources

Apthorpe, Major D. P., 'Diary of the British Sumatra Battalion', IWM (DPS 4/2)

Benford, E. S., 'The Rising Sun on My Back', IWM.

Benson, Lt. Col. H. C., 'Report on History of "L" Force POW Thailand', 1945, IWM.

Burma Intelligence Bureau, Govt. of Burma, Burma During The Japanese Occupation, Vols. 1 and 2, Simla 1943 and 1944, MOD Library.

Clarkson, Capt. J. F. N., 'Atrocities', IWM.

Crook, Lt. Col. P. E. *et al.*, 'A Report on RAPWI in Malaya and Singapore', MOD Library.

Escritt, C. E., (trans. and annotated), 'A Japanese Engineers Trace of the Thailand–Burma Rail Link', IWM.

———, 'The Thai–Burma Rail Link – The Death of General Shimoda (note based on Japanese sources), Escritt Collection.

———, Notes on the 'V' Organisation, (Oxford, 1982, IWM.)

Futamatsu, Yoshihiko, 'Recollections of the Thai–Burma Railway', (trans. and. annotated by C. E. Escritt, 1980), Escritt Collection.

———Across The Three Pagodas Pass, (trans. and annotated by C. E. Escritt, 1987), IWM.

Jones, Lt. Col. R. D. H., 'Notes on the Organisation of Japanese Railway Regiments', 1945, IWM.

Knights, Lt. Col. A. E., 'Personal Experience of 'V' Organisation', 1958, IWM.

Newey, Lt. Col. T. H., 'Report on H Force', IWM.

Operations Record Books, '99, 159, 215, 354–6 Squadrons RAF', PRO Air 27 Vols. 791, 1061, 1329, 1751–4, 178–9.

SEATIC Bulletin 242, 'Japanese Generals' Answers to Questionnaire', 1946, IWM.

SEATIC Bulletin 246, 'The Burma–Siam Railway', 1946, IWM.

Takeo, Kurahashi, 'Burma Operations Record: Outline of Burma Area Line of Communications', Japanese Monograph No. 133, HQ Armed Forces Far East, 1952, RMA Sandhurst Library.

Toosey, Lt. Col. P. D., 'Report on PW Camps in Malaya and Thailand', Bangkok, 1945, IWM.

Young, Capt. W. B., 'Report to Colonial Office', IWM.

Published Sources: Books

Adams, G. P., *No Time for Geishas*, (London, Leo Cooper, 1973).

———*The Thailand to Burma Railway*, (Poole, Ashley Press, 1978).

Aida Yugi, *Prisoner of the British*, (trans. H. Ishiguro and L. Allen), (London, Cresset Press, 1966).

Allbury, A. G., *Bamboo and Bushido*, (London, Robert Hale, 1955).
Allen, L., *The End of the War in Asia*, (London, Hart–Davis MacGibbon, 1976).
——*Sittang: The Last Battle* (London, Arrow, 1976).
——*Burma: The Longest War*, (London, Dent, 1984).
Apthorpe, A. A., *The British Sumatra Battalion* (Sussex, Book Guild, 1988).
Arasaratnam, S., *Indians in Malaysia and Singapore* (Kuala Lumpur, OUP, 1970).
Barnard, J.T., *The Endless Years*, (London, Chantry, 1950).
Blake, W. T., *Thailand Journey*, (London, A. Redman, 1955).
Boulle, P., *The Bridge on the River Kwai* (London, Secker and Warburg, 1954).
Bowden, T. *Changi Photographer*, (Sydney, ABC Enterprises, 1984).
Boyle, J., *Railroad to Burma*, (London, Allen and Unwin, 1990).
Braddon, R., *The Naked Island*, (London, Werner Laurie, 1952).
Bradley, J. B., *Towards the Setting Sun*, (Chichester, Phillimore, 1982).
Brailey, N. J., *Thailand and the Fall of Singapore*, (London, Westfield Press, 1986).
Brodrick, A. H., *Beyond The Burma Road*, (London, Hutchinson, 1945).
Burton, R., *The Road to Three Pagodas* (London, Macdonald, 1963).
Caffrey, K., *Out in the Midday Sun*, (London, A. Deutsch, 1974).
Carter, N., *G-String Jesters*, (Sydney, Currawong, 1966).
Charles, H. R., *Last Man Out* (Marlborough, Crowood Press, 1989).
Clarke, H. *et al.*, *Prisoners of War*, (Sydney, Time Life, 1988).
Clarke, H. V., *A Life for Every Sleeper* (Sydney, Allen and Unwin, 1986).
Coast, J., *Railroad of Death*, (London, Commodore Press, 1946).
Coombes, J. H. H., *Banpong Express* (Darlington, Dresser, 1948).
Craven, W. F. and Cate, J. L., *The Army Air Forces in World War Two*, Vols. 4 and 5, (Chicago, Chicago University Press, 1950 and 1953).
Crew, F. A. E., *Army Medical Services Campaigns, Vol. 2 Malaya*, (London, HMSO, 1957).
——*Vol. 5 Burma*, (London, HMSO, 1966).
Crosby, J., *Siam: The Crossroads* (London, Hollis and Carter, 1945).
Cruickshank, C., *SOE in the Far East* (Oxford, O.U.P., 1983).
Davies, P. N., *The Man Behind the Bridge*, (London, Athlone, 1991).
Dewey, J. and S., *POW Sketchbook*, (Cholsey, Pie Powder Press, 1985).
Donnison, F. S. V., *British Military Administration in the Far East 1943–46*, (London, HMSO, 1956).
Dunlop, E. E., *The War Diaries of Weary Dunlop*, (Melbourne, Nelson, 1986).
Elsbree, W. H., *Japan's Role in S.E. Asia Nationalist Movements 1940–45*, (Cambridge, Mass., 1953).
Falk, S., *The March of Death*, (London, Robert Hale, 1964).
Fleming, P., *The Siege at Peking*, (London, Hart–Davis, 1960).
Foot, M. R. D. and Langley, J. M., *MI9: Escape and Evasion 1939–45* (London, Futura, 1980).
Ford, C. and MacBain A., *Cloak and Dagger, The Secret Story of OSS*, (New York, Random House, 1946).
Futamatsu, Yoshihiko, *Account of the Construction of the Thai–Burma Railway*, (trans. C. Escritt), Escritt Collection, (Mainichi Shimbunsha, 1955).
Gamba, C., *The National Union of Plantation Workers*, (Singapore, Donald Moore, 1962).
Garrett, R., *POW: The Uncivil Face of War* (Newton Abbott, David and Charles, 1981).
Gilchrist, A. *Bangkok Top Secret* (London, Hutchinson, 1970).
Gill, H. C., *Royal Australian Navy 1939–42*, (Canberra, Australian War Memorial, 1957).
Gullick, J. M., *Malaysia* (London, Ernest Benn, 1969).

Gordon, E., *Miracle on the River Kwai* (London, Collins, 1963).

Hall, E. R., *Burma-Thailand Railway of Death*, (Armadale, Graphic Books, 1981).

Hammond, R., *The Flame of Freedom*, (London, Leo Cooper, 1988).

Hardie, R., *The Burma-Siam Railway* (London, IWM, 1983).

Harrison, K., *The Brave Japanese*, (London, Angus and Robertson, 1957).

Haseman, J. B., *The Thai Resistance Movement in the Second World War*, (Bangkok, Chalermnit Press, 1988).

Hastain, R., *White Coolie*, (London, Hodder and Stoughton, 1947).

Higham, R. and Williams, C. (eds.), *Flying Combat Aircraft of the USAAF and USAF*, (Ames, Iowa State U.P., 1978).

Hla Pe, U., *Narrative of the Japanese Occupation of Burma*, (Cornell U.P., 1961).

Howard, M. (ed.), *Soldiers and Governments*, (London, Eyre and Spottiswoode, 1957).

Hoyt, E. P., *Japan's War*, (London, Hutchinson, 1987).

Kaur, A., *Bridge and Barrier: Transport and Communications in Colonial Malaya 1870-1957*, (Singapore, O.U.P., 1985).

Kennedy, M., *The Military Side of Japanese Life*, (London, Constable, 1924).

Kennedy, P., *The Rise and Fall of the Great Powers*, (London, Unwin Hyman, 1988).

Kirby, S. W. *et al., The War Against Japan*, 5 vols., (London, HMSO, 1958-69).

Leasor, J., *Singapore: The Battle That Changed The World*, (London, Hodder and Stoughton, 1968).

Lee, E., *To The Bitter End*, (London, Viking, 1985).

Malayan Union, *Annual Report of the Malayan Union*, (Kuala Lumpur, Govt. Press, 1947).

Mamoru, Shinozaki, *Syonan – My Story*, (Singapore, Times Books, 1982).

Martin, A. C., *The Concentration Camps 1900-1902: Facts, Figures and Fables*, (Cape Town, Timmins, 1958).

Mason, W. W., *Prisoners of War*, (Wellington, Dept. of Internal Affairs, 1954).

Maw, Ba, *Breakthrough in Burma: Memoirs of a Revolution*, (London, Yale U.P., 1968).

Miller, H., *The Story of Malaysia*, (London, Faber and Faber, 1965).

Moon, P. (ed.), *The Viceroy's Journal*, (London, O.U.P., 1973).

Moorehouse, G., *India Britannica*, (London, Paladin, 1984).

Morrison, I., *Malayan Postscript*, (London, Faber and Faber, 1942).

———*Grandfather Longlegs*, (London, Faber and Faber, 1947).

Nelson, D., *The Story of Changi*, (West Perth, Changi Publication Co., 1974).

Nelson, H., *Prisoners of War: Australians Under Nippon*, (Sydney, ABC, 1985).

Nicholson, W. N., *The Suffolk Regiment 1928-46* (Ipswich, East Anglia Magazine Co. Ltd., 1948).

O'Brien, T., *The Moonlight War*, (London, Collins, 1957).

Onn, Chin Kee, *Malaya Upside Down*, (Singapore, Jitts and Co., 1946).

Pakenham, T., *The Boer War*, (London, Weidenfeld and Nicholson, 1979).

Parkin, R., *Into the Smother*, (London, Hogarth Press, 1965).

Pavillard, S., *Bamboo Doctor*, (London, Macmillan, 1960).

Peacock, B., *Prisoner on the Kwai*, (London, Blackwood, 1966).

———*Peacock's Tales*, (Wallington, Fleetwing, 1970).

van der Post, L., *The Night of the New Moon*, (London, Hogarth, 1971).

Probert, H., *History of Changi*, (Singapore, 1965).

Rawlings, L., *And the Dawn Came Up Like Thunder*, (Rawlings, Chapman, 1972).

Rivett, R., *Behind Bamboo*, (London, Angus and Robertson, 1946).

Rust, K. C., *Tenth Air Force Story in World War Two*, (Temple City, 1980).

Saburo, Ienaga, *Japan's Last War*, (Oxford, Blackwell, 1979).

Sandhu, K. S., *Indians in Malaya, Immigration and Settlement 1786-1957*, (Cambridge, Cambridge U.P., 1969).

Sastri, C. S. R., *Congress Mission to Malaya*, (Tenali, 1947).

Satow, H. and Lee, M. J., *The Work of the Prisoners of War Department during the Second World War*, (London, Foreign Office, 1950).

Searle, R., *To the Kwai and Back*, (London, Collins, 1986).

Shaw, R., *Brother Digger, The Sullivans 2nd AIF*, (Richmond, Greenhouse, 1984).

Stanistreet, J. A., *The Malayan Railway*, (Oakwood Press, 1974).

Stewart, I. McA., *History of the Argyll and Sutherland Highlanders, 2nd Bn. 1939–45*, (London, Nelson, 1947).

Stewart, J., *To The River Kwai: Two Journeys 1943, 1979*, (London, Bloomsbury, 1988).

Taylor, E., *Richer by Asia*, (London, Secker and Warburg, 1948).

Thomas, M., *In the Shadow of the Rising Sun*, (Singapore, Maruzen Asia, 1983).

Thorne, C., *The Issue of War*, (London, Hamish Hamilton, 1985).

del Tufo, M. V., *Malaya: A Report on the 1947 Census of Population*, (London, Crown Agents, 1949).

Wigmore, L., *The Japanese Thrust*, (Canberra, Australian War Memorial, 1957).

Articles

Beaumont, J., 'Gull Force Comes Home', *Journal of the Australian War Memorial*, (April 1987).

British Red Cross and St John Organisation, *Prisoner of War*, (May 1942 onwards).

Chatrabandhu, K., 'Force 136 and the Siamese Resistance Movement', *Asiatic Review*, 43, (April 1947).

Coox, A., 'High Command and Field Army: The Kwantung Army and the Nomonhan Incident 1939', *Military Affairs* 10, (1969).

Davidson, R. A. N., 'POW on the Siam–Burma Railway', *News Bulletin of 4th Gurkha Rifles Officers' Association*, (1987).

Davies, W. L., 'The Bridges on the River Kwai', *Aerospace Historian*, (Spring 1973).

Drea, E. J., 'In the Army Barracks of Imperial Japan', *Armed Forces and Society*, (Spring 1989).

Escritt, C. E., 'The Thai–Burma Railway', *Royal Corps of Transport Review*, (June 1988).

Fisher, C. A., 'The Thailand–Burma Railway', *Economic Geography*, (1947).

Fritsche, C. H., 'Liberators on the Kwai', *Aerospace Historian*, (Summer 1983).

Henderson, W. A., 'About That Bridge On The River Kwai', *Air Force Magazine*, (February 1972).

Hugh, C., 'The Last Journey', *Blackwoods Magazine*, (April 1946).

Kublin, H., 'The "Modern" Army of Early Meiji Japan', *Far Eastern Quarterly*, IX, (1949).

McIntosh, I. R., 'The Selarang Barracks Incident', *Royal Artillery Journal*, (1953).

Nelson, H., 'A Bowl of Rice for Seven Camels', *Journal of the Australian War Memorial*, (1989).

Ramsey, W. G. (ed.), 'The Death Railway', *After The Battle* No. 26, (1979).

Ripley, S. D., 'Incident in Siam', *Yale Review*, (Winter 1947).

Snelling, A., 'Notes on Some Administrative Aspects of the Campaign of the Fourteenth Army, 1943–44', *Army Quarterly* (July 1965).

Thorne, C., 'Racial Aspects of the Far Eastern War 1941–45', *Proceedings of the British Academy* LXVI, 1980.

Towle, P. A., 'Japanese Treatment of Prisoners in 1904–1905 – Foreign Officers' Reports', *Military Affairs*, (Oct. 1985).

Tyler, P. A., 'Water Chemistry of the River Kwai, Thailand', *Hydrobiologica* III, (1984).

Vlieland, C. A., 'The 1947 Census of Malaya', *Pacific Affairs*, Vol. 22, (1949).

Watt, I., 'Bridges over the Kwai', *The Listener*, (6 Aug 1959).

Index